THE
CITY ON
A HILL

THE
CITY ON
A HILL

FULFILLING RONALD REAGAN'S
VISION FOR AMERICA

MICHAEL REAGAN
WITH
JIM DENNEY

A
JANET
THOMA
BOOK

THOMAS NELSON PUBLISHERS
Nashville•Atlanta•London•Vancouver
Printed in the United States of America

Published in Nashville, Tennessee, by Thomas Nelson, Inc., Publishers, and distributed in Canada by Word Communications, Ltd., Richmond, British Columbia.

The Bible version used in this publication is THE NEW KING JAMES VERSION. Copyright © 1979, 1980, 1982, Thomas Nelson, Inc., Publishers.

Library of Congress Cataloging-in-Publication Data

Reagan, Michael, 1945–
    The city on a hill : fulfilling Ronald Reagan's vision for America / Michael Reagan.
        p.   cm.
    Includes bibliographical references.
    ISBN 0-7852-7236-4
    1. United States—Politics and government—1993–   2. United States—Politics and government—1981–1989.   3. United States–Economic policy—1981–1993.   4. Reagan, Ronald—Philosophy.   I. Title.
E885.R426   1997
973.927—dc21   97-21555
                                                                                                              CIP

Printed in the United States of America.

1 2 3 4 5 6 BVG 02 01 00 99 98 97

To my father

CONTENTS

ACKNOWLEDGMENTS

"When I'm not here," as I say on my radio show, "I'm there." That is, when I'm not on the radio, you can find me at my Internet website (www.reagan.com) or in the pages of my monthly newsletter or in my books, *The City on the Hill* and *Making Waves*. Thanks to the twenty-four-hour-a-day power of the Internet and the printed page, you can access the truth about your government anytime you wish. There are a lot of people who make this nonstop information interchange possible.

Much of the credit for bringing this book into existence goes to my teammates (past and present) on "The Michael Reagan Talk Show," Paul Wilkinson and Silva Mergerditchian; my newsletter publisher and Internet webmaster, Andy Beal of MediaFAX; Jeremy Locke and Lara Post, who keep my website fresh, up-to-date, and exciting; and Mary Mostert, the prolific editor of *The Michael Reagan Monthly Monitor* and constant contributor to the website.

Thanks also goes to my friends at various think tanks and grass-roots organizations who keep my fax machine humming and my airwaves buzzing: Amy Moritz of the National Center for Public Policy Research; Brannon Howse of the American Family Policy Institute; Grover Norquist of Americans for Tax Reform; Tom Schatz of Citizens Against Government Waste; John Goodman of the National Center for Policy Analysis; Frank Gaffney of the Center for Security Policies; Karen Mazzarella and Gary Stewart of Speak Out America; Brent Bozell III of Media Research Center; Conna Craig of the pro-adoption Institute for Children; and my good friends at The Heritage Foundation. Thanks also to Tom Denney for access to his vast research library.

A special thanks goes to Congressman George Radanovich of California. He graciously permitted me to adapt the visual aid of the four-legged chair from his Blueprint to Renew Society. In fact, Congressman Radanovich told me that his concept of American society as four sectors—Family, Religious-Civic, Business, and Government—was based in large part on Ronald Reagan's vision of America as a Shining City on a Hill. It was only natural that

ACKNOWLEDGMENTS

those four sectors of society should become the four divisions of our Shining City—the Neighborhood, the Corner of Faith and Charity, Main Street, and the City Square. I am indebted to Congressman Radanovich for the idea that inspired the structure of this book.

Thanks to Jim Denney who transformed my thoughts, convictions, and stories into words on paper; to my editor, Janet Thoma, who believed in this book and helped shape it; and to managing editor Todd Ross, who shepherded this book through the publishing maze.

A special thanks to my cheerleading section—Colleen, Cameron, and Ashley—who have taught me so much about the meaning of words like *faith, love,* and *family.*

Finally, thanks go to Dad for his vision and love for America. More than any other human being I know, he was able to see the greatness of this land and its people—not merely as they are, but as they could be. He saw the Shining City on a Hill, and he drew up the blueprint.

Now it's up to you and me to go build it.

Michael Reagan
Sherman Oaks, California

WE SHALL BE LIKE A CITY ON A HILL;
THE EYES OF ALL PEOPLE ARE ON US.

—RONALD REAGAN

CHAPTER ONE

THE
NEW AMERICAN
MILLENNIUM

"THE WORLD IS QUIET TODAY, MR. PRESIDENT"

We raised a banner of bold colors—no pale pastels. We proclaimed a dream of an America that would be a Shining City
on a Hill.

Ronald Reagan
Acceptance Speech
Republican National Convention
Dallas, Texas, August 23, 1984

I keep remembering all those magazine photo essays of past
presidents. There's always that one shot of the president
standing in the Oval Office, silhouetted against the window.
He's always alone, and the picture is always taken from behind. And the caption invariably quotes the president as saying that this is the loneliest job in the world or some such
thing. Well, I never felt that way. I enjoyed it. I haven't been
lonely one minute.

Ronald Reagan
Farewell to the White House staff
January 18, 1989

1

After eight years as the leader of the Free World, Ronald Reagan was ready to go home. Unlike his predecessor, Jimmy Carter, who had aged visibly in a mere four years in the White House, Ronald Reagan seemed unchanged, and even invigorated, at the end of his two terms in office. He not only loved the job of being president, he had succeeded in the job, confounding his critics and excelling even the wildest expectations of his friends and supporters. But at noon on January 20, 1989, it would be over—and that was fine with him. He was ready to return to California and resume his private life as Ronald Reagan, citizen.

At a little before 10:00 A.M., "Rawhide" (his Secret Service code name) stepped into the Oval Office for the last time. He stood cowboy-straight and cowboy-tall, impeccably dressed in a black suit and striped tie. Also in the Oval Office with him were his personal assistant Jim Kuhn, press secretary Marlin Fitzwater, personal secretary Kathy Osborne, and a White House photographer. The photographer hung around the edges of the office, trying to blend into the ivory-white walls as his camera clicked off the waning seconds of the Reagan presidency.

Ronald Reagan paused in the center of the carpet that bore the seal of his presidential authority, and he took in his surroundings. The office looked naked and unfamiliar to the outgoing president, having been cleared of all his photos, mementos, and other personal effects. Even his large, comfortable executive chair was gone, replaced by a worn secretary's chair that had been moved in from another office. The desktop was bare of everything but a single telephone.

The president sat down at the desk, picked up the phone, and asked the White House operator to place a call for him. It was the last phone call he would make from the Oval Office. Typically for Ronald Reagan, this call was to give a personal word of comfort. Sue Piland, the daughter of the president's longtime friend and aide, Lyn Nofziger, was dying of cancer, and after trying unsuccessfully to reach Sue at the hospital, he called Lyn's wife, Bonnie, and talked with her for about ten minutes. As he was on the phone, chief of staff Ken Duberstein came into the office, along with national security advisor Colin Powell.

After Ronald Reagan said his good-byes to Bonnie Nofziger and hung up the phone, he leaned back and chatted with his aides who had gathered around him. He talked about his favorite room in the White House residence, the Yellow Room, and mentioned the note he had left in the desk drawer for George Bush on a notepad with the printed heading, DON'T LET

2

THE TURKEYS GET YOU DOWN. Someone suggested that the president carve his initials in the Oval Office desk. A chuckle went around the group, and they all felt the bittersweetness of the moment.

Ken Duberstein stepped forward and briefed the president on the schedule for his last day in office—where he was to stand during the inauguration ceremony, when he would board the helicopter that would take him to Andrews Air Force Base for his final flight on *Air Force One*, when he would give his speech to the well-wishers at Los Angeles International Airport. As Duberstein finished his briefing, the president reached into his coat pocket and pulled out a plain white, plastic-coated card, like an unmarked credit card.

"Well, I guess I won't be needing this anymore," he said, holding the card out in General Powell's direction. "Whom do I give it to?"

It was the nuclear authentication code card that Ronald Reagan had carried throughout his presidency. That thin plastic wafer, when inserted into a black leather briefcase carried by a military aide, had the power to unleash Armageddon upon the world.

"Just hold on to it, sir," said Jim Kuhn. "You're still the commander in chief. You can turn it in after Mr. Bush is sworn in as president."

Ronald Reagan nodded and placed the card back in his pocket.

Then Colin Powell stepped forward and gave the president the most succinct national security briefing of Ronald Reagan's entire presidency. "The world is quiet today, Mr. President," said Powell.

The photographer snapped a few more pictures, including some group shots with the staff clustered around their boss, who was still seated at his desk. After the pictures, Jim Kuhn said, "It's time, Mr. President."

Ronald Reagan stood and faced the door that led through the Rose Garden to the car that waited to take him to the Capitol for the inauguration of his successor. Kuhn opened the door and moved aside. The president stepped forward—then paused at the threshold for one last glance at the room that had been his workplace and sanctuary for eight years. He paused for a few seconds, thinking his private thoughts. His aides waited in silence.

Then Ronald Reagan turned and stepped out of the White House and into history.

PERIL AND OPPORTUNITY

We are too great a nation to limit ourselves to small dreams. We are not, as some would have us believe, doomed to an inevitable decline. I do not believe in a fate that will fall on us no matter what we do. I do believe in a fate that will fall on us if we do nothing. So, with all the creative energy at our command, let us begin an era of national renewal. Let us renew our determination, our courage, and our strength. And let us renew our faith and our hope.

We have every right to dream heroic dreams.

Ronald Reagan
First Inaugural Address
January 20, 1981

Ronald Reagan is my father.

As his presidency was drawing to a close, I was three thousand miles from Washington, D.C., having just started my new job as a news coanchor on Radio KSDO in San Diego. So I witnessed this transition in my father's life the same way everyone else in America did: I watched it on television.

The Monday morning before Friday's inauguration—my first day on the job, right in the middle of the news broadcast—Dad called me from the White House. He told my radio audience and me how much he was looking forward to coming home to California. He closed with the words, "Nancy sends her love, and please give our love to Colleen and the children."

"You take care, Dad," I said in return. "Love you."

"Well . . . love you."

A few days earlier, on January 11, he had gone on television and radio and given his last speech as president. In that farewell address, delivered live from the Oval Office, Ronald Reagan summed up his two terms in these words:

It's been quite a journey this decade, and we held together through some stormy seas. And at the end, together, we are reaching our destination.

4

THE CITY ON A HILL

The fact is, from Grenada to the Washington and Moscow summits, from the recession of 1981 to 1982, to the expansion that began in late 1982 and continues to this day, we've made a difference. The way I see it, there were two great triumphs, two things that I'm proudest of. One is the economic recovery, in which the people of America created—and filled—nineteen million new jobs. The other is the recovery of our morale. America is respected again in the world and looked to for leadership. . . . Once you begin a great movement, there's no telling where it will end. We meant to change a nation, and instead, we changed a world. . . .

Ours was the first revolution in the history of mankind that truly reversed the course of government, and with three little words: We the People. We the People tell the government what to do; it doesn't tell us. We the People are the driver; the government is the car. And we decide where it should go, and by what route, and how fast. Almost all the world's constitutions are documents in which governments tell the people what their privileges are. Our Constitution is a document in which We the People tell the government what it is allowed to do. We the People are free. This belief has been the underlying basis for everything I've tried to do these past eight years.

But back in the 1960s, when I began, it seemed to me that we'd begun reversing the order of things—that through more and more rules and regulations and confiscatory taxes, the government was taking more of our money, more of our options, and more of our freedom. I went into politics, in part, to put up my hand and say, "Stop!" I was a citizen politician, and it seemed the right thing for a citizen to do. I think we have stopped a lot of what needed stopping. And I hope we have once again reminded people that man is not free unless government is limited. There's a clear cause and effect here that is as neat and predictable as a law of physics: As government expands, liberty contracts. . . .

The past few days when I've been at that window upstairs, I've thought a bit of the "Shining City upon a Hill." The phrase comes from John Winthrop, who wrote it to describe the America he imagined. What he imagined was important because he was an early Pilgrim. . . . He journeyed here on what today we'd call a little wooden boat; and like the other Pilgrims, he was looking for a home that would be free. I've spoken of the Shining City all my political life, but I don't know if I ever quite communicated what I saw when I said it. But in my mind it was a tall, proud city built on rocks stronger than oceans, windswept, God-blessed, and teeming with people of all kinds living in harmony and peace; a city with free ports that hummed with commerce and creativity. And if there had to be city walls, the walls had doors, and the doors were open to anyone with the will and the heart to get here. That's how I saw it, and see it still.

And how stands the City on this winter night? More prosperous, more secure, and happier than it was eight years ago. But more than that: After two hundred years, two centuries, she still stands strong and true on the granite ridge, and her glow has held steady no matter what storm. And she's still a beacon; still a magnet for all who must have freedom, for all the pilgrims from all the lost places who are hurtling through the darkness toward home.

We've done our part. And as I walk off into the City streets, a final word to the men and women of the Reagan revolution, the men and women across America who for eight years did the work that brought America back: My friends, we did it. We weren't just marking time. We made a difference. We made the City stronger, we made the City freer, and we left her in good hands. All in all, not bad; not bad at all. . . .

Eight years earlier, Ronald Reagan had defeated Jimmy Carter with a politically devastating question: "Are you better off today than you were four years ago?" And on Election Day 1980, with inflation nearing 13 percent, with the prime rate hovering at more than 15 percent, and with unemployment topping 7 percent, Americans knew the answer to that question. The Carter years were America's darkest days since the Great Depression. Cans on supermarket shelves were topped with ten layers of price stickers, because food prices leapfrogged every few days. Economic growth had stalled, median family income was falling, and the Keynesian economic theories that had produced this crisis couldn't find any solution.

By the end of Ronald Reagan's two terms in office, inflation was tamed to a mere 4.4 percent, the prime rate stood at 9.32 percent, and unemployment was down to 5.5 percent. He presided over the greatest peacetime economic expansion in American history—a time in which nearly every economic indicator demonstrated unparalleled economic health and vigor. The economy grew by a third. The gross national product nearly doubled. Except for a brief, but scary, crash in 1987, the stock market roared through the 1980s. The Dow-Jones industrial average stood at 2235.36 on January 20, 1989—up from 960.68 the day Ronald Reagan took office.

Clearly, my father had made a difference. The Shining City he left in the hands of his successor was a more prosperous, secure, and happy City by far than the one he had inherited from Jimmy Carter. The incoming president, George Bush, had a golden opportunity to consolidate the achievements and public confidence passed down from Ronald Reagan—but Bush got in the way of his own success. Instead of building on that foundation, George Bush distanced himself from the Reagan legacy.

Though communism collapsed on his watch, Mr. Bush was a mere observer of events already set in motion by Ronald Reagan. By pledging to be "the education president" and "the environment president," he signaled his intent to reverse Ronald Reagan's efforts to shrink government spending and regulation. And, as everyone knows, he betrayed his "read my lips, no new taxes" pledge. Bush's one great achievement in office was Operation Desert Storm; all else is mere footnote.

My first inkling that George Bush intended to break faith with the Reagan revolution was his constant use of the campaign slogan "A kinder, gentler America." It nagged at me. I wondered, *Kinder than what? Gentler than whom? Kinder and gentler than Ronald Reagan? Impossible! Preposterous!* Unfortunately, that's exactly what George Bush meant. After eight years as Ronald Reagan's understudy, he never truly grasped what the Reagan revolution was about. In the 1980 campaign primaries, Bush—then my father's nearest Republican rival—called Ronald Reagan's supply-side theory "voodoo economics." Eight years of Ronald Reagan in the White House proved that supply-side Reaganomics was not voodoo—it was *miraculous.* Bush was there; he watched it happen. He saw that while Ronald Reagan cut top marginal tax rates from 70 percent in 1981 to 28 percent in 1986, overall tax revenues rose from $599 billion in 1981 to nearly a *trillion* dollars in 1990.

Why did George Bush decide in 1990 that you and I were undertaxed? Because he didn't believe in Reaganomics. He was still thinking, *That's a lot of voodoo.* He supported a massive tax hike because he thought higher taxes would close the gap in the deficit by $100 billion. In the end, the Bush tax hike didn't close the *federal* deficit at all—but it did contribute to a lot of middle-class *family* budget deficits. Worse, it produced the recession that tragically hurt American businesses and families, corroded Bush's lead in the polls, and gave Bill Clinton his winning campaign issue. If George Bush hadn't been so eager to distance himself from the Reagan legacy, he almost certainly would have been a two-term president.

To make matters worse, Mr. Bush also betrayed the defense agenda of Ronald Reagan. Immediately after using America's Reagan-restored military might against Iraq in Desert Storm, he proceeded to slash defense spending, supposedly in response to a reduced threat from the former Soviet Union following the collapse of communism. Bush's cuts in defense spending were coupled with massive increases in domestic social spending. The domestic budget—which had consumed 15.3 percent of the gross national product (GNP) under Jimmy Carter, and which Ronald Reagan had cut to 13.0 percent of the GNP—swelled to 15.8 percent (worse than Carter's) under George Bush. *That* was what George Bush meant when he announced a "kinder, gentler" America.

Domestic spending rose faster under Bush than under other so-called big spenders such as Lyndon Johnson, Richard Nixon, and Jimmy Carter. In his first two years, Bush launched dozens of new spending programs while increasing many existing programs—$34 billion for housing and related programs, $5.5 billion for agricultural programs, $4.7 billion for the Department of Education, $2.5 billion for the Department of Energy, and on and on. Whereas Ronald Reagan had tried to abolish the education and energy departments, Bush enlarged their budgets and their bureaucratic power over our lives.[1]

In 1994, the Republican Party stormed the halls of Congress, armed with the Contract with America—a Reaganesque agenda that included the balanced budget amendment, the line-item veto, anticrime legislation, welfare reform, pro-family tax cuts and education reform, a restored national defense, raising the senior citizen's earning limit, regulatory rollbacks, commonsense legal reform, and congressional term limits. Grassroots America read the Contract and threw a party! At last, the Republicans were the party of Ronald Reagan once more!

But then came the election of 1996. At the Republican National Convention in San Diego, it was as if the Contract with America never existed! The agenda that took the Congress by storm was suddenly no longer even whispered about among Republicans. Believe it or not, if you wanted to hear about the Contract with America, you had to go to the Democratic Convention! There, in Chicago, Bill Clinton cited achievement after achievement during his first term—*and virtually every one of those achievements was a provision of the Republican Contract with America!* It was ludicrous! Bill Clinton ran *on* the Contract with America—and the Republicans ran *away* from it!

During the 1996 primary campaign, every Republican candidate, from Bob Dole to Bob Dornan, tried to position himself as the heir to Ronald Reagan. Yet out of the entire 1996 campaign cycle, only one candidate emerged who truly ran a Reaganesque campaign—the Democratic incumbent, Bill Clinton! Here was Bill Clinton, committed to dismantling everything Ronald Reagan stood for—yet he shamelessly modeled his campaign after the campaign style of Ronald Wilson Reagan.

If Ronald Reagan's Shining City fell into disrepair in the hands of George Bush, it is becoming a slum in the hands of Bill Clinton. By the end of Clinton's second term, it could well be a ghost town. We are experiencing the highest tax rates and slowest growth of any economy since the Carter administration. America is broke. Medicare and Social Security are going bankrupt. Our military has been hollowed out, and our national sovereignty has been surrendered to the United Nations. Our education standards and our children's test scores have fallen into the red zone. Teen drug use doubled in the first four years of Bill Clinton's presidency. The terror of crime keeps law-abiding citizens locked behind bars in their own homes.

Our society is approaching a meltdown—an economic meltdown, a cultural meltdown, and a moral and spiritual meltdown. We are poised at a moment of great peril and of great opportunity for American society. Are we witnessing the end or the rebirth of America? Ours is the generation that will answer that question.

THE BLUEPRINT TO RENEW SOCIETY

A growing economy and support from family and community offer our best chance for a society where compassion is a way of life.

Ronald Reagan
Second Inaugural Address
January 21, 1985

On June 18, 1996, Congressman George Radanovich (R-California) gave a talk before the Heritage Foundation in Washington, D.C., in which he laid out a vision for American society that he called "The Blueprint to Renew Society." As he spoke, he presented a simple, easy-to-grasp picture of what is fundamentally wrong with American government today—and how to fix it. Radanovich, president of the freshman class of the 104th Congress, pictured our society today as, quite simply, a chair.

Present Reality
Figure 1.1

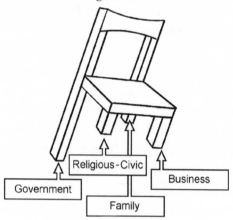

What's wrong with the chair in Figure 1.1? Obviously, it is wobbly, unstable, and unbalanced. It can't support weight. It is doomed to fail. The leg labeled *Government* is much longer than the other legs, labeled *Family*, *Religious-Civic*, and *Business*. This chair represents the fact that our society is unhealthy and unbalanced because it is dominated by the federal government, while the other pillars that support our society—family, business, and religious-civic—have become stunted.

A healthy society is a balanced society, built on four sturdy legs, each leg bearing an equal share of the load. See Figure 1.2.

Vision for the Future
Figure 1.2

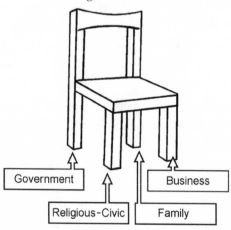

So how do we accomplish this vision for our society? Clearly, we have to saw off some of the leg that is too big—government. And we have to lengthen the legs that are too short. The roles of each of these pillars of American society have to be realigned:

- **Family.** The federal government's paternalistic intrusions into the American family must be halted, and families must be empowered (through sensible tax and education policies) to take complete charge of the raising of their children. Parental rights must be restored and respected. Neighborhoods and schools must be made safe from crime and drugs.

- **Religious-Civic.** The role of helping the poor and needy must be removed from the gray cubicles of the federal bureaucracy and restored to the caring, compassionate sanctuaries and shelters of our religious and civic organizations. We must commit ourselves, regardless of our political persuasion and religious convictions, to stop demonizing one another. We must work together and solve the problems of poverty, illiteracy, racism, teen pregnancy, AIDS, and abortion.

- **Business.** Both large and small businesses in America must be relieved of regulatory and tax burdens so that more jobs and individual opportunities can be created. Government must learn to work with business instead of against it, and our leading edge in technology and scientific research must remain a high national priority.

- **Government.** We must maintain our national sovereignty and restore our military strength. Domestically, we must not only balance the budget but also run surplus budgets so that we can begin to level the mountain of debt we have accumulated. We must work together to save Social Security and Medicare for future generations.

"The result," says Congressman Radanovich, "is a positive vision of what America should be, based on a new foundation: a society of four equal institutions—family, religious-civic, business, and government—to provide freedom, security, and prosperity to the American people."

From the Reagan era to the present day, one of the biggest roadblocks to shrinking the government has been *fear:* the fear that a downsized federal government will leave a vacuum in our society. The fear that if government gets out of the welfare business, the poor and needy will have nowhere to turn for help. The fear that businesses, state and local governments, religious and civic institutions, and families either can't or won't step up to the plate and shoulder their responsibilities. We have to allay these fears and meet these concerns. We have to make sure that the American people understand the enormous benefits that come with greater freedom and smaller government. We have to empower the nongovernmental sectors of our society to handle the job the government will no longer do (and has never done well). As Congressman Radanovich concludes, "The American people will not allow us to redefine the role of government unless they are assured the other institutions in this country will assume their rightful roles."

JUST AROUND THE CORNER

And how stands the City on this winter night?

Ronald Reagan
Farewell Address
The Oval Office, January 19, 1989

There is a clear contrast between what America is and what America could become, as the Radanovich chair model makes clear. Another way to illustrate this concept is with the image Ronald Reagan spoke of so often in his political career—the image of the City on a Hill. America today is not the Shining City that Ronald Reagan envisioned—"a tall, proud city built on rocks stronger than oceans, windswept, God-blessed, and teeming with people of all kinds living in harmony and peace." Here, at the brink of a new millennium, America looks more like a vast concrete fortress on a hill, surrounded by three squalid little slums, populated by bickering, contentious factions. The massive concrete fortress is the federal government— huge and imposing, bureaucratic and impersonal, cold and forbidding, demanding and intimidating.

The glowering gray fortress of the federal government is proof of Ronald Reagan's warning, "Man is not free unless government is limited. There's a clear cause and effect here that is as neat and predictable as a law of physics: As government expands, liberty contracts." The ponderous, hyperimmense Washington bureaucracy represents force and control, not freedom. And the three slums that huddle at the feet of the fortress? They are the family neighborhood, the religious and civic sector, the business district—and they are pitiful and shrunken in size and influence. As the gray fortress of government has expanded, these three other sectors have been forced to retreat. And the people who live in this place are at war with one another over who will receive the meager benefits dispensed from the fortress.

That is not Ronald Reagan's vision for America. His Shining City on a Hill is a beautiful, well-planned city divided into four equal, mutually supportive districts:

- **The Neighborhood**, where the American family lives free and grows strong.
- **The Corner of Faith and Charity**, where the religious and civic institutions of our City live out their beliefs and carry on their compassionate work.
- **Main Street**, bustling and prosperous, where the business and industry of the City are freely conducted; where the opportunities for individual success and achievement are truly limitless.
- **The City Square**, where the City's public servants govern according to the will of "We the People."

That is the Shining City in all its glory—a golden and joyous City; a beacon to all who seek freedom; a place of opportunity and compassion, of vital schools and safe streets; a place where people keep and enjoy the fruit of their labors—but also look out for the needs of their neighbors. This book is the blueprint for that City.

We don't have to live out our lives in the shadow of the gray concrete fortress. We can create a New America—the Shining City Ronald Reagan envisioned—and we can pass that City on to our children and to our children's children. In the pages that follow, we will look at this Shining City through the eyes of Ronald Reagan and hear it described in his words. We will see how, by joining together to build this City, we can meet the challenges and solve the problems of today and tomorrow.

We know that the principles and ideals presented in this book will work in the future because they have already been tried and proved in the past. Most Americans look back on the Reagan 1980s as a time of great hope, optimism, opportunity, and growth. It was the Great American Decade.

It was a good beginning—but somewhere along the way, during the Bush-Clinton 1990s, America got derailed. The hope faded, opportunity receded, the economy stalled. Our proud, flag-waving optimism soured to cynicism: "All politicians are scoundrels—so why not elect the scoundrel who promises us the most goodies from the public treasury?" We don't have to settle for that. America *can* be America again.

You may think because my name is Reagan and I'm writing about Ronald Reagan's vision for America that this book only presents a glowing, one-sided assessment of Ronald Reagan's presidency and views. But if you've listened to my radio show or read my previous books, *On the Outside Looking In* and *Making Waves*, then you know I've disagreed with Ronald Reagan before, and I'll do so a time or two in this book as well. And that's okay. The fact that I don't agree with everything he said and did in no way diminishes the respect I have for my father or the awe in which I hold his accomplishments.

When you get to the end of this book, I think you will find that you have just read one of the most honest assessments of President Ronald Reagan ever written. As a son, I have admired this man—and I have struggled with him. I have watched him up close and from a distance. I believe this experience has given me a unique perception of who Ronald Reagan is, what he believed, what he achieved, and what his vision for America's future truly is. And my experience as a political observer over the nation's airwaves has given me the ability to apply that vision to the realities of the fast-approaching new millennium.

Near the end of his presidency, before an audience in San Diego, California, Ronald Reagan said, "I hope that someday your children and grandchildren will tell of the time that a certain president came to town at the end of a long journey and asked their parents and grandparents to join him in setting America on the course to the new millennium, and that a century of peace, prosperity, opportunity, and hope had followed." I share the hope of Ronald Reagan—a hope for a new America in a new millennium. I'm sure you share that hope as well.

So let me be your guide to the broad, beautiful streets of Ronald Reagan's America, his City on a Hill. Let's visit the Family Neighborhood together. Let's stop at the corner of Faith and Charity to be inspired and to lend a hand to neighbors in need. Let's stroll through the shops and marketplaces on Main Street. And let's amble down to the City Square and talk things over with the men and women who serve us in the halls of government. Together, let's rediscover our Shining City and recapture her greatness. If we can restore this vision of America and make it real again, our greatest days, our shining new millennium, may be just around the corner.

PART ONE

THE

FAMILY

NEIGHBORHOOD

The first cornerstone
of the City on a Hill is the
Family

CHAPTER TWO

A CITY
MADE FOR
FAMILIES

THE NEIGHBORHOOD—
OR THE VILLAGE?

Many of us in government would like to know what parents think about this intrusion in their family by government. We're going to fight in the courts. The rights of parents and the rights of family take precedence over those of Washington-based bureaucrats and social engineers.

Ronald Reagan
Speech before the annual convention of the
National Association of Evangelicals
Orlando, Florida, March 8, 1983

Liberals love to quote the old African proverb "It takes a village to raise a child." And the fact is, there is actually a lot of wisdom in that proverb—if by the word *village* you mean neighbors helping neighbors, friends and grandparents and extended family getting involved with one another's families, going on camping trips together, baby-sitting one another's kids, getting involved in Boy Scouts and Girl Scouts, reading to kids at the local kindergarten or elementary school, coaching one another's kids in Little League and soccer leagues, shooting baskets with the kids on the school yard or down at the YMCA, or becoming youth group advisors at the local church or synagogue. These are all ways the village—the *local community* of

19

relatives, neighbors, teachers, pastors, scoutmasters, camp counselors, and friends—can pitch in and help families grow strong, healthy, happy kids. When we invest ourselves in the next generation—whether our own kids or our neighbors' kids—we help build this Shining City called America.

Unfortunately, when liberal leaders like Hillary Rodham Clinton say, "It takes a village to raise a child," they mean "It takes a bureaucracy" or "It takes a liberal government program" or "It takes higher taxes and more spending" or "It takes Child Protective Services." They don't just want your friendly neighborhood villagers helping you and supporting you as you raise your children; they want the big spear-toting *village chieftains* to make sure you raise your children according to the sacred, politically correct village laws and taboos. So before we accept this idea of the village being involved in the raising of our kids, let's make sure we understand one another.

I would like to open a dialogue with liberals on this issue, because I believe many liberals truly care about children and want what's best for our nation's kids. I'm not talking here about the Dick Gephardts, the Tom Daschles, and the Jesse Jacksons of the world—the demagogues who ruthlessly exploit our children as an issue rather than truly seeking their welfare. I mean the liberal rank and file—the average people of compassion and generosity who feel that children and poor people and old people sometimes just need a break from society in order to be okay. When you get away from the marble halls of Washington and the newsrooms of New York and Los Angeles, you find that deep down people are pretty much the same. Liberal or conservative, we all want to see stronger families and healthier kids. We all care about our neighbors and reach out to help people in need. We all want strong, involved "villages"—prosperous and well-protected *local* communities where kids can grow up in safety and security, knowing they are loved and valued.

So as we begin talking together—liberals, moderates, and conservatives—let's define our terms. Let's not speak in code words. Let's not call a government *bureaucracy* a *village*. A village gets to know and love your kids. A bureaucracy cannot. A village can spend time with your kids and impart values to your kids. A government program cannot. Your friends and neighbors in the village can be teachers, counselors, mentors, coaches, and role models to your kids. A government social worker cannot.

The liberal big-government "village" of Hillary Rodham Clinton does not merely want to *help* us raise our own children, because it does not trust parents to do a good job raising kids. In many cases, the "village" of liberal Big Brother seems bent on taking over the job of parenting our children and directing their lives. A recent case in point:

In March 1996, parents of fifty-nine sixth-grade girls at the J. T. Lambert Intermediate School in East Stroudsburg, Pennsylvania, were outraged to discover that their daughters had been spread-eagled naked on a table and subjected to forced genital exams without parental consent. The local pediatrician who performed the exam said that she checked the girls' genitals for warts, lesions, and other abnormalities. Some who investigated the case, however, are convinced that the exam was really a random screening for signs of sexual abuse by parents.

Before and during the examinations, many of the girls began to cry and asked to call their parents. One girl ran crying from the room and was forcibly restrained, returned to the room, and examined against her will. The school nurse berated the girls, calling them "babies." None were allowed to call home, and no parents were allowed to be present during the exams.

Though the doctor claimed it was an "external exam," she admitted there was "some touching" and retracting of the labia of some of the girls. Parents Paul and Katie Tucker said their daughter was definitely touched internally. "My daughter told me the doctor digitally penetrated her," said the mother. Other girls reported feeling pain and experiencing blood spotting from their vaginas the next day, and they did not return to school.

Think about it! As responsible parents, we teach our kids never to allow a stranger to touch them in a way that makes them feel uncomfortable. We teach them to assert their right to defend their own bodies against intrusion and tell them if they ever have a problem, they can come to us and we will help them. But these girls were isolated from their parents, placed in a position of utter powerlessness, and violated. Their bodies were violated, their rights were violated, and the rights of their parents were violated.

When Brannon Howse of the American Family Policy Institute (AFPI) brought this story to national attention on my show, a firestorm of controversy erupted nationwide. How did the doctor respond to this controversy? With incredible arrogance! "Even a parent doesn't have the right to say what's appropriate for a physician to do when they're doing an exam," the doctor told a reporter for the *Pocono Record*. A board of inquiry sided with the doctor—even though the board never interviewed even one of the fifty-nine girls.

This is not what life in the Shining City on a Hill is to be like. The strength and integrity of our City depend on the strength and integrity of our families. We do not override the prerogatives of parents. We do not violate the rights and innermost being of children. We do not allow social engineers and self-appointed do-gooders to perform their experiments on our children. We do not treat parents like outsiders who have no say over the treatment of their children. The East Stroudsburg case is an extreme case, but not an isolated one. It is only one of the more outrageous examples of a trend that has become all too common in America. For example:

In late September 1996, Brannon Howse received a phone call from Marlene Mitchell of Dallas, Texas. After hearing how Brannon, the AFPI, and *The Michael Reagan Talk Show* had come to the defense of the parents and children in East Stroudsburg, Marlene Mitchell knew she had to talk to Brannon about her friends, the Stout family. After confirming the facts of the case, Brannon publicized the story on his own radio airwaves and on my show.

In June 1996, ten-year-old Rachel Stout began experiencing rectal bleeding. Despite the best medical treatment, Rachel's condition rapidly worsened. By early July, she was down to fifty-two pounds and was experiencing constant weakness, cramping, and pain. At Cook's Fort Worth Children's Hospital, a colonoscopy was performed and the physician decided to remove her colon. The procedure would stop the bleeding and stabilize her condition, but it would also reduce the quality of her life and shorten her life span to a mere twenty-five years. Not surprisingly, Rachel's parents, Steve and Patricia Stout, wanted additional medical opinions. For three weeks, Rachel was on IV feedings and steroid medication while additional medical options were explored. The surgeon continued pressing the Stouts to consent to the operation. Meanwhile, Rachel developed additional problems, such as an insulin deficiency due to the high sugar content of her IVs.

One doctor the Stouts consulted, a specialist at Children's Medical Center in Dallas, was initially very encouraging that Rachel could be successfully treated without removing her colon. After consulting with the original doctor in Fort Worth, however, the Dallas doctor also began pushing for surgery. The Stouts, meanwhile, did extensive research on ulcerative colitis and Crohn's disease, and found a Toronto specialist, Dr. Devgan, who offered hope of a recovery without removing Rachel's colon. But when the Stouts attempted to move Rachel to another hospital in Texas or in Canada, the Fort Worth surgeon refused to okay the move.

Instead of working with the Stouts, the Fort Worth physician threatened to call Child Protection Services (CPS) and have their parental rights terminated if they refused to consent to the surgery. On Labor Day weekend, Steve Stout came to a decision: He had to act *now*—or lose his right to defend his daughter's life. So he arranged with an M.D. who was a friend of their family to wait in a van outside the hospital. Then he boldly walked into his daughter's hospital room, scooped her up in his arms (IV and all), and carried her out to the waiting van. They drove straight to the airport and boarded a plane for Toronto. Even the doctor went, so that Rachel would have the best possible care during the trip.

Clearly, these were not abusive parents and this was not a case for CPS. These were loving parents trying desperately to safeguard the life of their child. They were forced to "steal" their own daughter from the self-appointed village do-gooders who had decided that doctors and bureaucrats had more right to determine Rachel's welfare than Rachel's own mom and dad. It is *fundamentally wrong* for government and social engineers to come between a child and her parents in this way. If parents have been conclusively shown to be abusive or neglectful, that is one thing. But to the contrary, the Stouts had proven that they were committed to doing anything, to going anywhere, to spending any amount of money, to even defy government authority, in order to spare the life of their child.

As it turned out, the parental instincts of the Stouts were better than a lot of the medical judgment exercised in Rachel's case. As soon as she was removed from Texas, Rachel began to improve. The doctors in Toronto were able to gradually reduce the dosage of steroids she was receiving. She was removed from the IV feedings and allowed to eat a carefully balanced variety of foods. Her blood sugar stabilized. Her spirits improved. Her health improved. The Toronto specialist, Dr. Devgan, began treating Rachel on September 3; by September 5, all her bleeding had stopped.

Meanwhile, CPS in Texas conducted a hearing to terminate the Stouts' parental rights and take custody of Rachel, with a goal of bringing her back to Texas to have her colon removed. The judge in Texas ruled that another doctor at the Hospital for Sick Children in Toronto should evaluate Rachel. The Children's Aid Society (Canada's version of CPS) took Rachel to the Hospital for Sick Children for evaluation on Saturday, September 7, and she was found to be doing well. The hospital released Rachel to her father, Steve, who returned her to Dr. Devgan for her treatment. Everything seemed to be proceeding well. Rachel was happy. The Stouts were ecstatic. They had no idea that events were about to take a disastrous turn.

A specialist at the Hospital for Sick Children in Toronto called and wanted to conduct one more examination. Unbeknownst to the Stouts, the Texas surgeon was in contact with the Hospital for Sick Children. Later, when the Stouts learned of this contact, they became convinced that the Texas surgeon had prejudiced the Toronto doctors against them and their case. The doctors found a minor infection in Rachel's system, which they used as a pretext to keep her in the hospital. Against the Stouts' wishes, the doctors at the Hospital for Sick Children took over the treatment of Rachel's colon from Dr. Devgan, administering the same regimen of steroids, lipids, and IV feedings that had been used in Texas. Soon, she was again experiencing diarrhea, cramps, and rectal bleeding. She became depressed over becoming sick all over again. At one point, she asked her father, "Daddy, are they trying to kill me here?"

Facing pressure from the Canadian government to leave the country, Mr. Stout arranged to move his daughter to the Mayo Clinic in Rochester, Minnesota—perhaps the finest medical institution in the country. The Mayo doctors believed Rachel could be treated without the life-shortening surgery. But on October 1—before Steve Stout could complete the arrangements—officials of the Canadian government entered Rachel's hospital room and told her father, "You have twelve minutes to pack, and then you and your daughter will be taken from here and placed on an airplane for Dallas." There was no time to argue or appeal.

The moment Rachel and her parents stepped off the plane, Rachel became a ward of the state of Texas, by order of the court. She was whisked off to Dallas Children's Medical Center, kept in a room under guard, and her parents were not allowed to visit her except in the presence of a CPS social worker. In mid-October, under intense pressure by state authorities, and after being threatened with the loss of custody of their daughter, the Stouts finally relented and allowed surgeons at North Carolina's Duke University Medical Center to perform the surgery.

Throughout their ordeal, the Stouts repeatedly, consistently proved themselves competent to choose their daughter's care. Dr. Devgan of Toronto was able to stabilize and improve her condition without surgery. Yet doctors, courts, attorneys, and social workers were determined to separate Rachel from her parents and force a surgical procedure on her that would take decades off her life. The Stouts are not the kind of abusive or neglectful parents that child protection laws are written for. Rachel Stout never needed Big Brother to swoop down and "protect" her from her parents. The state of Texas had no business even taking notice of the Stouts' situation—much less bulldozing their way into it.

But this is what the liberal "village" intends for all our children: a world in which the almighty State, not parents, decides what's best for children—a brave new world in which children are "protected" from the love and nurturing of their own parents. Time after time, government makes itself the enemy of the American family, inserting itself where it is not wanted, not needed, and where it does vastly more harm than good. As Ronald Reagan has often said—and as these stories demonstrate—government does not solve problems. Government is the problem.

These cases are extreme, but the fact is that child protection agencies routinely treat parents as guilty unless proven innocent. CPS is an out-of-control government bureaucracy with gestapolike power to rip children out of homes without any trial, without any constitutional due process whatsoever. Every year, agencies remove 100,000 to 150,000 kids from their homes. In fact, there is actually an incentive for CPS to remove these kids, since these agencies receive taxpayer money every time a child is taken out of the home. And the child advocacy activists are on the warpath, pushing for ever more intrusive control over your family and mine. In Colorado, a bill called the Children's Welfare Act has been proposed, which would require all Colorado parents to allow a government "home visitor" into their house to assess the parents as potential abusers.

Obviously, we need to defend children against abuse. The problem is that in our current political climate, we have come to treat parents as the natural enemies of children. Big Brother agents of the CPS operate on the assumption that child abuse by parents is a routine occurrence, when the reality is that the percentage of abusive parents is actually quite small. Suddenly, perfectly decent, loving parents find themselves humiliated and their children traumatized or ripped away from them by the all-powerful village chieftains.

The Fifth Amendment to the Constitution states that "No person shall . . . be deprived of life, liberty, or property, without due process of law." The government can't put you in prison or take away your car without due process. Amazingly, however, the government can—without having to justify its actions in a court of law!—seize the most precious and important part of your life: your children. Our laws must be amended to require CPS to make a compelling case in court before a child can be removed. This action would defend the rights of innocent parents and the emotional well-being of their children.

But the laws should also be changed with regard to terminating parental rights. Once it has been proven in a court of law that a parent is unfit—guilty of physical abuse, sexual abuse, drug abuse, or neglect—that individual's parental rights should be terminated *swiftly* and *irrevocably,* so that the children can readily be placed in good homes. This would dramatically reduce the incidence of the scenario that has become all too common in our society: children being revictimized and even murdered while their parents are under the so-called supervision of Child Protection Services.

Those who use the child protective system as a way to punish enemies by knowingly filing false child abuse reports should be slapped down hard. Repeated offenses should be prosecuted as felonies. By reducing the incidence of false reports, CPS personnel would be freed up to investigate real abuse, so that more children could get the help they need.

We conservatives have long believed that the fundamental institution of our society is the family. It is in the family where children learn honesty, diligence, honor, self-discipline, self-respect, and respect for others—all the qualities that produce greatness in a society. Liberals believe that the fundamental institution of society is the government. I invite liberals to examine the evidence, to witness the excesses and pain caused by a too-large, too-powerful, too-intrusive government. The American family is under assault, and it is Uncle Sam who's kicking down the door.

FAIRNESS FOR FAMILIES

And what about fairness for families? It's in our families that America's most important work gets done: raising our next generation. But over the last forty years, as inflation has shrunk the personal exemption, families with children have had to shoulder more and more of the tax burden. With inflation and bracket creep also eroding incomes, many spouses who would rather stay home with their children have been forced to go looking for jobs. . . . We're going to make it economical to raise children again.

Ronald Reagan
On signing the 1986 Tax Reform Act
White House South Lawn
October 22, 1986

My friend Dana Rohrabacher, congressman from the Forty-fifth District in California and a former speechwriter for my dad, tells the story about an incident he witnessed when Dad was running in the 1976 primaries. On one occasion, Dad was speaking at a Reagan for President rally in North Carolina. A woman tugged on Rohrabacher's arm and said, "I've brought a group of blind children to the rally. Would it be possible for Governor Reagan to come shake hands with them after he gives his speech?"

"I'll see what I can do," Rohrabacher replied. After the speech, he went to the campaign bus and told Dad's aide, Mike Deaver, about the woman's request. Dad overheard and said, "Look, fellas, I don't want the press to get wind of this, because I don't want anyone to think I'm trying to exploit children in this campaign. Just bring the kids over to the bus and I'll talk to them."

So Rohrabacher got the kids—there were five of them, around ten to twelve years old—and he introduced them to Ronald Reagan. Dad chatted with the kids for a few minutes—and then he had an idea. "Would you children like to touch my face?" he asked.

Dana Rohrabacher was amazed. "I'll never forget that," he recalls, "because it would never have dawned on me to say that to those kids. But Ronald Reagan was so understanding and so sensitive that he knew those blind children could not 'see' him unless they touched his face."

And, indeed, all the kids wanted to touch my dad's face. These five sightless children gathered around my dad, and Rohrabacher was struck by the fact that here was a very public man giving these children a very private moment of his time. Rohrabacher recalls, "I thought to myself, *What politician in this country wouldn't give millions to have his picture on the cover of* Time *or* Newsweek *with all those small hands outstretched to touch him?* But Ronald Reagan didn't use children for his own personal gain. He reached out to them, and let them reach out to him. He genuinely cared about kids—not as window dressing for a photo op, but as people."

After he became president, Ronald Reagan felt that part of his job as president was to stay in touch with the people, so even though he could not

27

personally answer the enormous mountain of mail he received, he did have his chief of correspondence, Anne Higgins, bring him a selection of letters. Many of these letters he answered with handwritten notes. One such letter came from a single mother who lived somewhere in the nation's heartland. This woman had written to tell her president how hard her young son was working to keep his grades up in school, and that she hoped she would be able to afford to send him to college someday. My father was so touched by her letter, he took out his checkbook, wrote a personal check to the woman for several hundred dollars, and told her to use the money to start a college fund for the boy.

The woman was excited when she received the check and the letter from the president of the United States, and she took the check down to the bank to deposit. The banker, however, told her not to cash the check, advising her that the check itself would someday be worth far more than its face value. When my father learned of this, he called the woman and said, "Please go ahead and deposit the check. I'll make sure my accountant sends the canceled check back to you to keep."

That story was never reported in the papers, because that's not why Dad did things like that. He is a man of real compassion, real caring—no fanfare, no press releases, just quiet acts of kindness and involvement in the lives of families and children. Anyone can make a show of caring for children when the cameras are running—even a monster like Saddam Hussein had his picture taken patting a little boy on the head. But Ronald Reagan's compassion is not a show. It's real. What he did in a small way for a group of blind children and for a single mother and her boy, he also did on a much larger scale for *all* American families: He touched their lives, and he improved the quality and affordability of family life.

The Reagan 1980s were the Wonder Years for the American family. The combination of lower taxes, low inflation, increased economic growth, and increased job opportunities meant that families were affordable once more—thanks to Ronald Reagan. The economic policies of the Reagan administration had a direct and tangible impact on every American family's earning power, spending power, and sense of security. After the corrosive 1960s and 1970s, which gave us Vietnam, Watergate, and the economic tribulation of the Ford-Carter years, the Reagan 1980s gave the American family reason to feel positive about the present and hopeful for the future. The economic indicators show us why we felt so positive in the 1980s—and why families are feeling less hopeful and more worried in the 1990s.

Figure 2.1. Economic Indicators

	The Reagan 1980s	The Bush-Clinton 1990s
Jobs Created	10.4 million (1981–88)	5.8 million (1989–96)
Annual Increase	3.2 percent per year	1.5 percent per year
Increase in the Gross Domestic Product	4.9 percent per year	2.9 percent per year
Increase in Disposable Family Income	3.8 percent per year	2.4 percent per year
Increase in Worker Compensation	1.6 percent per year	0.7 percent per year
Net Increase in Business Formation	7.6 percent per year	4.3 percent per year
Increase in Family Net Worth	3.2 percent per year	1.9 percent per year

(Figures are adjusted for inflation. Source: *National Review*.)[1]

How did Ronald Reagan do it? First and foremost, he did it with tax cuts. Ronald Reagan cut top marginal rates from 70 percent to 50 percent in 1981, and from 50 percent to 28 percent in 1986—and the result was ninety-six consecutive months of economic growth. All income groups— rich, middle-class, and, yes, even the poor—experienced real income gains during the Reagan 1980s. From 1983 to 1989, the total number of people below the poverty line decreased by 3.8 million as an unprecedented number of jobs were created under Reaganomics.

Who benefited most from the Reagan 1980s? The American family— dads, moms, and their kids. And who has been hit hardest since Ronald Reagan left office? Again, it is the American family.

Both George Bush and Bill Clinton have signed huge tax hikes into law—tax hikes that were devised and inflicted on us by Democratic-controlled Congresses. True to their Contract with America, the Republicans in Congress passed a major plan for tax reform and tax relief—but Bill Clinton *vetoed* it, and he used the money taxed out of our family budgets to buy votes and pay off special interests. The centerpiece of the Republican plan was a $500 per child tax credit—a feature that was clearly aimed at improving the life of the cash-strapped, overtaxed American family—and Bill Clinton *vetoed* it.

My friend Gary L. Bauer, president of the Family Research Council and an advisor to my father during his administration, is very concerned about the economic viability of the American family. He put it this way in a speech before the Heritage Foundation:

> The key fact of the American economy is this: It is getting harder, not easier, for working families to make ends meet. . . . It isn't just a problem of slow economic growth. The real problem is that the take-home pay of workers has fallen behind the growth of the economy. They get to keep less and less of what they earn. Here's a stunning fact: We have created ten million-plus new jobs, but only eight million more workers are now employed. Every three workers are holding down four jobs. One income used to provide for a family. Then it took two. Now, increasingly, it takes three![2]

Now, this is not to say that a family's take-home pay is the most important aspect of a healthy family life—far from it! But when we promote economic fairness for families, we create a climate in which families can grow stronger, closer, and more secure. Time spent working at extra jobs is time spent away from the family, time robbed from children, time that can never be repaid once a child has outgrown the formative years. A parent who is gone too much or is tired from too many hours at work simply cannot be there for a child's emotional, spiritual, and physical needs. That means the child will not get read to, talked to, listened to, prayed with, hugged, or cuddled as much as he or she needs.

There was a time, just a generation or two ago, when a middle-class family could live comfortably on a single salary. Not anymore. What has changed in all that time? One of the biggest factors is the family tax burden.

In 1913, the family breadwinner worked from January 1 to January 30 to pay taxes—after that, he got to keep everything he earned for the benefit of the family. By 1925, taxes had risen to the point where a breadwinner had to work until February 6 just to pay taxes. By 1940, FDR's New Deal tax-and-spend programs had extended the breadwinner's bondage to Uncle Sam to March 8. By the end of World War II, it was April 1. In the 1950s and early 1960s—the era of *Father Knows Best* and *Leave It to Beaver*—Tax Freedom Day hovered around the end of March or beginning of April. LBJ's Great Society programs and the Vietnam War pushed Tax Freedom Day all the way to April 14 in 1965 and to April 30 by 1969. Under Jimmy Carter, the tax bite on the American family reached a then record high, forcing breadwinners to work until May 5 just to pay Uncle Sam's cut. The Reagan tax cuts rolled Tax Freedom Day back into April throughout the 1980s. But two huge post-Reagan tax hikes—the Bush tax disaster of 1990 and the Clinton tax monster of 1993—have set new records for Tax Freedom Day— May 7 in 1995 and 1996 (the May 7 in 1996 is actually a day later than 1995, because 1996 is a leap year) and May 9 in 1997 (the latest Tax Freedom Day in U.S. history). Because of liberal tax-and-spend policies crafted by Democratic Congresses and signed by presidents Bush and Clinton, American families now spend more on federal, state, and local taxes than on shelter, food, clothing, and transportation *combined,* according to the Tax Foundation, a nonprofit, nonpartisan policy research organization founded in 1937.

The idea that you should keep the money you have earned through the expenditure of your own time and labor, the liberals claim, is pure selfishness. So they have anointed and appointed themselves to take nearly half of everything you earn, to spend it on the people, programs, and issues they think are important. Most of all, they have engineered the tax code in such a way as to force you to order your life according to the dictates of the Internal Revenue Service. Every time you spend a dollar here, make a dollar there, or contribute a dollar to this or that cause, you have to worry about the tax impact, and you have to pay an accountant to tell you what to do. If you use your money in a way the government disapproves of, it's gonna cost you—and that's how the social engineers in Washington keep us under their control.

The American family can no longer afford to support the scheming social engineers in Washington in the style to which they are accustomed. When the government took its greedy bite out of your paycheck and spent it on some new and wasteful bureaucracy, it meant that you couldn't afford that new computer, those braces, those violin lessons, that vacation, or that set of encyclopedias that would have made life a little better for you and your children. It's wrong for American families to strain, suffer, and do without so that Uncle Sam can throw a big party for lobbyists and bureaucrats. I would much rather see the politicians have to strain and sweat and cut back so that American children have what they need, and so that their parents can enjoy the good things they've earned by their own ingenuity and hard work.

Economic fairness for families was one of the great, guiding dreams of Ronald Reagan. During his two terms in office, he made great strides in his quest to make it economical to raise children again. Since he left office, however, the American family has been steadily losing ground, while the federal tax bite has been getting bigger and bigger. For too long, we have allowed Uncle Sam to take away our economic freedom. It's time we restore Ronald Reagan's dream, reclaim our freedom, and put Uncle Sam back in his place.

A VISION OF FAMILY

I would like to be president because I would like to see this country become once again a country where a little six-year-old girl can grow up knowing the same freedom that I knew when I was six years old, growing up in America.

Ronald Reagan
"To Restore America"
March 31, 1976

All great change in America begins at the dinner table.

Ronald Reagan
Farewell Speech, Oval Office
January 11, 1989

Ronald Reagan's critics have tried to paint him as a hypocrite because of his resolute defense of the American family. "Reagan claimed to be for traditional family values," they sneered, "but look at him. He's divorced. His children are mad at him. His life contradicts what he preaches." Yes, he was divorced once, and, yes, he has had struggles in his relationship with his four children. But the critics are wrong in trying to find a contradiction there. Ronald Reagan's family life may be a paradox in many ways, but it's not a sham. His belief in the ideal of the family has always been a deeply held conviction. Throughout his political career, he believed in the family and fought for the family precisely because he always yearned so deeply for something he never fully knew as a child and couldn't always achieve as a father: strong, healthy family relationships.

If you've read my first book, *On the Outside Looking In,* you know about my early struggles as the son of famous divorced parents. My entire childhood—especially after I learned I was adopted and began to wonder if I was a full-fledged member of the family—was spent trying to get from my father the very things he was unable to give, such as a hug or the words, "I love you, Son." I know now that I have always had my father's love and approval, even though it was hard for him to demonstrate it. In my dad's era, men just didn't hug other men.

What made it even harder for Dad to be emotionally demonstrative with me—and, indeed, with his other kids, Maureen, Patti, and Ron—is the fact that his own father was an alcoholic. Dad has rarely talked about the pain or shame of having an alcoholic father, but I know it hurt him. John Edward Reagan—everybody called him Jack—was not a mean or violent alcoholic, but his drinking and inability to keep a job for very long were an embarrassment to his devoutly Christian wife, Nelle, and his two sons, Ronald and Neil. Sometimes Jack would disappear for days, and Nelle would explain to her two sons that their father had a "sickness" that he couldn't control, and they shouldn't love him any less because of it. They should simply remember what a good man he was when he was sober.

Once, at the age of eleven, Ronald Reagan returned home from the YMCA. It was a cold, wintry night, and Nelle was away from home on one of her jobs as a seamstress. As he came up the steps, he found his father, Jack, lying in the snow on the porch, reeking of whiskey, completely passed out in full view of the neighborhood. So young Ronald Reagan bent down, dragged his father into the house, and closed the door—shutting the family's hurt and shame inside.

Experts in the recovery field will tell you that it's common for children of alcoholics to wall themselves off emotionally in order to shield themselves against emotional pain. Adult children of alcoholics, like my dad, also have a tendency to consciously reject some aspects of an alcoholic parent while unconsciously copying other aspects. My father was no different. He consciously rejected Jack Reagan's taste for drink, and throughout his life he has avoided alcohol except for an occasional glass of wine.

But in other ways, he absorbed and repeated the parenting style of his emotionally unavailable father—the only male parenting model my father ever knew. As a male role model, Jack Reagan conveyed to his son that it's just not manly to show emotion or to say "I love you." Since that was the only example of fathering Ronald Reagan ever knew, that example shaped the kind of father Ronald Reagan became. Ronald Reagan was a very caring, gentle, compassionate dad, and he always did the best he could—but the fact remains that while he could give his heart to the world, it was hard for him to hug his own children.

Peggy Noonan, one of my dad's White House speechwriters, tells of the time that a reporter interviewed my father, before he was elected president. The reporter asked Dad about the fact that his father, Jack Reagan, had never gone to any of Dad's football games when he was in school. "Yes, that's true," said Dad.

"Well," said the reporter, "do you ever see your father in you?"

Peggy Noonan says that my father blinked and looked away—as if he was surprised by a sudden realization.[3]

In his own way, my dad has always tried to show me he loves me. As a disciplinarian, he was very easygoing—never raising a hand to me, and hardly ever raising his voice. I desperately hated to disappoint my father, because I deeply admired him and wanted to be like him.

Maureen (we called her Merm) and I lived with my mother, actress Jane Wyman, in a big white house on South Beverly Glen. I always looked forward to Saturdays when Dad would come and take us to the ranch. Those memories are the best of all, because it was only there, at the ranch, that I could really have my father all to myself. Every Saturday, I would walk down the big circle driveway of Mom's beautiful southern-style mansion and sit on the curb, waiting for Dad to come around the corner from Sunset Boulevard. He lived near the beach, in Pacific Palisades, and he'd drive up Sunset in his big red station wagon, make a right-hand turn on Beverly Glen, follow the curve of the road, and there I'd be, watching and waiting for him.

At the ranch, Dad was always working with his hands, always building—putting up barns or fences or jumps for his horses, cutting horse trails through brush, mending, painting, repairing. I would watch him, awestruck and admiring, as he did the physical chores he enjoyed so much. If he wasn't building, he was splitting wood or working with his jumping horses or teaching Maureen and me how to ride. The best days of my childhood were spent at the ranch—though I often wished he'd take me to a baseball or football game instead (I didn't understand that he avoided such places to keep from being mobbed by fans).

When his chores were done in the late afternoon, we'd go for horseback rides, and then for a ride in a jeep. If it was a really warm day, we'd play tag in the pool. He didn't want us running too fast around the pool, so the rule was that as we scurried around the deck, we always had to stop at each corner and dip one foot into the pool. Because the ranch was watered by a well instead of city water, minerals always clouded the pool.

Dad was an incredibly strong swimmer. In his younger days, he had been a lifeguard at Lowell Park, a rough and dangerous section of the Rock River north of his hometown of Dixon, Illinois. During the summers of 1927 through 1932, he saved seventy-seven people from drowning. So he could not only swim like a fish, he could hold his breath forever. He'd go down in one corner of the pool while Maureen and I were trying to catch him, and because the water was so cloudy, we couldn't find him. Maureen and I would thrash all over the pool, coming up for air three, four, five times, before he'd finally pop up in some other corner. We'd play this game till it was time to go home.

On the way back home, we'd sometimes go via the Pacific Coast Highway, and we'd stop at the Foster's Freeze at the Malibu Pier for some ice cream. They'd serve it up any way you wanted—cup or cone, shake, malt, chocolate dipped, banana split, or a sundae with any topping you could imagine—incredible! Other times, we'd go through the San Fernando Valley, via Ventura Boulevard, over the Sepulveda Pass. We'd roll down the windows and breathe in that wonderful fragrance from the orange groves and apple orchards in the Valley, and we'd stop at a roadside stand—usually the one at Ventura and Topanga—and buy a jug of fresh apple cider.

At the end of the drive, Dad would drop us off with Mom, and we wouldn't see him again until the next Saturday. Sunday night, it was back to boarding school—Chadwick or St. John's Military Academy or Loyola High School. I would endure my days at school, and live for Saturdays at the ranch with my dad.

All four of Ronald Reagan's children—Maureen, Patti, Ron, and I—have been very open and public with our struggles to be as close to our father as we truly wanted to be. Maureen, in her memoir titled *First Father, First Daughter*, talked about how hard it was to get either Dad or Mom to "go below the surface" explanation and tell her why their marriage broke up when she was only seven. Patti spent many years in well-publicized rebellion—frequently to the shock and embarrassment of Ronald and Nancy Reagan. The youngest of the Reagan children, Ron, probably had the fewest problems of all of us in relating to Dad, yet he once told reporter Lou Cannon, "You know, there is something that [Dad] holds back. You get just so far, and then the curtain drops, and you don't go any farther."[4]

Yet whatever our problems in relating to Dad or understanding him, all four of us genuinely love this great man and treasure every memory of our time together with him. All of us except Patti have campaigned for him—and despite her political differences with him, she understands and appreciates the strength, love, and quiet greatness of Ronald Reagan. In 1995, after Dad was diagnosed with Alzheimer's disease, she wrote a book called *Angels Don't Die*, a beautiful tribute to Dad.

So those who criticize my father's defense of the American family are wrong. There was no contradiction between his private life and his public crusades. However imperfectly he achieved it in his own life, his idealized vision of the American family was always before him. "What do we want for ourselves and our children?" he asked an audience at the dedication of the library at Eureka College, September 28, 1967. "Is it enough to have material things? Aren't liberty and morality and integrity and high principles and a sense of responsibility more important?" Throughout his career, he has preached that the American family must remain not merely prosperous, but free and morally strong.

Yes, his childhood was clouded by unhappiness, his first marriage failed, and his relationships with his four children by two marriages were clearly strained at times. Those experiences troubled him deeply because the idea of family was so deeply ingrained in him. The image of the family as a place of belonging and security was burned into Ronald Reagan's soul. Whatever his faults and limitations, Ronald Reagan loved his own family, and he fought for the rights and the vitality of the American family.

FAMILY IS THE FOUNDATION

You and I have a rendezvous with destiny. We will preserve for our children this, the last best hope of man on earth, or we will sentence them to take the first step into a thousand years of darkness. If we fail, at least our children and our children's children can say of us we justified our brief moment here. We did all that could be done.

Ronald Reagan
"A Time for Choosing"
Televised speech on behalf of
presidential candidate Barry Goldwater
October 27, 1964

36

When I was about forty years old, I received an unexpected gift from my dad. It was a package, mailed to me from my father's former business manager, containing two pieces of paper—a letter and a forty-dollar U.S. War Bond. Ronald Reagan, in the name of Michael Edward Reagan, had purchased the bond on April 4, 1945—just a few days after my birth. The letter said that the War Bond was "in celebration of your coming home." Opening that package was a powerfully emotional event in my life. Having spent years doubting my father's love for me, it was a profoundly moving experience to see that bond and picture my father purchasing it and bringing it home to celebrate the fact that I was being added to the family. Here I was, forty years old, still feeling that in relationship with my father and my family, I was *on the outside looking in.*

In all those years, neither Mom nor Dad knew about the struggle that I went through, feeling unlovable and unloved. I never talked to them about it. Mom was not easy to talk to about feelings and personal issues, and I didn't want to wreck my few weekends with my dad by bringing up this kind of unpleasantness. For all his gentleness and kindness as a father, I often felt an emotional distance between us. I know now that Dad loved me all along, but for years I felt disappointed and resentful because my father didn't express a fatherly pride and affection toward me. On some level, I assumed that if my father didn't hug me, it was because there was something wrong with me.

Then one day, the thought hit me: *Mike, when was the last time you hugged your dad?* Answer: I had *never* hugged my dad. He didn't initiate—and neither did I. So I decided the next time I saw my father, I would give him a hug.

That opportunity came in 1991, when my father came to San Diego to make an exclusive appearance on my local show on Radio KSDO. He was on a national book tour for his autobiography, *An American Life.* It was a fascinating experience, interviewing my father about his book. The studio was filled with people from the press—local news crews, *Time* magazine, the *LA Times*, and more. After the interview, Dad and I walked out to the reception area of the radio station—and it hit me: Dad needed a hug.

I went to him right in front of all the station personnel, the reporters, the Secret Service agents, and all, and I wrapped my arms around him and hugged him. I felt him tense up, and he was like, *Whoa! What's going on here, a guy hugging a guy—in front of all these people!* But I didn't let that bother me. I just gave my dad a hug.

Though it didn't seem to do much for my dad at the time, it was a tremendously healing experience for me. I had made a decision that I wasn't going to let my emotions be ruled by the fact that my dad was not a huggy kind of guy. I was through using that as an excuse to be mad at my dad.

To this day, every time I see him, I give Dad a hug hello and a hug good-bye, and he's not only okay with that, but he looks forward to it. These days, because of the Alzheimer's, he doesn't always know my name when I come to visit him, but he knows who I am. I'm the guy who always gives him a hug. When I walk into the room and we see each other, he opens his arms, and we come together, and I *grip* him! And when I leave, he opens his arms, and I hug him good-bye.

I'm glad I finally stopped fuming and agonizing about the problem between my dad and me. I'm glad I finally became part of the solution. And I think the same principle applies to the problems that exist in so many American families today. We have a lot to complain about, a lot to be mad about, and a lot to agonize about as parents, trying to raise healthy kids in America. The government overtaxes families. We see the institution of marriage scorned and ridiculed in our media. We see unmarried and gay couples demanding to be given all the legal rights and privileges of marriage. We see families destroyed by welfare and other liberal social policies. And we see these destructive social experiments being paid for with our money. Here in the Neighborhood, the residential section of our somewhat tarnished Shining City, we're angry. *Righteously* angry.

But anger is not enough. We can't just gripe at the problems, we have to become the solution. We have to take our society back and make it family-friendly once more. America can once again become a gleaming City where families are nurtured and protected, where kids go to good schools with great teachers, and where parents can afford to be parents. Following are some of the solutions we can begin implementing today.

BEWARE OF MISLEADING CHILD ADVOCACY RHETORIC

Liberal child advocacy organizations claim to be the only people on the planet who care about children. "Nobody speaks for children," accuses Ann DeRose of the Fort Myers Children's Action Team. "Children aren't there to represent themselves. If we don't represent them, children's needs are a very easy place to cut money."[5]

And that's what it's really all about, isn't it? Government money. Government-funded childcare. Government-funded healthcare and immunization programs. Government-funded welfare.

Liberal child advocacy spokespeople like Marian Wright Edelman of the Children's Defense Fund have made their careers demanding government money to support their child advocacy organizations. How many children have actually benefited in any direct way from these groups? It seems that the primary function of these organizations is not so much to improve the lives of children as it is to enlarge the budgets and political muscle of their own organizations. I would submit to the Marian Wright Edelmans of the world that it's not enough to shout, "We care about children!" at a Stand for Children rally in Washington, D.C. We have to make sure that families take care of children, not the government. Those who claim to care about our kids while perpetuating a system that harms kids are either deluded or they are exploiting children for their own gain. Either way, they must be stopped.

A good example of how government child advocacy programs fail our kids is the massive child-immunization disaster launched by Marian Wright Edelman's good friend, Hillary Rodham Clinton, in 1994. Hillary devised a costly federal vaccination program to respond to a crisis that never existed. Though the program was sold as a way to target at-risk children—the poor, the uninsured, the underinsured, and Native Americans—these so-called at-risk kids were never truly at risk. They have always had access to free vaccinations through public health clinics—and they were receiving the proper vaccinations without any further help from Uncle Sam and Aunt Hillary.

The fact is, state and local efforts were already assuring that roughly 96 percent of America's children were vaccinated. Yet the Clinton administration in true socialist fashion sought to distribute free vaccine nationwide from a single, centralized, government-run warehouse in New Jersey. When vaccine manufacturers discovered that the White House had not even supplied adequate refrigeration in the warehouse, they warned that the vaccine supplies would likely go stale just sitting on warehouse shelves and become dangerous to kids. Moreover, by placing the entire nation's supply of vaccine in a single storage facility, the government put all of America at risk in the event of a warehouse fire or other catastrophe. When the warehouse idea became such a bureaucratic nightmare that the Clintons finally abandoned it, states such as New York and Texas, which had counted on the federal warehouse being in place, were thrown into a panic, rushing to set up their own makeshift distribution systems.[6]

The result of this debacle was that the vaccine program was delayed for months, forcing thousands of kids who would have otherwise been vaccinated by state and local programs to go unprotected while the Clinton administration tried to get its act together. The *Wall Street Journal* noted,

> There has not been a social program in recent history so badly flawed as [Hillary Clinton's] Vaccine for Children. The administration's initiative is based on misleading information about immunization levels in the U.S. It is determined to create an entitlement even though immunization rates are at record levels. At a time when local health officials have more free vaccine than they can use, it is spending money to set up a government-run delivery service of unknown cost and questionable utility. . . .
>
> In fact, a number of states, including Arkansas, have told the Centers for Disease Control that the Vaccine for Children program will actually hurt immunization efforts by taking time and staff away from their own vaccine initiatives. The Centers for Disease Control is understaffed and cannot keep up with the state and local health officials' demand for technical assistance.[7]

The Clinton administration blew a cool $460 million on a fatally flawed vaccination plan that not only stuck it to the kids, but needled the taxpayers too. The government bought about 23 million doses of oral polio vaccine (41 percent more than needed) and 13 million doses of measles-mumps-rubella vaccine (60 percent more doses than all the unvaccinated children in America). Even the Clintons' usual supporters, such as Senators Dale Bumpers (D-Arkansas) and Ted Kennedy (D-Massachusetts), labeled the vaccination plan as "crazy" and a "train wreck." Yet the Clintons stubbornly clung to their plan, demanding an additional $891 million for Vaccine for Children in the 1996 budget,[8] prompting *Newsday* to observe,

> The Clinton administration's nationwide child immunization program could be viewed as good intentions gone awry. That would be charitable. Realistically, it is a political and administrative failure that is emblematic of a blockheaded commitment to liberal ideology that sometimes characterizes this administration. . . . The Clintons insisted that cost, driven by price gouging by pharmaceutical companies, was the reason many low-

income and uninsured families failed to get their kids shots. In reality, free vaccines already were available through various federal and state programs. . . .

Now a highly critical General Accounting Office study has determined (to almost no one's surprise) that the cost of vaccines isn't a big problem and that the best solution may be an outreach program, increasing parents' awareness of the need to have their children immunized and making clinics more accessible. Amazingly, the administration still clings to its program.[9]

In order for America to truly become the Shining City that Ronald Reagan foresaw, we must have more family, less government. We have to drive out the village chieftains and village idiots who are systematically destroying the future of our kids. We have to make the case to our society that what children need is not more government childcare and welfare, but family care. Everything these "children's defense" advocates want for our children are poor substitutes for what kids really need. In place of fathers, the village chieftains offer food stamps, welfare, and WIC (supplemental nutrition for Women, Infants, and Children). In place of mothers, they offer daycare centers.

Today, the government is more involved in the raising of children than at any other time in our history—and the result is that kids are more abused, more troubled, more neglected, and more mistreated than at any other time in our history. This is not a coincidence. This is a simple cause-and-effect relationship. People who would never dream of putting their dog in a kennel when they go on vacation have no qualms about placing their children with strangers in a "kiddie kennel" day in and day out, five days a week! It's insane! What will they do when these kids develop emotional problems and behavioral problems because they have never bonded, because they feel rejected and unwanted by their parents? Pack them up and send them to the village headshrinker for therapy!

I come back to that statement by the child advocacy activist in Fort Myers, Florida: "Nobody speaks for children." You know what? That is such an insulting statement. And arrogant. And infuriating. Because a lot of people speak for children. I speak for children. You speak for children. Every responsible parent in America speaks for children. We speak for children by working hard, providing for our families, spending time with our kids, and donating time and money to kids through neighborhood programs and national charities. No, we don't go to rallies and scream into bullhorns about who does and does not speak for children. We don't have time to put on a show of our compassion—we're too busy just doing it. We're too busy driving kids to school and piano lessons, volunteering in the youth group at the church or synagogue, coaching Little League, helping out in our local schools or Boys Clubs and Girls Clubs or Big Brothers and Big Sisters. Sorry we can't come to your rally and listen to your speeches, but we're too busy tutoring and baking cookies and hugging and applying Band-Aids and drying tears and listening to kids.

But we speak for the children whenever we can. In fact, I believe we speak most loudly for children by demanding that the government cut spending and balance the budget, so that America's kids won't be facing an 83 percent tax rate when they grow up. And, of course, we speak for children whenever we stand up to these smug, self-righteous activists who claim to be the only people in America who care about kids.

We don't need more *child* advocacy in America. We need *family advocacy*. Only by supporting the family can we make sure that America's kids get the love they need and the care they deserve.

OPEN YOUR HEART AND HOME TO KIDS WHO NEED ADOPTION OR A FOSTER HOME

The liberal village chieftains have a slogan: "Make every child a wanted child." In other words, if a child is unwanted, abort her, kill her, destroy her. Lovely sentiment, don't you think? The fact is, abortion not only destroys the lives of the unborn, but it wreaks havoc on the lives of America's children as well. Abortion cheapens the lives of children, generating the attitude in our society that children are expendable and should be discarded if they get in the way. These cultural attitudes subject children to increasing rates of abuse, sexual exploitation, and child murder—all of which have risen dramatically since *Roe v. Wade* legalized abortion nationwide.

The village idiots stubbornly refuse to acknowledge, even when the fact is staring them in the face, that *every child is already a wanted child* —wanted by someone. Go to any adoption agency and they will tell you that there is a waiting list of eager, loving parents—not just for kids who are physically perfect, but even for kids with Down's syndrome and other physical and mental deformities. America is full of love for children—but the village chieftains would rather sacrifice these children than give them to loving homes.

As a citizen of the Shining City, contact your representatives and support reforms that would make it easier, less risky, and less costly for families to adopt. For example:

- Support legislation that will simplify and streamline adoption procedures for infants and children who have been abandoned by birth parents, and who are stuck in institutional, group, or foster homes.
- Support legislation that will require the government to treat adoptive families with the same rights as birth families, free of intrusion by government agencies.
- Support legislation that will make it easier to terminate parental rights of those who have repeatedly shown a pattern of violence, sexual abuse, drug abuse, or neglect—so that children can more readily be placed in healthy, loving homes.
- Support legislation that will require that voluntary surrender of children for adoption be made final and irrevocable beyond a limited period of time (ideally, no more than three days).
- Support legislation that will require courts to prioritize the best interests of the child above all other considerations in child custody cases—and particularly to favor family environment and emotional bonding over a mere genetic connection. Courts need to recognize that two people are not parents just because they spent twenty minutes together in the backseat of a Chevy.
- Support legislation that will prohibit the consideration of race or ethnicity as a qualification for adopting or fostering children (racial litmus tests have often prevented white couples from adopting nonwhite babies—and the shortage of nonwhite adoptee parents forces these children to remain in institutions rather than be placed in loving families, where kids belong).

As one who is grateful to have been adopted rather than aborted, I encourage you to consider the option of adoption or foster parenthood. I especially encourage you to consider taking on the special problems posed by the few hard-to-place kids in the system—kids who come from tough backgrounds, who are older, who may not be as cute and cuddly as newborns, but who need the love and the security of a family as much as any kid.

Here is a special opportunity for single parents or older couples who are looking to adopt: If you are up to the challenge, check into the possibility of providing a home for a kid who, at age five or nine or eleven, is stuck in the bureaucratic system. Consider making a place in your home for a child who has never known a home. Get counseling from adoption professionals and child psychologists so you are prepared for the challenges—and then, if you are ready and willing, open your heart and your home.

UPHOLD THE SANCTITY AND THE DEFINITION OF MARRIAGE AND FAMILY

Write letters to newspapers and legislators, call talk shows, and support pro-family candidates. Challenge the growing notion in our society that the definitions of *marriage* and *family* can be stretched and distorted in any direction that happens to appeal to people at any given moment. Marriage is the legal union of one man and one woman, no more, no less. Oppose all efforts to redefine family relationships in terms of *spousal equivalents* and similar sociobabble terminology. There is no equivalent to marriage but marriage.

DEMAND THAT GOVERNMENT REVISE THE TAX CODE TO MAKE FAMILIES AFFORDABLE

And that includes all families—birth families, adoptive families, and foster families. The present tax system punishes families and penalizes marriage.

The marriage penalty in the present tax code is particularly unfair to working married women. The first $16,000 earned by the primary bread-winner—usually the husband—is taxed at progressively higher rates. The earnings of the secondary breadwinner—usually the wife—are taxed at the rate where the primary breadwinner's earnings left off. In other words, instead of having the first $16,000 of her earnings exempt as her husband does, she starts out paying the higher rates on every dollar she earns. So, for example, if she earns $20,000 a year and files jointly with her husband, she will pay about $3,000 in taxes (she'd pay even more as married filing separately). But if she were single filing as an individual (which, being married, she is not allowed to do), her tax would only be $1,500. That's how the tax code penalizes marriage. (These examples refer only to income tax, and do not include Social Security taxes.)

High tax rates force both parents to work just to pay the government, and make child rearing and adoption too expensive. In the Shining City on a Hill, tax rates are low and both the federal budget and family budgets are balanced.

DEFEND GENUINE COMPASSION AND HEALTHY FAMILIES—NOT MORE GOVERNMENT SPENDING

When you talk over the back fence or by the watercooler with friends, neighbors, and coworkers, be bold and outspoken about the solutions we need to implement as a society. We have spent hundreds of billions of dollars over the last thirty years on government-run welfare, yet our social problems have gotten worse, not better. More money is not the answer. More government is not the answer. The answer is the American family itself. What children need is something money can't buy, something government can't provide. Children need loving hands, understanding hearts, listening ears, and they can't find these things in a government office. They can only find them in a family.

In the name of compassion, the Great Society programs of the welfare state fed a generation on food stamps and WIC, yet the children in these programs continued to starve for hope, care, and parental love. Why? Because these children didn't need a government program. They needed a *family*—and the welfare state provided dollar incentives for families to break up. Women received more benefits as single mothers, so the fathers of their children were driven away by the "compassionate" rules of the welfare bureaucracy. The rhetoric of helping mothers and children sounded so good, but the results were disastrous.

In government and society, as in all other areas of life, the road to the abyss is paved with good intentions. What good are good intentions if they produce a society with the highest illegitimacy rate, the most one-parent families, the most murders, the most abortions, the highest infant mortality

45

rate, the most incarcerated children, and the most children on government aid of any industrialized nation in the world? If that isn't a description of hell on earth, I don't know what is.

Tell your friends and neighbors, "If you do what you always did, you'll get what you always got. We've tried liberal 'solutions' for thirty years, and look what we've got to show for it. Let's demand that government get on the side of social restoration for a change. Let's focus on solving America's problems by raising up and empowering the family."

DEMAND REFORM OF DIVORCE LAWS

Let me tell you about a big mistake Ronald Reagan made. As governor of California, he signed the first no-fault divorce law in America, and it quickly became a model for divorce laws throughout the nation. I know that at the time, his goal was a conservative one: Get government out of people's lives. If a couple want a divorce, they shouldn't have to justify their reasons to some judge in a courtroom. I know the issue of divorce was not something he approached lightly.

The breakup of Dad's first marriage to my mother, Jane Wyman, was something he never sought, and something that hurt him deeply. It was definitely *not* the kind of casual Hollywood divorce you hear about so often. His mother, Nelle, was a deeply religious woman who brought up her sons in the conservative Disciples of Christ Church, and she instilled a strong faith and moral sense of responsibility in them. Ronald Reagan grew up viewing divorce as unthinkable. There were undoubtedly many factors leading to the breakup of my parents' marriage, but the catalyst for the divorce was probably the unresolved pain and grief that followed the death of my younger sister Christina. She was born four months prematurely in June 1947 and died three days later. Dad was in the hospital, literally fighting for his life with pneumonia when Christina was born (it took him four months to recover), and I suspect Mom unconsciously faulted him for not being there when she needed his support. Statistically, it's very common for marriages to break up after the death of a child.

Maybe his own divorce played a role in his decision to sign California's no-fault divorce law; maybe not. But I can tell you this: Looking back over the devastation caused by easy divorce laws, I truly believe Ronald Reagan would make a different decision on no-fault divorce today. The family is the foundation of our society, and when we permit the careless destruction of the family, we hasten the destruction of our Shining City. We are witnessing that destruction right now. Here are some of the disturbing facts according to analysis by the U.S. Census Bureau:

- The proportion of two-parent families in America fell from 87.1 percent in 1970 to 71.9 percent in 1990 (from 89.9 percent to 77.4 percent among white families and from 64.3 percent to 39.4 percent among African-American families).
- The rate of growth of female-headed single-parent families (the family category representing the highest concentration of poverty in America) accelerated from 3 percent a year during the Reagan 1980s to 4 percent a year in the first four years of the 1990s.

These growth rates of family destruction and poverty are compounding like a vicious inflation rate in our society, promising a catastrophe for American society in the not-too-distant future.

As families dissolve at an ever-increasing rate across our land, we can expect to see an increase in intensity in today's social crises—the teen pregnancy crisis, the juvenile crime crisis, the drug crisis, the education crisis. The evidence shows that all these terrible plagues in our society are actually subcrises of the one fundamental crisis in America—the crisis of broken families. Following is a sampling of that evidence.

Children of single-parent families have lower grade point averages and poorer classroom attendance than the general population. They're twice as likely to drop out of high school as kids from two-parent families. Daughters in single-parent homes are 2.5 times as likely to become teenage moms. And crime? Studies show that 70 percent of jailed juveniles come from single-parent households, though single-parent households make up only 28 percent of all American households. Three-fourths of all teenage murderers were raised in single-parent homes.[10]

So-called no-fault divorce laws gained in popularity throughout the 1960s, 1970s, and 1980s, and it is no coincidence that the divorce rate nearly doubled over those very decades. Before that time, couples had to show cause—such as desertion, cruelty, or adultery—for a divorce action. Today, breaking a marriage contract is little more than a ribbon-cutting ceremony—snip, snip, and you're on your way.

Divorce law is a state-by-state issue, so it is at the level of our state legislators and governors where divorce policy must be affected. As a society, we need to make it harder for people to destroy their families. We need to replace the permissiveness of our "no-fault" society with an expectation of accountability, responsibility, and caring for children, who are the innocent victims of divorce. Divorce causes incalculable pain to children—why should it be painless for adults? We could help couples put the brakes on their downhill slide to family destruction by building a few guardrails into our divorce laws:

- Making cooling-off periods mandatory.
- Categorizing all property as family property, so that the welfare of children would be adequately weighed in the distribution of assets.
- Dismantling no-fault divorce laws and requiring couples to show cause or fault for divorce.
- Reinstating fault as a requirement for determining the terms of a divorce settlement.

None of these provisions would prevent divorce per se, but they would give couples pause on the way to the divorce court and force parents to consider the needs of their children before they push the plunger and blow their family sky-high.

The religious community has a crucial role to play in rolling back the tide of divorce. One national movement that is doing something about the problem is Marriage Savers, which began in the central California community of Modesto in 1986. "In this ministry, there is zero tolerance for divorce," says Pastor Michael Douglass, one of the founders of the movement. "If there's any doubt in someone's mind that divorce is not an option, I won't marry them." That's the position of over a hundred pastors of some sixty Modesto-area churches that take part in Marriage Savers, plus pastors and churches in dozens of other communities where the Marriage Savers concept has spread. During the ten years the organization has operated in the Stanislaus County community of Modesto, the county's divorce rate has plummeted 40 percent.

The Marriage Savers program puts couples through a demanding "prenuptial boot camp" of counseling and seminars on subjects ranging from communication skills to conflict resolution to family budgets to sexual fulfillment in marriage. Couples agree to a minimum four-month waiting period and abstaining from premarital sex. They also take personality inventories that compare their answers to questions in thirteen categories. Over time, these inventories have proved to be accurate indicators of marital compatibility. About one in ten couples who undergo the boot camp decide to call off the wedding, and a marriage that never was beats a divorce any day, especially if children are involved.[11]

As a society that claims to care about kids, it's time we start speaking the truth about divorce. I'm not saying that divorce is always avoidable. In some cases, where there is abuse or other risk to the child, divorce may actually protect the child. In most cases, however, divorce is the result of selfishness, stubbornness, immaturity, and irresponsibility. I'm not saying divorced people are bad people. Hey, I've been divorced and my parents were divorced, so I know what divorce is about for both kids and adults. Take it from one who knows: Divorce stinks. We need to discourage it as much as possible.

RENEW YOUR COMMITMENT TO YOUR MARRIAGE AND YOUR FAMILY

If you are thinking about adultery, separation, or divorce, stop! Think it over. Think about your kids. Think about the hurts and problems that separate you from your mate. Are they insoluble? Or could it be that you haven't tried hard enough to make your relationship work? Have you looked at your marital problems from every conceivable angle? Have you sought counseling? Have you used the counselor's office as a place to gain insight and solve problems, or have you used it as a place to unload your grievances and justify yourself?

According to the *Washington Times*, a 1951 survey showed that 51 percent of Americans agreed with the statement, "Parents who don't get along should not stay together for the children." When that question was asked again in 1985, 86 percent agreed.[12] Let me ask you this: What's wrong with staying together for the children? What better reason could two people have for keeping a marriage together than for the sake of the emotional health and security of their children?! Good grief, people! What's wrong with loving your kids enough to give them a home, even if it costs you some work, some sacrifice, some pain?

I know the words *obligation* and *responsibility* sound archaic to our ears today, but I assure you, they are as valid now as they have ever been. And you have an *obligation* and a *responsibility* to keep your family together and, if possible, make the marriage better. Don't make your kids pay for your mistakes.

If you are considering divorce, understand that what you do isn't just about you. It's about your kids. It's about the example you set for them and the kind of emotional security you build for them. And it's about your responsibility to the society you live in. Are you going to contribute to the decline of our society or help to rebuild the Shining City? If we are going to make it as a nation, then all of us must make a renewed commitment to strengthen our marriages and protect the integrity of our families.

In June 1971, I married a young woman who was eighteen years old and fresh out of high school. I was twenty-six, and no more mature than she was. The marriage took place in Hawaii, and while Mom and Maureen were there to help plan the wedding, Dad didn't attend. I was very hurt by that. But just a few days before the wedding, I received a letter from Dad. It was, in fact, the first letter he ever wrote me. Here's what he told me:

Dear Mike:

You've heard all the jokes that have been rousted around by all the "unhappy marrieds" and cynics. Now, in case no one has suggested it, there is another viewpoint. You have entered into the most meaningful relationship there is in all human life. It can be whatever you decide to make it.

Some men feel their masculinity can only be proven if they play out in their own life all the locker-room stories, smugly confident that what a wife doesn't know won't hurt her. The truth is, somehow, way down inside, without her ever finding lipstick on the collar or catching a man in the flimsy excuse of where he was till three A.M., a wife does know, and with that knowing, some of the magic of this relationship disappears. There are more men griping about marriage who kicked the whole thing away themselves than there can ever be wives deserving of blame.

There is an old law of physics that you can only get out of a thing as much as you put in it. The man who puts into the marriage only half of what he owns will get that out. Sure, there will be moments when you will see someone or think back on an earlier time and you will be challenged to see if you can still make the grade, but let me tell you how really great is the challenge of proving your masculinity and charm with one woman for the rest of your life. Any man can find a twerp here and there who will go along with cheating, and it doesn't take all that much manhood. It does take quite a man to remain attractive and to be loved by a woman who has heard him snore, seen him unshaven, tended him while he was sick, and washed his dirty underwear. Do that and keep her still feeling a warm glow and you will know some very beautiful music.

If you truly love a girl, you shouldn't ever want her to feel, when she sees you greet a secretary or a girl you both know, that humiliation of wondering if she was someone who caused you to be late coming home, nor should you want any other woman to be able to meet your wife and know she was smiling behind her eyes as she looked at her, the woman you love, remembering this was the woman you rejected even momentarily for her favors.

Mike, you know better than many what an unhappy home is and what it can do to others. Now you have a chance to make it come out the way it should. There is no greater happiness for a man than approaching a door at the end of a day knowing someone on the other side of that door is waiting for the sound of his footsteps.

Love, Dad.

P.S. You'll never get in trouble if you say "I love you" at least once a day.

The letter was straight from Dad's heart—honest and old-fashioned. I cried when I read those words, and I reread that letter several more times during the honeymoon. That marriage didn't last.

But four years later, on November 7, 1975, I married Colleen, and she has been my friend, my lover, my cheerleader, my spiritual inspiration, my prayer partner, my business partner, and the mother of my two children. I don't know where I would be today without her. I have committed myself to living out the wise advice from my father's letter every day of my married life with Colleen. I guarantee you, just as I have promised Colleen, this marriage is for keeps. It's for life.

I truly believe that none of us live in isolation from the rest of society. What you do in the privacy of your home sends ripples out into the neighborhood and the nation. Your attitude and behavior toward your marriage, your mate, and your kids affect the society we all live in. So be a good citizen of the Shining City. Make a commitment to keep your family healthy, secure, and intact—and keep that commitment.

The family is the foundation of society. When the family is finished, America is finished. Only when the American family is strong will the Shining City on a Hill be truly secure.

CHAPTER THREE

A City
of Knowledge
and Wisdom

THE HIGH COST
OF BAD EDUCATION

Four years ago I didn't know precisely every duty of this office, and not too long ago, I learned about some new ones from the first graders of Corpus Christi School in Chambersburg, Pennsylvania. Little Leah Kline was asked by her teacher to describe my duties. She said: "The President goes to meetings. He helps the animals. The President gets frustrated. He talks to other Presidents." How does wisdom begin at such an early age?

Ronald Reagan
Acceptance Speech
Republican National Convention
Dallas, Texas, August 23, 1984

The purpose of an educational institution is to teach not only knowledge, but also wisdom.

Ronald Reagan
Eureka College Library Dedication Speech
September 28, 1967

A few years ago, I took my son, Cameron, to a California public middle school in Sherman Oaks, to be tested for attention deficit disorder. While I was there, I decided to check into the possibility of enrolling him in that school. So I sat down with the principal and talked with her about the programs offered there. We had a pleasant and informative visit, but near the end of our conversation she dropped a bombshell.

"If you decide to enroll your son at our school," she said, "there's one thing we ask you to be aware of."

"What's that?"

"We would encourage you to make sure your son goes to the bathroom before coming to school, and waits to use the bathroom until after school."

"Excuse me?" I asked. I thought she was kidding.

"We don't like the children going to the school rest rooms," the principal continued, "because it's not safe in there. The gangs have taken over the rest rooms. If you look at the rest rooms, you'll see they're covered with graffiti, inside and out, because the gangs have marked those rest rooms as their turf. They do their drugs in there, and it's just not safe for the schoolchildren to use the rest rooms during lunch break and recess."

She wasn't kidding. I couldn't believe it. I wondered, *Who's in charge of the public school system? The gangs?*

We kept Cameron in his private school. But if we had decided to send him to the public school, I would have made sure that he and all the other kids in the school could use the bathroom anytime they needed to. If necessary, I would have volunteered time from work to patrol the rest rooms, and I would have encouraged other parents to volunteer, and together we would make those rest rooms safe for kids and dangerous for druggies and gangsters.

We are the parents, we are the taxpayers; the schools belong to us, and we can't wait for the government to do it all. The school system is not a baby-sitting service, it's an educational institution, and it exists to prepare our children for life. It's up to us to be involved in the PTA, the school board meetings, the playground, the classrooms, and if need be, even the rest rooms. We need to be involved in the schools for the sake of our children.

The decline of America's education system has been gradual but steady since the early 1960s. Hardly anyone noticed as test scores began to slip, as school discipline grew lax, as taxpayers spent more and more while their children got less and less of an education. But Ronald Reagan noticed. As long ago as the mid 1970s, Ronald Reagan noticed that the quality of education was deteriorating, and he put his finger on the fundamental problem:

increasing control and interference at the federal level. He understood the principle expressed so long ago by George Washington: "Like fire, government is at best a dangerous servant, and at worst a fearful master." In his speech "To Restore America," March 31, 1976, he said,

> In America we created at the local level and administered at the local level for many years the greatest public school system in the world. Now through something called federal aid to education, we have something called federal interference, and education has been the loser. Quality has declined as federal intervention has increased. . . . Control of education should be returned to local school districts.

There is not one sentence, not one word, not even one comma or apostrophe in the Constitution that gives federal government authority over education in America. If you think I'm wrong, read the Constitution for yourself and show me. Washington interference in education is a recent development in our history—not a constitutional power. In order to get the government out of education, all we have to do is return to the principles this nation was founded on.

Scholastic Aptitude Test scores were steadily rising in America until 1965, and then they began to fall steeply. Is it mere coincidence that 1965 was also the year Lyndon Johnson's Elementary and Secondary Education Act (ESEA) federalized America's public schools? Reasonable people would be inclined to think that maybe, just maybe, the federal government *is* the problem! Yet the response of the education establishment, the teachers' unions, and President Clinton is to propose *more* of what got us into this mess in the first place! More federal control. More federal spending. More federal programs. Instead of returning our public schools to local control so they can become great once more, the only solution the education establishment and liberal politicians can come up with is to spend more money.

In his 1997 State of the Union speech, Bill Clinton proposed a whole slate of new education initiatives. Topping the list is his $2.45 billion program to send a corps of "paid volunteers" into the schools to teach reading. Could someone suggest to Bill Clinton that instead of propping up a failed educational system with paid noneducators, perhaps we should simply fix the system and make it work again?! Kids used to learn how to read in school, back in the days before there was a Department of Education, and kids can still learn to read in school without expensive "volunteers" if we would only return to what has worked in the past.

Then there's Bill Clinton's proposal that we spend more federal money connecting every American high school to the Internet. Simple question: "Why?" Most schools in America already have computers and phone lines. If those computers have modems, they are ready to go on-line. There are already low-cost, school-oriented Internet access services in most communities, so access is not a problem. Why do we need a *federal* school Internet program, when schools can already get info-wired very cheaply without help from Washington?

I have no problem with kids learning on-line—as long as there is adequate supervision to keep adolescent web surfers out of (*ahem!*) certain web sites. Fact is, I would love to see kids logging on to my website at www.reagan.com, because it is one of the most informative, educational sites on the World Wide Web. It's not only packed with the latest hot topics in the news, but with downloadable history such as the Federalist Papers, the Declaration of Independence, the Constitution, the great speeches of Ronald Reagan, plus links to other informative sites. But face it, most of what kids need to get out of school is found right in their own classrooms and school library, not on the Internet. Let's not be so technodazzled that we forget what real learning is all about. Above all, let's not make a federal case about it. If schools want to plug into the Internet, fine, but not with dollars from Washington.

These are just two of a whole host of programs Bill Clinton offers in his scheme to pump an additional $50 billion into an already overpriced education system, and that amounts to a two-thirds increase in the federal takeover of our kids' learning. According to a 1995 report prepared by Congressmen Pete Hoekstra, Mark Neumann, Sam Brownback, and Mark Sauder, the Washington education bureaucracy consists of 760 separate programs. Only 3.6 percent of these 760 programs are science-related, 1.8 percent are reading-related, and 1.1 percent are math-related. At the same time, these programs spend federal education dollars on such projects as closed captioning for TV shows (including such important "educational" shows as *Baywatch, All My Children,* and *Ricki Lake*) and lurid sex-ed videos like *Hot, Sexy, and Safer.*

We must demand of our leaders, "Stop dumping more money into a broken educational system. Cut out what doesn't work. Restore what used to work. Fix what's broken. We can't afford bad education anymore. We can't afford it as taxpayers, as parents, or as a society. Make good education affordable again."

A report in *Investor's Business Daily* shows exactly what kind of education you get when you only throw money at the problem. The Financial Control Board for the city of Washington, D.C., conducted a study of the city's public schools titled "Children in Crisis: A Report on the Failure of D.C.'s Schools." The city spent a whopping $7,655 per student during the 1994–1995 school year—26 percent more than the national average. Much of that money went to administrative overhead. For example, the school superintendent's office in D.C. outspent the superintendents' offices in neighboring Fairfax County, Montgomery County, and the city of Baltimore *combined*. Yet test scores of D.C. students were more than 20 percent below the national mean, and over half of D.C. students dropped out before reaching their junior year in high school. The study found that the *longer* a student remains in school, the *less* likely he or she is to succeed in life. In other words, that Cadillac-priced D.C. education actually does more harm than good!

Awash with funding yet shockingly dilapidated, D.C. schools deploy metal detectors and armed guards to quell violence in these educational war zones, yet are chronically short of such basic school necessities as books, paper, pencils, crayons, toilet paper, and even teachers. During the rains in February 1997, students at Tyler Elementary School in Southeast Washington were sent to makeshift classes in other schools and nearby churches because water from a leaky roof drenched most of the classrooms. Many D.C. students have never been to such national treasures in their own city as the Smithsonian Institution or the Library of Congress—because there's no money for field trips.

"The school system has ample resources to educate children. It's the management of resources and the lack of any plan or guide on how to use those resources that is the problem," explains Jim Ford, former staff director of the D.C. Council's Education and Libraries Committee, in an interview with the *Washington Post*. Where does all that money go? Some of it goes to graft, political payoffs, and mismanagement—and a lot of it is soaked up in salaries paid to people who have little or nothing to do with the process of educating children. In 1979, the D.C. school system had 113,000 students and 511 workers in the central office. By 1992, the school system had lost 33,000 students—about a quarter of its student body—yet the number of central office workers had nearly doubled, to 967 workers—clerks, secretar-

ies and administrative assistants, coordinators, directors, deputy superintendents, assistant superintendents, assistant directors, and on and on. This is
what you get when you throw money at a bad education system.

Are there solutions to these problems? You bet! In fact, Republicans in
the 104th Congress tried to implement one such solution—school choice—
in 1996. The House passed a plan to create scholarships for low-income
children that would have allowed them to attend the school of their
choice—public, private, or parochial. Who blocked the plan on the Senate
side? Senator Ted Kennedy. He sent his kids to private schools; President
Clinton sends his daughter to a private school; almost every liberal politician in Washington sends his or her kids to private schools. But the poor
children of Washington, D.C., are condemned by the liberal elite to the
squalor, crime, and failure of the D.C. public school system.[1]

Government education represents an ocean of money that is drained
out of American taxpayers and sloshed into elementary schools, secondary
schools, state universities, and community colleges. All that money has
made the two largest teachers' unions—the National Education Association
(NEA) and the American Federation of Teachers (AFT)—the most powerful
political lobbies in America. They use their political muscle to wring gobs of
money from the federal treasury, and those federal dollars go to buy still
more political muscle for the unions. It's a vicious cycle of power that keeps
the education establishment firmly in control of the education agenda in
America while locking out parents who pay the taxes and whose kids' futures are at stake.

And so it grows. If money were the answer, America would have the
best educational system in the world. But America doesn't have the best,
only the most expensive. Most of that money simply fails to "trickle down"
to the kids. It buys more administrative salaries, funds research, and gener-
ates experimental programs—but it does not hire more teachers or purchase
books, computers, and supplies for the classroom. The facts clearly show
that pouring *more* money into our education problems is like trying to put
out a fire by pouring more gasoline on it:

- The U.S. already spends more on public education than any other
  industrialized nation—roughly $240 billion a year—yet ranks near the
  bottom in surveys of student achievement. Today, 30 percent of all
  students entering college must take remedial education classes.

- Private schools (such as Catholic schools) spend roughly half as much per student as public schools (about $2,800 per private school pupil compared with $5,300 per pupil in the public schools), yet private school students routinely outperform public school students on standardized tests.

- Average reading proficiency of fourth graders has declined steadily ever since Jimmy Carter created the Department of Education so that today roughly 40 percent of fourth graders fail to meet basic reading standards.

- As federal spending on education has gone up, Scholastic Aptitude Test (SAT) scores have gone down. Before the federal government intruded into the education process, SAT verbal scores were showing steady, gradual improvement. In 1952, the average SAT verbal score was 476; ten years later, in 1962, it had edged up two points to 478. Then in 1965, Lyndon Johnson pushed through his massive Elementary and Secondary Education Act (ESEA), which brought the federal government into public schools in a big way. Five years later, in 1970, SAT verbal score averages showed a steep drop to 460. By 1980, SAT verbal scores declined to an average of 424; by 1994, it settled to 423.

- In the twenty-two-year period from 1972 to 1994, the number of students scoring higher than 750 on the SAT verbal test dropped from 2,817 to 1,438—*even though 28,000 more students took the test in 1994 than in 1972!* On average, U.S. students score worse in math than students from all other large countries except Spain.

- Title I of LBJ's ESEA of 1965 was intended to help the children of the poor learn to read through remedial education. After spending more than 120 billion dollars over three decades, illiteracy was worse, not better, under Title I. The program was renewed again and again by Congress, despite a 1974 Rand Corporation analysis of Title I that declared, "Without exception, all of the large surveys of the large national compensatory education programs have shown no beneficial results on average as measured by achievement tests or IQ scores." Despite the spectacular, costly failure of Title I, Congress reauthorized ESEA in 1995, including $6.9 billion for a so-called New Title I that stresses experimental teaching methods sure to produce even greater illiteracy.[2]

The dumbing-down of the schools by the federal education establishment is a disaster not only for our kids, but also for the future of our nation. As John Gaston, former director of the Human Engineering Laboratory in Fort Worth, observed, "The present generation knows less than its parents. All of our laboratories around the country are recording a drop in vocabulary of one percent a year. In all our fifty years of testing, it has never happened before. . . . Can you imagine what a drop in knowledge of one percent a year for thirty years could do to our civilization?"[3]

The government policies and programs that fatten the wallets of the education establishment do not deposit more knowledge and wisdom in the minds of our young people. With all this evidence, why would President Clinton propose yet another federal education program to the tune of $2.8 billion?

Clinton himself gave us the answer in a speech before the NEA: "I won't forget who brought me to the White House." In other words, it's a political payoff. The NEA's political action committee donated $5.5 million to the Clinton war chest in 1996, and sent more members to the Democratic National Convention in Chicago (405 delegates and alternates) than any other independent organization. He owes the teachers' unions big time—and the unions always collect on political debts.[4]

A study conducted by Caroline Hoxby of Harvard University shows that student dropout rates are higher in unionized schools than in nonunionized schools. The study, "How Teachers' Unions Affect Education Production," appeared in the August 1996 issue of the *Quarterly Journal of Economics*. Some of the observations and conclusions of that study include:

- Teachers' unions have gained enormous power in the last three decades; the number of students in unionized public schools has grown from 1 percent in 1960 (when collective bargaining by teachers was illegal in many states) to 43 percent in 1992.
- Per-pupil spending is 12 percent higher in union versus nonunion school districts.
- The student dropout rate is 2.3 percent higher in union versus nonunion schools.[5]
- According to Richard Vedder of the Center for the Study of American Business, the productivity of public school employees in the 1990s is about half what it was in the 1950s, although overall output per

American worker has tripled during the same period. In 1950, there were 1.55 nonteaching public school employees per 100 students; by 1993, there were 5.28.[6]

Teachers' unions claim to be focused on helping kids learn, yet the evidence shows that union involvement tends to have a negative rather than a positive impact on the learning process. Why? Unions look out for the welfare of their members, not the children. Unions create pressure to divert school resources into the things they care about—larger employee rolls, higher pay, easier working conditions—not better student performance.

It's time we realize that the interests of the education establishment and the interests of children are not necessarily parallel. Let the unions look out for the interests of their members. That's fine, that's their job. As parents, however, it's our job to look out for the welfare of our kids.

THE LITTLE RED SCHOOLHOUSE IN THE VILLAGE

Just as surely as we seek to put our financial house in order and rebuild our nation's defenses, so too we seek to . . . end the manipulation of our schoolchildren by utopian planners.

Ronald Reagan
Speech before the
Conservative Political Action Conference
Washington, D.C., March 20, 1981

You know what they're teaching kids in school these days? They're teaching kids to be more "tolerant" of the Big Bad Wolf.

Oops. Scratch that. Can't say *bad*. That's too judgmental. Let's just call him the Big Culturally Deprived Wolf. After all, he's misunderstood. He's confused. He doesn't know any better. That's why he wants to eat those nice little pigs. We need to understand him and be nice to him. If we show him we like him, he'll learn to like himself more, and he won't be so mean to the Three Little Pigs.

That's what kids are learning in school today. It's called "diversity training." In these exercises, children are encouraged to role-play or rewrite a classic fairy tale—but with a twist: The students are to put themselves in the role of the wolf in "The Three Little Pigs." They are told to identify with the villain of the story and to try to understand the circumstances that made him so nasty. Maybe the wolf didn't really mean to blow down the pigs' houses—maybe he just had a cold and sneezed too hard. Maybe he ate little pigs because he was from a poor neighborhood and couldn't afford to eat at McDonald's. The message kids take away is that wolves are victims of circumstance; they may be misguided, but they are not bad; they are not responsible for their actions, and even wolves have rights.

This exercise gives kids a basis for "understanding" the behavior of graffiti taggers, gangsters, muggers, terrorists, thieves, drug dealers, and other people who do unpleasant things. The classic fairy tales, with their good-versus-evil moral absolutes, have been stood on their heads. Through these exercises, kids learn that there are *no* moral absolutes, *no* good guys and bad guys, *no* right or wrong, *no* personal responsibility or accountability. There are only some poor misguided predators in need of tolerance, inclusion, understanding, and a government program or two.

Welcome to the little red schoolhouse in the village.

This exercise is typical of a relatively new approach to education that has rapidly become entrenched throughout the nation's schools: outcome-based education (OBE). The godfather of outcome-based education (and the man who coined the term) is Dr. William Spady, director of the High Success Network on Outcome-Based Education in Eagle, Colorado. He once predicted that America's schools would soon be totally changed from everything you and I remember from our school days—and his prediction is rapidly coming to pass. OBE is taking over our classrooms so fast that we may soon see the end of grades, traditional curricula, semesters, honor rolls, and other features of education as we once knew them. OBE deliberately saws across the grain of all the beliefs and assumptions that once formed the foundation for American education: traditional Judeo-Christian values and absolutes, local control, respect for family privacy, and an emphasis on instilling knowledge and skills rather than ideology.

OBE is not an educational experiment being conducted in a few schools here and there. It is a national education reform movement and is already being implemented to some degree in virtually every state in the union. Odds are, your local public school is already heavily influenced by OBE. Whereas traditional education placed its emphasis on cognitive or thinking skills—the three Rs of reading, 'riting, and 'rithmetic—OBE dramatically de-emphasizes thinking skills and focuses on attitudes, self-esteem, and affective (emotional) learning. The main thrust of OBE is the child's worldview, attitudes, and feelings, and its goal is to produce a generation of politically correct global citizens.

Another feature of OBE is that it replaces traditional phonics with a "whole-word" or "whole-language" approach to reading. Common sense tells us that our language was designed to be decoded as a series of phonetic units called syllables. The outcomers have scrapped common sense in favor of an approach that supposedly teaches kids to recognize whole words rather than decode the words, syllable by syllable. Obviously, when you and I read as adults, we read in a whole-word way. We don't have to decode words like *character* or *president* when we see them because repetition has enabled us to recognize them at a glance. But a child needs to be given the language decoder—phonics—at the beginning of the learning process or he/she will never be able to recognize multisyllabic words. If a child is only taught to recognize whole words and is never given a language decoder, that child will grow into adulthood knowing nothing but a few common one- or two-syllable words. The substitution of a whole language approach in place of phonics is widely blamed for pulling California's fourth-grade reading scores down to forty-eighth in the nation—just above Mississippi.[7]

Outcome-based education also stresses group activities, cooperative activities, and coercive learning strategies instead of individual achievement and initiative. For example, a class will often be divided into groups of five or six children. The children in each group work together as a unit, and all the children in the group receive a single collective grade. This process suppresses the individuality of the higher achievers, and enables the lower achievers (and even the nonachievers) to take a free ride and get a free grade. This collectivist approach to education is designed to channel a child's worldview, to discourage a child's competitive drive, to cause the child to see the group as more important than the individual, and to introduce the concept of global cooperation instead of individual sovereignty and self-reliance.

Outcome-based education was supposedly designed to provide a safety net for children determined to be "at risk" for failure. The problem is that OBE does not accomplish this noble end by improving the child's ability to compete. Rather, it does so by removing all risk of failure. Imagine saying to a pole-vaulter, "Take your pole, go over to that sand pit, and vault away. And don't worry about failing. We took away the bar!" Dr. Spady himself once said that the reason so many American children fail in school is "because we make failure available." In other words, if we just remove all possibility of failure from the schools, voilà! Instant 100 percent success!

Read through OBE literature and you will find again and again such phrases as "consistent, high expectations of 100 percent success" and "every child can learn." The goal of OBE is literally "100 percent student outcome success." The outcomers have decreed that *no* student will *ever* fail in school! How do these OBE utopians expect to completely eliminate the risk of failure in our schools? Obviously, there is only one way this can be accomplished: Completely do away with all objective measurements and performance standards. Once success or failure can no longer be measured, all risk of failure will have been removed. Failure has become unavailable. And that's exactly what the outcomers propose.

OBE has solved the problem that has plagued educators since the mid-1960s—steadily declining student performance and test scores. We simply replace grades and test scores with subjective "outcomes." The problem is, when nobody fails, nobody succeeds. When you remove the possibility of failure, you remove incentives and motivation. Genuine learning stops. The future of our children and of our City on a Hill is riding on a vast and very shaky educational experiment.

OBE also enables the indoctrination of our children on a national scale. Examine the outcomes that educators look for in any OBE program. They are drenched with a liberal political agenda—political correctness, socialism, radical environmentalism, multiculturalism, and the promotion of a one-world government. Since the education establishment can set the education agenda for the entire nation through the Department of Education, OBE can be implemented on a nationwide basis rather than state-by-state, district-by-district, school-by-school. We have come to an extremely dangerous moment in our history in which government has acquired the power to dictate mass political and social opinion through centralized education.

Our founding fathers foresaw the danger of giving the compulsory power of the state to any one religious group, which is why they guaranteed freedom of belief, thought, speech, and conscience in the First Amendment to the Constitution. Today, the liberal social utopians have set themselves up as America's new "state church," trampling our freedom of conscience by ramming down our throats their own doctrines of political correctness, multiculturalism, radical environmentalism, bans on "insensitive speech," "values-neutral" sex education, and campus contraception. These doctrines are truly religious in nature, reflecting a worldview that is agnostic or New Age–influenced and actively hostile to Judeo-Christian traditions and beliefs.

Under OBE, kids are taught to question the values and beliefs they are taught at home. Patriotism is undermined in OBE, because love of country runs counter to being a good global citizen. Whereas you and I were taught that American culture is the great melting pot, kids today are taught that America is a balkanized collection of distinct cultures. Whereas you and I were taught to be good stewards of the world God created, students today are taught that animals have rights and forests have feelings.

Reading OBE literature is like entering a foreign culture, where the outcomers babble in such incomprehensible jargon as "clarity of focus around culminating exit outcomes of significance," and "expansion of available time and resources so that all students succeed in reaching the exit outcomes," and "reaching the transformational zone." Outcomers don't teach, they "deliver instruction." They don't set achievement goals; they "develop performance indicators." They don't plan lessons and curricula; they "design learning experiences and determine instructional strategies." They don't give tests and grade performance; they "document results and determine advancement." This kind of jargon helps to keep outsiders like us in the dark.

OBE is the centerpiece of Bill and Hillary Clinton's Goals 2000 scheme for nationalizing, centralizing, and directing all aspects of education from Washington, D.C. Though the public face the Clintons put on Goals 2000 involves only such noncontroversial features as school safety, discipline, and high standards, Hillary and her friends in the liberal education elite are bent on a Washington-based takeover of every aspect of our children's indoctrination. One of the catchphrases of the Goals 2000 crowd is "a curriculum of inclusion," a strategy to break down our kids' belief in a distinctly American society. Outcomers seek to instill a "multiculturalist" view of America:

- Immigrants should not have to assimilate into our society, but should maintain a separate culture.
- Those who fail to succeed in America are victims of an oppressive, racist majority.
- All the resources and machinery of the government should be bent toward accommodating various cultures rather than encouraging these cultures to become part of our American culture.

As multiculturalism increasingly takes over as the driving force in American education, much of the old, traditional curricula is being discarded to make room for the new. The Clinton administration's Goals 2000 Act created the National Education Standards and Improvement Council (NESIC) to decide what parts of American history would be tossed in the Dumpster to make way for the curriculum of inclusion. As a result, students under Goals 2000 will no longer learn about the First Continental Congress, Robert E. Lee, Alexander Graham Bell, Thomas Edison, the Wright Brothers, Albert Einstein, or Jonas Salk. The NESIC standards omit all mention of the Federalist Papers, but include extensive discussion of the 1848 Seneca Falls "Declaration of Sentiments," which many radical feminists consider the charter document of the women's movement. The NESIC guidelines substitute the phrase "the American peoples" (plural!) in place of the constitutional phrase "We the People." Instead of being taught that the American people are (in the words of the Declaration of Independence) "one people," our kids would be brainwashed by Goals 2000 into viewing the United States as a loose collection of diverse cultures, "the American peoples."

The American culture has been enriched by ethnic contributions from all over the world, but America is not a multicultural nation. It is multiethnic, but it is one culture. We are not many peoples—we are *one* people, the American people, We the People.

OUR KIDS, OUR CHOICE

Let me welcome all of you spellers to the White House and let me compliment you—that's compliment with an "i," not complement with an "e." I want to compliment you with an "i" on your accomplishments. . . . All of us are proud not only of your spelling ability but of your determination to increase your knowledge. I wish all American students were as interested in their studies as you evidently are and have been. And I wish all teachers and parents took an interest in their children's educational development as your parents and teachers have taken in yours. . . .

So, enjoy the competition and enjoy your trip to Washington. . . . And remember, "i" before "e" except after "c."

Ronald Reagan
Greeting to finalists
of the National Spelling Bee
White House Rose Garden, June 6, 1983

While governor of California, my father received this letter from a Sacramento schoolteacher:

Dear Governor Reagan:

I thought you might enjoy hearing about something that happened today in my kindergarten class. I was telling the children about the field trip we are taking tomorrow to various sites around Sacramento, including the governor's mansion. I asked the children, "Does anyone know who is the governor of California?" Complete silence. "I'll give you a hint. His first name is Ronald." Instantly, twenty-three hands shot up and twenty-three voices shouted, "Ronald McDonald!"

My father wrote back:

Thanks for your letter—I did get a kick out of it. Please tell your students, "Hello," from the governor—and tell them I don't mind being Ronald McDonald at all.

In early 1981, while my father was recuperating from the assassination attempt that nearly took his life and which left three other men wounded, he received a letter that brightened his day. It was penciled in large block letters on lined paper by a second grader from Long Island, New York. He enjoyed the letter so much that he quoted it often in interviews and speeches:

Dear President Reagan,

I hope you get well quick or you might have to make a speech in your pajamas.

Your friend,

Peter Sweeney

P.S. If you have to make a speech in your pajamas, I warned you.

Ronald Reagan loves schoolchildren. He has always wanted the best for America's children, not only because of his big, warm heart, but because he has always been a man who looked to the future. He clearly understood that if America is to have a future, we must invest in our children. But he also understood, years before he was elected president of the United States, that investing in our children doesn't necessarily mean dumping bales of tax-payer dollars into a centralized education system. As early as 1976 he was urging the return of the school system to local control, and in his very first State of the Union address, January 26, 1982, he proposed eliminating the Department of Education. Today, at the end of the century, as the decline of education accelerates, these are still the solutions America needs.

And there is more that each of us can do as parents, as taxpayers, and as citizens of the Shining City to restore our education system to its former state of health. We've talked about the problems. Now let's look at the solutions, solutions that can be implemented on a national level and a grassroots level.

WORK FOR LOCAL CONTROL OF PUBLIC SCHOOLS

Support conservative candidates who believe in local control. Speak out and tell your friends and neighbors how the decline of education directly parallels the rise in centralization and federal control of education. We have to stop funneling education money through Washington, D.C., because that money has a way of evaporating along the way. For example, in my home state of California, we have migrant education programs funded through Washington. The money goes from California taxpayers to Washington, which takes a 15 percent or 20 percent cut for overhead; Washington sends what's left to Sacramento; Sacramento takes a 15 percent or 20 percent cut of that and sends it to the county; the county takes its 15 percent or 20 percent and sends the money to the school where what's left (less than half the cash that originally left the state) is finally spent on migrant education, thank you very much! That's the federal bureaucracy doing what it does best: generating waste, diminishing returns.

The supply of this most vital service to our society—the dispensing of knowledge and wisdom to an entire generation—is controlled by a monopolistic education cartel. This must change. The survival of our republic demands that education become more customer driven, so that it meets the real and varied needs of students, families, educators, and local communities. By decentralizing education and returning it to local control, we will see more diverse kinds of schools, more diverse teaching methods and techniques, higher standards, greater family involvement, and greater accountability of schools to the parents and communities they serve.

That means we must abolish the Department of Education, and that won't be easy. The Republicans in the 104th Congress proposed doing away with the Department of Education and were bashed by the Democrats and the liberal media for it. Candidate Bob Dole promised to abolish the Department of Education and was soundly trounced for it at the voting booth. The problem Republicans have faced in abolishing the Department of Education is twofold:

1. We conservatives have done a terrible job of explaining to the public why the Department of Education should be abolished. Polls showed that the education issue was a major factor in the gender gap, which helped swing the 1996 presidential election in Bill Clinton's favor. Over half of women voters cited education as a major factor in their vote. Republicans are on the right side of the education issue but allowed it to slip through their fingers. Why? Because Bob Dole and the Republicans of the 104th Congress failed to go directly to the people and make the case that centralized federal control of education has been the single most destructive force in American education.

   While the liberals kept talking about how they were defending schools, we should have been talking about *defending children*. If all the voters ever hear is that the Republicans are "attacking teachers" and want to "tear down the Department of Education," they will naturally question our commitment to education. It won't be easy to get our message through the clamor of liberal politicians, teachers' unions, and dominant media, but we have to assure the public that we are intensely committed to educating our children and that federal control of education harms the education process and harms our kids.

2. The education establishment and liberal politicians have successfully created the impression that education is the rightful burden of the federal government, and that education in America must have a cabinet-level Department of Education in Washington, D.C. The liberal accusation is that anyone who would do away with the Department of Education must hate children and love ignorance. It's an absurd caricature, but it works. The public has a short memory and forgets the fact that the Department of Education was only created a couple of decades ago by Jimmy Carter. The teachers' unions helped put Carter in office, and the Department of Education was his political payoff to the unions. Political payoff—not better education—continues to be its primary function.

For two centuries, this country provided kids with a quality education, the kind of education that made America the most incredibly successful and innovative society in the history of the planet, and we did it all without the help of a federal Department of Education. Tell your elected representatives that you do not want federal control, national standards, or tests that gauge students' beliefs, attitudes, or family experience. You want Washington to keep its nose out of your local school, out of your child's thoughts and feelings, and out of your family.

DEMAND SCHOOL CHOICE

Write or call your elected representatives and tell them you want school vouchers, opportunity scholarships for the poor, school rebates, and charter schools. Tell them you want the right to choose how and where your child will be educated, whether in public school, private school, or home school. Don't be fooled by politicians who mouth the words *school choice* but do not support vouchers and charter schools. Bill Clinton, for example, claims to support school choice while opposing vouchers. He spent seven years in private school, sends his daughter to the most prestigious private school in D.C., but only allows the rest of us the choice of one public school or another. And that's no choice at all.

At a speech on behalf of Eisenhower College on October 14, 1969,

Ronald Reagan talked about the role competitive education has to play in building the Shining City on a Hill:

> On the deck of the tiny *Arabella* off the coast of Massachusetts in 1630, John Winthrop gathered the little band of pilgrims together and spoke of the life they would have in that land they had never seen: "We shall be as a City Upon a Hill. The eyes of all people are upon us, so that if we shall deal falsely with our God in this work we have undertaken and so cause Him to withdraw His present help from us, we shall be made a story and a byword through all the world."
>
> To you who are considering what you can do to support Eisenhower College, I tell you that without such [private] schools, this shining dream of John Winthrop's may well become the taste of ashes in our mouths. They are an educational whetstone, serving to hone the educational process, helping to improve the public, tax-supported system, keeping it competitive in the drive for excellence. By that very competition they help preserve the public institutions from political interference, guaranteeing a measure of academic freedom they could never attain by themselves.

Though Ronald Reagan was addressing the need to support private education at the college/university level, the principle holds true at every level of education: Competition hones and improves the overall educational system. Private schools force public schools to work harder, smarter, more economically, and more effectively. Competition preserves academic freedom and guarantees academic excellence.

Instead of a federally mandated diversity (which is really an enforced multicultural sameness from one school to the next), let's demand true diversity, competitive diversity. Instead of schools that are designed and controlled by a D.C.-based educational elite, why not have schools that are locally designed, locally controlled, and that reflect the needs and character of the local community? If one group of parents wants a school that focuses on the three Rs while teaching morality, chastity, patriotism, and good citizenship, shouldn't they be able to have it? If other parents want to send their kids to a school that teaches Afrocentrism or multiculturalism, then why not give them that choice? How about a school that specializes in music and the arts, a little Julliard for kids? Or a school that's specially structured for kids with behavior problems? Or a school for kids with learning disabilities?

Researchers from Harvard and the University of Houston studied the results of the nation's first school-voucher program, located in Milwaukee, Wisconsin, and found that students in the voucher program scored higher over a four-year period than students who remained in public schools. The program began in 1990, offering tax-free tuition vouchers of up to $3,600 for low-income children to attend private schools; 97 percent of the students were black or Hispanic. The study compared the progress of 1,034 voucher students versus 407 low-income students who applied for vouchers but were turned down because of insufficient space in the program. Change takes time, and the first two years showed little change in test scores. But by year three, voucher students were scoring 5 percentage points higher in math and 3 percentage points higher on standardized reading tests; by year four, voucher kids were 11 points higher in math, 5 points higher in reading.[8]

The standard argument against vouchers for private education is that private schools get high test scores and low dropout rates by accepting only the best and most gifted students. The facts show otherwise. Private education actually offers an astounding range of options in specialized schools and programs for kids who are at-risk or disabled or have special needs. Over 100,000 children with disabilities are currently enrolled in more than 3,000 private schools nationwide. And many other private schools fill specialized niches in the community, including schools for recovering alcoholics, for teen moms, and for chronic truants.

Sobriety High School near Minneapolis is one of nineteen private Minnesota high schools specializing in giving kids a fresh start and helping them recover from drug and alcohol abuse. State-funded vouchers to Sobriety High cost taxpayers $3,500 per student per year—roughly half what it would cost to send that same kid to public school!

The High Road School in New Jersey serves kids with emotional problems and learning disabilities. When kids fail scholastically and socially in public school, they can go to High Road and find specialized care and a new beginning. Critics claim vouchers would turn the public schools into dumping grounds for kids with special needs, but High Road shows that there is a big, broad welcome mat in the private sector for such kids.[9]

Any program that allows real school choice must include church-affiliated parochial schools. Liberals argue that giving a child voucher money to be spent at a parochial school violates the First Amendment, in that the voucher somehow constitutes "state-sponsored religion." But how is the government establishing a state religion when parents can spend that voucher at any school they freely choose? The reality is that it is a violation of a family's First Amendment rights for the government to say to them, "Because you are poor, you must send your children to state-approved schools. Because you are poor, you cannot educate your kids according to your faith. You must educate them in a secular environment." As Patrick Fagan of the Heritage Foundation observes, "The United States of America and the now-defunct Union of Soviet Socialist Republics are the only major modern states to deny funding to faith-based schools."[10]

Parochial schools work, and they give hope to kids who otherwise might grow up without a future. Here are the facts: Minority children from troubled or poor families are less likely to drop out of parochial school than public school. They score higher on SAT tests; they are more likely to go to college; and they earn 27 percent more than their public school counterparts when they become adults.[11]

A charter school is a public school that is run like a private school, with fewer government controls and restrictions. The charter school concept is designed to meet the special needs of poor and other at-risk children who are not well served by the federally controlled cookie-cutter public school. In charter schools, parents have more say and more choice in the education of their kids, while educators have more freedom to innovate and design programs that meet the unique needs of their students. In states where charter schools are already in operation, attendance and standardized test scores have soared, as compared with the regular public schools.

DEMAND LITIGATION REFORM

Unions aren't the only factor driving up costs in the public schools. Other factors are litigation and the high cost of liability insurance. We need litigation reform to keep costs in check. It used to be that if you expelled a kid, he stayed expelled, end of story. Nowadays, if you expel a kid from school for being disruptive or even dangerous, he shows up the next day with his lawyer. That creates two problems: First, it drives up the cost of running a public school, because attorneys and litigation are very expensive. Second, it destroys order in the classroom by giving power to disruptive kids and taking disciplinary authority away from teachers and administrators. Educators must be given the power to maintain order in the classroom. We need to make it harder for children to disrupt and bankrupt our schools. One possibility is the loser-pays system now in place in the civil courts of England: If a plaintiff knows he has to pay all the other side's legal expenses and court costs if he loses, he will be a lot less likely to bring a frivolous action to court.

GET INVOLVED WITH YOUR LOCAL SCHOOL

Volunteer in the classroom. Go on field trips with the kids. Get to know the teachers, aides, counselors, and administrators who are the daily mentors and role models for your kids. Get involved with the PTA. Go to school board meetings. Run for the school board yourself. Become an active participant in your child's education.

The more we as parents take an active partnership role in the education of our kids, the sooner schools will adopt a new and healthier view of their relationship with us, the parents. We need to be working within the education system, encouraging and supporting a cooperative relationship between educators and parents, encouraging schools to join with us in promoting values of self-respect and chastity, and discouraging schools from condoning promiscuity with "values-neutral" sex education, condom distribution, and free trips to the abortion clinic behind parents' backs. If we want to defend our parental rights, the best place to begin is within the education system itself. If we are not actively, positively involved in the education of our kids, we have abdicated our parental responsibilities.

KEEP COMMUNICATION OPEN BETWEEN YOU AND THE TEACHER

Avoid being confrontational or accusing, even if you see signs of outcome-based education being conducted in the classroom. Understand that many teachers and administrators would rather not be involved in OBE but feel they have no choice. The OBE system is often mandated from the federal level on down, and teachers and administrators are required to learn it and teach it—or possibly lose their jobs.

I don't blame teachers for what has happened to our schools. Most teachers are caring, committed people who have devoted their lives to serving kids. They got into teaching because they wanted to make an investment in the lives of young people. I respect and honor that.

But let's say you take the most skilled, caring, dedicated builder, and you hand him a blueprint and say, "I want you to build a schoolhouse." He unrolls the blueprint and says, "Just a moment! This is all wrong! This is a blueprint for an outhouse, not a schoolhouse! And look, the way these plans are drawn, this outhouse will lean to the left." And you reply, "I say it's a schoolhouse, and I want you to build it according to this blueprint, right down to the last nail." He scratches his head and says, "Okay, you're the boss." What are you going to get? You're not going to get a schoolhouse, no matter how great a builder he is. If you give him a blueprint for a left-leaning outhouse, you're going to get a left-leaning outhouse every time.

That's what's happening to our schools. We have great American kids; we have great American teachers; we have plenty of money to build and equip great American schools. But the people who have drawn up the blueprint for education in America have given us a left-leaning outhouse. Instead of blaming teachers for doing a bad job, let's work on giving them a better blueprint to build with.

STAY INVOLVED WITH YOUR KIDS

Talk to your children every day. To really find out what they're thinking and what's going on in their lives, avoid asking them questions that can be answered with a simple yes or no. Involve them in a dialogue. Find creative ways to interact with them about what's going on in their lives and their schoolwork. When they come to you and talk to you, put down the newspaper or mute the TV and really listen. Give them eye contact and verbal feedback. Spend time building relationships with them—taking trips to the park, going on picnics, working on projects and hobbies with them, going to their soccer games, and watching TV with them and discussing what you see together.

As parents, we must create a learning environment for our kids. We need to make sure they have a place to do homework every evening, free of distractions and interruptions. What's more, we need to set a good example for them, showing them that learning doesn't stop once we become adults. Instead of seeing us zoned out in front of the TV every night, they need to see us reading good books, watching stimulating shows on TV, listening to stimulating talk radio (*ahem!*), and going to concerts, museums, and libraries. Learning must be continuous and vital to our lives. If our approach to learning is lazy and haphazard, how can we expect more from our children?

Make sure your kids can read, perform mathematics, and reason logically. And make sure they are growing wiser, not just smarter. Read to them, and have them read to you. Make sure your child is being taught phonics, not whole-word or whole-language approaches to reading. If the school is not responsive to your child's educational needs, don't wait—get help. Order a reading aid to learning phonics. Get a private tutor. Put your child in a private school. If you have no confidence in your public school and you are qualified to do so, home school your child. Whatever the malfeasance, misfeasance, or nonfeasance of the people in charge of your child's public school, the ultimate responsibility for your child's education rests with you, the parent. Make sure the job gets done one way or another.

KEEP YOUR MARRIAGE STRONG

Studies conclusively demonstrate that children from one-parent families are twice as likely to drop out of school as are children from two-parent families. That fact spells big trouble for America's future, because the number of children living in one-parent homes is steadily rising, from 17.5 percent of all kids in 1960 to nearly 50 percent today. The increasing absence of dads in the home has been linked to increases in teen promiscuity, teen substance abuse, and teen suicide. Recent studies show that the absence of fathers is also linked to the seventy-five-point average decline in SAT scores from 1960 to 1990. David Popenoe, professor of sociology at Rutgers University and author of *Life Without Father*, observes,

> Fathers' involvement seems to be linked to improved verbal and problem-solving skills and higher academic achievement. Several studies found that the presence of the father is one of the determinants of girls' proficiency in mathematics. And one pioneering study showed that along with paternal strictness, the amount of time fathers spent reading with them was a strong predictor of their daughters' verbal ability.
>
> For sons the results have been equally striking. Studies uncovered a strong relationship between fathers' involvement and the mathematical abilities of their sons. Other studies found a relationship between paternal nurturing and boys' verbal intelligence.[12]

When parents divorce, they don't just shatter their own marriage—they shatter their children's world. So unless there is something so terrible going on in the marriage that the children are being harmed—such as abuse, addiction, or adultery—parents owe it to their kids to do whatever it takes to keep the family together.

TEACH YOUR CHILD VIRTUES, VALUES, AND CHARACTER

Faith, patriotism, self-reliance, self-control, responsibility, integrity, honesty, loyalty, respect for others, kindness, and civility. Make sure your children understand their freedoms and how America came to be founded as a free nation. Let them know that America was built on a foundation of faith, liberty, and equality of opportunity—not multiculturalism, political correctness, and equality of outcome. This, in fact, was Ronald Reagan's final challenge to America before he left office. In his farewell speech from the Oval Office, January 11, 1989, he said:

> All great change in America begins at the dinner table. So tomorrow night in the kitchen I hope the talking begins. And children, if your parents haven't been teaching you what it means to be an American, let 'em know and nail 'em on it. That would be a very American thing to do.

Outcomers view the American classroom as the place where they can seize control of American society and American minds, instill political correctness, and impose their utopian solutions. That's not what education is for. Education should teach a child how to function in society, how to read and appreciate literature, how to understand his place in history, how to appreciate the mental discipline of mathematics, how to make wise and responsible choices, how to sift through new ideas and to separate the good ideas from the bad.

As far back as the late 1800s, education reformer John Dewey advocated using the public education system as a tool for creating a "new social order." William Spady and his fellow outcomers are well on their way to achieving the New World Order through OBE, an order that more resembles the nightmare societies of George Orwell and Aldous Huxley than the shining dream of Ronald Reagan. The liberal utopians want to change the world. So do Reagan conservatives. But there's a big difference between the liberal and conservative approaches to social change. Liberals seek to change society though political manipulation, indoctrination, big-government control, and a complete takeover of the education process. Conservatives seek to change society by setting our schools free, by maintaining academic liberty and choice, by returning schools to local control, and by fighting bureaucratic intrusion into the schools and the family.

New World Order or Shining City on a Hill—where would you rather raise your children?

CHAPTER FOUR

A
CITY WITHOUT
FEAR

NO SAFE STREET

We no longer walk in the countryside or on our city streets after dark without fear. The jungle seems to be closing in on this little plot we've been trying to civilize for 6,000 years.

Ronald Reagan
Eisenhower College Fund-Raiser Speech
Washington, D.C., October 14, 1969

If our crackdown on crime could produce the sharpest drop ever in the crime index, then we can keep cracking down until our families and friends can walk our streets again without being afraid.

Ronald Reagan
Campaign "Stump Speech"
Republican Rally, Fairfield, Connecticut
October 26, 1984

On March 30, 1981, I was in my office at Dana Ingall's Profile, a small Burbank aerospace company where I worked as vice president of sales and marketing. I was meeting with a few clients when we heard a knock at my office door. Mike Luty, one of the Secret Service agents assigned to my family, opened the door and said in his businesslike Secret Service voice, "There's been an assassination attempt on your father. One man is down, but your father is okay." Then he closed the door, and I was left sitting at my desk with my mouth hanging open.

For several long, silent seconds, I just sat there looking at the door, and the other people in the room did the same. Finally I asked, "What was that all about? Did he say somebody tried to shoot my dad?"

"I think that's what he said," one of the clients replied uncertainly.

"Excuse me," I said, getting up. I went out and found Mike Luty in the hall. "Mike," I said, "would you say that one more time?"

"There's been an assassination attempt," he told me. "One man is down—"

"Down? You mean wounded?"

"Right. But your father is fine. He's headed back to the White House."

"When will you have more information?" I asked.

"When I get it, you'll get it," he replied.

"Okay," I said, and went back into the office. I quickly concluded my business with the people inside, then turned on the radio. There was no TV in the building. The radio news bulletin said pretty much the same thing as Mike Luty had said, only it was becoming clearer that three men were down, not just one: my father's press secretary, Jim Brady, who had been shot in the head; Secret Service agent Timothy McCarthy, who had thrown himself into the line of fire between Dad and the gunman; and D.C. police officer Thomas Delahanty, who was not supposed to be on duty that day, but was filling in for a fellow officer who was sick. The news reports also said that Dad was returning to the White House.

So I picked up the phone and called the White House. Because of the churn of White House activity that would naturally follow an assassination attempt, I didn't know if I could get through to Dad, but I thought I could at least talk to Nancy. I was told, however, that Nancy had left the White House. Instantly, I knew things were more serious than I had been told. If Nancy had left the White House, then Dad was certainly not on his way there. If Nancy was headed elsewhere, then Dad was headed elsewhere, too—and the only place that made sense was the hospital.

I decided to make one more attempt to find out what was going on. I called the office of Mike Deaver, Dad's longtime aide and White House deputy chief of staff. When they told me that Deaver had left his office, alarm bells went off in my head. I just *knew* Dad had been shot. I went out in the hall were Mike Luty was sitting and said, "Something's wrong. Dad's not going back to the White House. They're taking him to the hospital. I'm sure he's been shot too."

"He must be going to check on Jim Brady and the others who were shot," Luty assured me. "He wants to make certain they're all right."

I shook my head. "I'll just bet Dad's been shot too."

"Can't be," Luty countered firmly. "I'm in touch with CP"—the command post—"and they told me Rawhide is definitely not hurt."

But as it turned out, I was right. Rawhide had indeed been shot. The reason I couldn't reach him or Nancy or Mike Deaver was that he was being rushed to the medical center at George Washington University in Washington, D.C. Here is what happened.

At just after 2:30 in the afternoon, on the rain-soaked sixty-ninth day of Ronald Reagan's presidency, a disturbed young man named John W. Hinckley Jr. stood on the sidewalk along the gray stone wall of the Washington Hilton. His head was filled with fantasies inspired by the movie *Taxi Driver*. His hands were thrust into his pockets. In one fist was a pistol loaded with explosive-tipped Devastor bullets. The young gunman watched as the president emerged from the hotel with his entourage of aides and protective escort, having just delivered a speech before the AFL-CIO. As the president paused by the limousine and waved to the crowd, the young man pulled the gun and began firing wildly, hitting Jim Brady, Agent McCarthy, Officer Delahanty, and Ronald Reagan.

The scene was played over and over on television—in slow motion, stop motion, frame by frame: Ronald Reagan standing by the limousine, his left hand raised in a wave, smiling his usual jaunty smile as he turned to a reporter who had just asked a question—and then wincing as the pop-pop-pop of gunfire rang out, as people shouted and men fell stricken to the ground. In those moments, one of the bullets glanced off the flank of the bulletproof limousine, flattened out, and entered beneath Ronald Reagan's raised left arm, making a tiny slit, seemingly more like a paper cut than a gunshot wound. At that moment, no one realized how seriously wounded Ronald Reagan was, not even Ronald Reagan himself.

Time seems to dilate at such moments, and for years afterward, Dad had a vividly etched recollection of a brief moment of time when he saw his longtime friend and aide, Jim Brady, lying on the sidewalk, facedown in a spreading pool of blood. Then, in the very next instant, the chief of Dad's Secret Service detail, Jerry Parr, slammed him hard from behind, forcing him into the limousine where he landed atop the transmission hump. Jerry threw himself on top of Dad, and yelled to the driver, "Go, go, go!" And the limousine roared off in the direction of the White House.

"You broke my ribs!" Dad complained as Parr got up and lifted him off the floor of the car. Dad began coughing, and Parr handed him his own handkerchief. After Dad coughed into the handkerchief a few times, he noticed spots of bright red oxygenated blood on it. When Parr saw the blood, he immediately ordered the driver to take the president to George Washington University Hospital. Parr's swift decision probably saved Dad's life. Had the limousine taken him to the White House first, he never would have made it to the hospital. It was that close.

Dad walked into the hospital trauma unit under his own steam, but he was bleeding internally. The bullet had entered his chest beneath the left arm, glanced off the seventh rib, and penetrated the left lung, stopping within a quarter inch of his heart. Though White House officials played down the seriousness of the wound in public statements, Dad was gravely injured. He was laboring for breath as they cut the suit off his body. His blood pressure had fallen alarmingly, indicating a serious internal loss of blood. In fact, his pleural cavity was filling with blood, and he was rapidly going into shock.

Through it all, he displayed enormous courage and good humor, and as usual, his thoughts were focused more on others than on himself. Seeing how shocked and scared Nancy looked when she arrived at the hospital, he joked, "Honey, I forgot to duck." He knew that others had been shot, and he asked how they were doing as the doctors examined him. Before they wheeled him into the operating room, his comment to one of the doctors was typical Gipper: "Please tell me you're a Republican."

Ronald Reagan is the only president who ever survived being shot by a would-be assassin's bullet. He knows what it's like to be the target of a violent crime and to see others, including a close friend, also targeted. If a criminal can shoot the American president while he is on an American street surrounded by the best security force in the world, then who in America can truly feel safe from the bad guys?

Drive through any American city today and it can be instantly seen that something is terribly wrong with our society: The wrong people are behind bars! Honest, law-abiding Americans live in houses with iron bars on the windows. Criminals roam the streets at will, graffiti-tagging, raping, robbing, car-jacking, murdering, and laughing at the criminal justice system. Only a generation ago, many Americans could go to bed at night with their windows open and their doors unlocked. Today, most Americans are afraid to sit on their front porch on a summer evening. Our homes have become prisons; our schools have become battlefields; and crime robs America of half a trillion dollars every year. We have grown to accept fear as a way of life, but we don't have to. We can choose to live in a City without fear. We can take back our homes, our streets, our parks, and our neighborhoods through a combination of tough legislation, community action, grassroots activism, and individual crime-curbing efforts.

According to the Heritage Foundation's Index of Leading Cultural Indicators, violent crime rose 159 percent over the twenty-year period from 1970 to 1990—from 738,820 violent crimes in 1970 to 1,911,770 violent crimes in 1990. The liberal response to the rising fear of crime in our nation is embodied in the $33 billion Violent Crime Control and Law Enforcement Act of 1994, the Clinton crime bill, which proposed to solve the youth crime problem with midnight basketball programs, solve the murder problem by banning categories of guns that account for only 2 percent of the murder statistics, and solve the fear in our cities by putting 100,000 more cops on the street. (After being in effect for two years, the crime bill had hired fewer than a tenth that many cops, and some of the money authorized for community policing was diverted by Bill Clinton to state parks and environmental projects.)

We have already endured decades of such "solutions" to the worsening problem of crime and fear. We cannot endure any more. We can do better. We must do better.

THE RIGHT TO BEAR ARMS

I don't think that making it difficult for law-abiding citizens to obtain guns will lower the crime rate—not when the criminals will always find a way to get them.

Ronald Reagan
"To Restore America"
March 31, 1976

One Sunday evening in 1933, a nursing student named Melba Lohmann got off a bus in Des Moines, Iowa, and began walking toward Broadlawns General Hospital. She had just returned to Des Moines after a visit to her parents' home in Sheffield, and she carried a purse in one hand and a suitcase in the other. Less than a block from the hospital, she heard heavy footsteps rushing up behind her and felt the nudge of cold, hard steel in her back. A rough male voice spoke into her ear. "Gimme the suitcase and the purse, lady," said the man, "or I'll shoot ya, so help me."

A jolt of terror went through the young woman. "Don't hurt me," she pleaded, handing over the purse and suitcase. "Please don't be mad—there's only three dollars in the purse."

Just then, both she and the robber were startled by a male voice coming from the window of the second-floor apartment above them. "Leave the lady alone," said the strong, self-assured voice from above. Looking up at the window, the young woman saw a man with dark hair, sturdy features, and keen eyes. He had a pistol in his hand, and he was sighting down the barrel. "Leave her alone, mister," the man in the window repeated, "or I'll shoot you right between the shoulders."

The stunned robber dropped Miss Lohmann's purse and suitcase, then took off running. In seconds, he was gone. Moments later, Miss Lohmann's rescuer dashed out of the apartment building and rushed to her side. After making sure the nursing student was unharmed, the man walked her the rest of the way to the hospital, carrying the suitcase for her.

That rescuer's name was Ronald Reagan.

As president, Ronald Reagan didn't need studies or statistics to prove that, in the hands of law-abiding citizens, guns stop crime. He knew it because he himself had used a gun to stop a crime. He had seen the wisdom of the Second Amendment in action, and that kind of experience shaped his belief in a sensible gun policy, which trusts law-abiding citizens with the right to keep and bear arms.

It's a simple, commonsense fact: Society is a lot safer when criminals don't know who is armed and who is not. When law-abiding citizens are legally allowed to carry concealed weapons, violent crime is reduced. An armed citizenry is a powerful deterrent. An FBI statistical study conducted by University of Chicago law professor John R. Lott Jr. analyzed crime patterns in every county in America from 1977 to 1992. He compared incidences of crime in the thirty-one states that allow citizens to carry concealed weapons to states that do not. Lott's conclusions:

- By conservative estimate, states that permit responsible citizens to carry concealed handguns reduced the murder rate by 8.5 percent, rape by 5 percent, aggravated assault by 7 percent, and robbery by 3 percent.
- According to these findings, if nongun states had changed their laws to allow responsible citizens to carry concealed handguns in 1992, the murder rate would have dropped by about 1,570 that year, rape by about 4,177, robbery by 12,000, and aggravated assault by 60,000.
- In major cities (population 250,000 and up), laws allowing citizens to carry concealed weapons reduced the murder rate an average of 13.5 percent.
- The most dramatic drop in murder rates occurred in areas where it was publicized that increased numbers of women were carrying firearms. The study found that for every woman who carried a concealed handgun, the murder rate dropped by three to four times more than if one more man carried a concealed handgun.
- The drop in crime was not primarily due to people using guns for self-defense, but merely to the deterrent value of the law. Bad guys quickly catch on to the fact that the risks of their chosen profession have been ratcheted up. The next guy they say "Stick 'em up" to may reply, "Bang! Bang! You're dead!" Perhaps the best news of all in this study is the fact that increased freedom to carry concealed guns did *not* result in increased gun *use*—just greater avoidance of criminal confrontation.
- Researchers found no evidence whatsoever of any increased incidence of accidental killings or suicides in states with relaxed concealed handgun laws.

"The policy implications are undeniable," Lott concluded. "If you're interested in reducing murder and rape, then letting law-abiding, mentally competent citizens carry concealed weapons has a positive impact."[1]

The Second Amendment to the Constitution guarantees us the right to arm ourselves in order to defend ourselves and our society: "A well regulated Militia, being necessary to the security of a free State, the right of the people to keep and bear Arms, shall not be infringed." Some people who have never actually read the Constitution will argue, "The Second Amendment says it's okay for people to have guns for hunting, but not handguns and assault rifles and guns that are actually designed to kill people." Wrong. There's not one word in the Second Amendment about sport shooting or hunting. Others argue, "The Second Amendment talks about 'a well regulated militia,' so that means only the National Guard or a state militia can have guns." Wrong. The amendment specifically says "the right of the people . . . shall not be infringed." The people—that's individual people, you and me. The government is not allowed to infringe on your right to keep and bear arms.

The Second Amendment cannot be removed from the overall context of the Constitution. It is an extension of the Preamble. The Second Amendment is a specific guarantee of the right to bear arms, which is an extension of the government's constitutional responsibility to "establish justice" and "insure domestic tranquility." We are guaranteed the right to bear arms so that we can defend ourselves and our society against bad guys, both foreign and domestic.

YOUTHFUL PREDATORS

Half of those who commit crime have not yet reached the age of eighteen, and half of all the crimes are committed in a desperate frenzy to finance addiction to narcotics.
Ronald Reagan
Eisenhower College Fund-Raiser Speech
Washington, D.C., October 14, 1969

In the summer of 1996, the LAPD obtained an extraordinary court order permitting police to publicly announce the name of a vicious murder suspect who was—are you ready for this?—eleven years old. Despite state laws that protect the anonymity of juvenile offenders, this boy was considered so dangerous, so violent, that the police went to extra lengths to publicize his name and warn the public that this little monster was on the loose. He was the leader of a group of kids who had kidnapped a thirteen-year-old girl, raped and tortured her, then tried to burn down the abandoned house where they had committed the crime and trapped the girl. In the process, they also murdered the eighty-two-year-old woman next door.

This is only one extreme example of what is becoming an increasingly dangerous trend in America. Children make up the fastest-growing segment of today's criminal population. The juvenile arrest rate for violent crime has tripled from 1965 to 1996, and homicide deaths among children up to the age of eighteen more than quadrupled from 1960 to 1991. Homicide is by far the leading cause of death among African-American teenagers. Fully 20 percent of all American high-school students now carry a concealed gun, knife, razor, or other weapon with them at all times—including at school.

Each new wave of juvenile criminals is younger and more vicious than the wave before, and today's wave of young, inexperienced thugs will become tomorrow's avalanche of seasoned, expert killers. According to a report in *USA Today,* a recent study of jailed boys in California found that 94 percent were rearrested as adults—82 percent for major felonies. Of those adult criminals, 42 percent had more than nine arrests as adults over the eight-year follow-up period.[2]

The juvenile justice system spends $20 billion a year arresting, jailing, and attempting to rehabilitate youthful offenders, yet fully 70 percent of these young criminals go out and get arrested all over again. The system is not very effective at turning young lives around. What's the answer? Following are some suggested reforms.

Treat youthful offenders much as adult criminals should be treated. Keep records of juvenile arrests, and make those records available to the police agencies and adult court system. This will help ensure that juvenile career criminals will no longer be treated as first-timers at age eighteen. The old system of sealing and expunging juvenile arrest records was created for an era when the average youth crime was stealing apples from a street vendor, not for today's young murderers and rapists.

Introduce legislation to remove the arbitrary age threshold at which children can be charged as adults for such crimes as murder, assault with a deadly weapon, or rape. Punishment should be based on the nature of the offense, not on chronological age.

Offenders should be dealt with swiftly and severely, and punishment should always include restitution to victims and community service. Juveniles who fail to perform their community service should be sent to institutional "boot camps" where they are subjected to a rigorous routine with few privileges and very strict accountability.

Many communities and states are experimenting with laws that penalize parents for the criminal acts of their children—so-called parental responsibility laws. The experiment seems to be working. In 1995, after the town of Silverton, Oregon, cited fourteen parents for the criminal acts of their children, juvenile crime nose-dived 39 percent. In California, over 1,000 parents of wayward youth have been court-ordered to receive counseling or attend classes in responsible parenting—or be prosecuted for contempt. Louisiana parents convicted of "improper supervision of a minor" can be fined up to $1,000 and sentenced up to six months in prison for allowing their children to associate with felons, drug dealers, or gang members.[3]

Prosecutors in California have successfully slapped street gangs with civil suits and injunctions to halt youth crime. Gang members who violate the injunctions can be prosecuted for criminal contempt, and contempt convictions are much easier to get than convictions on most other crimes. The civil suits are built on the assertion that gang activity constitutes a "nuisance." These suits halted the practice of a Van Nuys–area gang that intimidated residents, ordering people to leave their doors unlocked so members could hide from the police. Since the court injunction, gang members no longer have a place to hide, and crime rates have dropped dramatically.

While gang-related violent crime rose sharply in LA County from 1986 (over 3,500 felonies) to 1994 (over 17,000 felonies), violent crime and gang activity are sharply down in areas where injunctions have been obtained. Under these injunctions, gang members may not possess knives, cellular phones, pagers, police scanners, spray paint, or burglary tools in public; they may not drink alcoholic beverages on public property; they are not allowed on the roofs of buildings (a popular place to post lookouts). Small-claims suits—and sometimes just the threat of lawsuits—have forced slumlords to clean up drug houses and gang meeting sites.[4]

It may be that some young criminals, like the eleven-year-old rapist-murderer in LA, are beyond all hope of redemption. No doubt, there are reasons why that child has become a vicious predator at such an early age. I have no problem with those who try to understand these predators, but first we must get the predators off the streets and make sure they can't ever hurt anyone again. Protecting the safety of the innocent and the law-abiding comes first. That means we must punish, we must deter, and we must hold the guilty accountable for their crimes.

JUST SAY NO

Drugs are menacing our society. They're threatening our values and undercutting our institutions. They're killing our children. From the beginning of our administration, we've taken strong steps to do something about this horror. Tonight I can report to you that we've made much progress. . . .

But we still have much to do.

Ronald Reagan
"Campaign Against Drug Abuse"
Televised address
The White House residence
September 14, 1986

On June 15, 1992, candidate Bill Clinton went on MTV to answer questions from young people. This was after the uproar over his claim that he had tried marijuana two or three times at Oxford but he "didn't inhale." One teenage boy asked, "If you had it to do over again, would you inhale?"

"Sure, if I could," Clinton answered jovially. "I tried before." The teen audience laughed.

But it wasn't funny.

Former Drug Enforcement Agency agent Wayne Roques goes to schools and talks to kids about drugs, and he's angry over the way Bill Clinton has undercut the antidrug effort in the schools. "Since Clinton took office," he said, "I haven't gone to one school where some of the kids didn't laugh at drugs because of the president's comments."[5] Whereas the slogan of the Reagan administration was "Just Say No to Drugs," the attitude of the Clinton administration seems to be, "What's the Big Deal About Drugs?"

Presidents and other public figures have an enormous responsibility to set an example for the nation. The things they say and do, the attitudes they display, and the lifestyle they represent can have a huge influence, especially among young people. During Ronald Reagan's presidency, the public learned of his fondness for jelly beans—and sales of jelly beans shot up 1,000 percent. Sometime later, basketball star Ervin "Magic" Johnson revealed that he had the AIDS virus. Overnight, sales of condoms shot up 400 percent.

When Bill Clinton went on MTV, instead of warning young people about drugs, he told them he wished he had inhaled! And drug use among America's teenagers has blown sky-high! Coincidence? Hardly. A simple matter of cause and effect. Bill Clinton inspires a flippant and casual attitude toward teen drug use, and the result is that many young people are throwing their lives away on drugs. Ronald and Nancy Reagan launched a war on drugs in the 1980s. The war still rages today. The difference is that Ronald and Nancy Reagan sounded the battle cry in the war on drugs—and Bill Clinton is leading the retreat. The drug lords are winning. Just look at what has happened to teen drug use since Bill Clinton took office:

- In 1994, 2.9 million kids ages twelve to seventeen admitted using marijuana within the past year—1.3 million more than in 1992, the last year of the Bush administration.
- Among fourteen to fifteen year olds, marijuana use has doubled since 1992. This upswing is all the more shocking since teen marijuana use had been declining throughout the previous eleven years of the Reagan-Bush administrations. (Source: National Household Survey on Drug Abuse, Department of Health and Human Services, 1995.)
- Hospital emergency rooms reported the highest level of cocaine-related incidences in 1994. Hospital emergency room reports of cocaine use rose 33 percent from 1992 to 1994; heroin-related incidences rose 77 percent during that same period; marijuana-related incidences jumped 118 percent; and methamphetamine/speed–related incidences skyrocketed 308 percent. (Source: Drug Abuse Warning Network Advance Report, Department of Health and Human Services, 1995.)

Bill Clinton's outrageous and irresponsible performance on MTV was just the beginning of the problem. Once in office, Clinton unilaterally disarmed America in its war against drugs. In February 1993, he cut 83 percent of the staff at the Office of National Drug Policy. When Clinton's surgeon general, Joycelyn Elders, stated in a December 1993 speech that America's crime rate would subside if drugs were legalized, Clinton stood by her. His attorney general, Janet Reno, announced a plan to reduce mandatory sentences for drug trafficking—and that was okay with Bill.

Another troubling part of the equation is that Bill Clinton has long had cozy relationships with people who are known to be involved in organized crime and the drug trade. One of his longtime close friends is a convicted drug dealer named Dan Lasater, who served time (along with Clinton's brother, Roger) for distributing cocaine to women and underage girls in return for sex.[6] While governor, Clinton pardoned Lasater after he had served six months of a thirty-month sentence. Then, when he became president, Clinton hired as one of his top aides a woman named Patsy Thomason. She ran Lasater's bond business while he was in prison.

Shortly after taking office as president, Bill Clinton took the abrupt, unprecedented, and never explained action of firing every U.S. Attorney in Justice Department offices around the country, an action that may have been intended to thwart investigations into the Whitewater land deal. The firing of the U.S. Attorneys removed some of our most experienced and dedicated prosecutors and derailed hundreds of ongoing investigations of drug smuggling. Clinton replaced the fired U.S. Attorneys with liberal prosecutors, many of whom refused to prosecute drug traffickers, smugglers, and child pornographers. The flow of drugs onto America's streets dramatically increased while drug prices dropped, making the stuff more available to teens.

Under Bill Clinton, prosecutions for federal drug violations declined 12 percent, from 25,000 in 1992 to 21,900 in 1994 (source: Administrative Office of U.S. Courts, 1994), and the number of federal marijuana defendants fell 18 percent, from 5,500 in 1993 to less than 4,100 in 1995 (source: U.S. Sentencing Commission). Clinton's budget for 1995 cut 621 drug enforcement agents from various services, including the Drug Enforcement Agency, the Federal Bureau of Investigation, Immigration and Naturalization, Customs, and the Coast Guard. Clinton also cut 150 positions from the Organized Crime and Drug Enforcement Task Force Program. The Office of National Drug Control Policy was cut by 80 percent. Soon after taking office, Bill Clinton cut military drug interdiction efforts by eliminating almost 1,000 positions. Because of Clinton-ordered budget cuts, the number of drug trafficking aircraft seized by Customs fell from 37 in 1993 to just 10 in 1995. Coast Guard vessel seizures dropped from 152 in 1989 to 19 in 1995 (an 88 percent drop), and cocaine seizures fell 73 percent below 1991 levels.

As part of his grubby, greedy scramble to trade access to the White House for campaign contributions, President Clinton hosted about a hundred White House coffee klatches, including one with a Chinese Communist weapons merchant named Wang Jun, whose company, Poly Group, is charged with smuggling 2,000 fully automatic AK-47 machine guns into the States for sale to American street gangs and drug dealers. Poly Group is a wholly owned subsidiary of the Chinese Communist government, long known to our government as a supplier of guns, missiles, tanks, jets, and even nuclear weapons technology to such unstable Third World countries as Iran and Pakistan. At the very time Wang was meeting with Clinton at the White House in early 1996, the U.S. government was engaged in a heated war of words over Chinese arms sales around the world. Wang was escorted to the meeting with Clinton by Charlie Trie, who also laundered $640,000 in donations to the Clinton Whitewater–Paula Jones legal defense fund.[7] Clinton claims he had no idea that Wang was a highly placed communist arms merchant. But I know firsthand how tight White House security is. Trust me, Wang Jun didn't just slide past the best security and intelligence apparatus in the world.

After considerable foot-dragging, public outrage, and quiet insistence by the Secret Service, the White House finally instituted a drug-testing program for administration staffers known to be recent users of illegal narcotics. Many staffers were unable to get security clearances to work at the White House because of extensive drug abuse problems, but that was not a problem. They simply ignored the law and continued working at the White House *without* a security clearance.

Bill Clinton deceitfully certified that Mexico has cooperated with U.S. drug interdiction efforts, despite the fact that Mexico has ignored 165 extradition orders for major drug traffickers. Our southern borders are as porous as a slice of Swiss cheese. Seventy percent of drugs smuggled into the U.S. come across the border from Mexico. Hundreds of suspected drug smugglers have been stopped at the border and then allowed to go free under the relaxed Clinton immigration rules and drug policy.

What will it take to turn back the tide on drug abuse in America?

First, we need strong national leadership—*moral* leadership—that can look America's youth in the eye and say with conviction and integrity, "Drugs are wrong. If you take them, you'll regret it." We can't afford any more leaders who smirk and wink and say, "I wish I had inhaled."

Second, we need a firm, unbending drug policy that rejects legalization of drugs and refuses to make excuses for drug abuse. We need tough drug interdiction, prosecution, and prison terms for those who enrich themselves over the broken lives and dead bodies of our young people. Our intelligence efforts against drug traffickers should be intensified so that we can break the back of the drug distribution network, seize the assets of drug thugs, and make the drug business unprofitable and unhealthy to be in.

At both the state and federal levels, we need strong penalties and mandatory minimum sentences for drug trafficking and other drug-related crimes. Those in the white-collar community who are involved with money laundering must be dealt with as harshly as distributors and street pushers.

Drug testing should be a normal part of the criminal justice system, both juvenile and adult. Experience shows that substance abusers rarely begin to turn their lives around until they start feeling the consequences of their choices. The criminal justice system will only be doing drug abusers a favor by pounding those consequences into them as soon as possible. Test results that show ongoing drug abuse should be factored into such matters as release on bail, sentencing, and probation—and the consequences for not getting clean and sober should be severe.

Funding for drug interdiction, investigation, and prosecution, so severely cut by the Clinton administration, must be restored. Antidrug efforts must be intensified, not abandoned. A special effort must be made to secure and seal up our southwestern borders. Our national security and our American way of life are at stake. This is war. Let's wage it to win.

But remember that government can't do it all. Religious and private social organizations have an opportunity to make a difference in society—and in individual lives—by setting up twenty-four-hour hot lines for drug abusers. Many people—including many young people—feel trapped, have hit bottom, and are on the cusp between suicide and salvation. They are ready for change, and they'll do anything to kick the habit and turn their lives around. They can be saved from destruction if caring people will make themselves available to point the way to a cure.

You and I, as individuals, also have a part to play in the war on drugs. We have to be bold and up front with our kids about the dangers of drugs. That may be hard for you, especially if you experimented with drugs in your past. This is a problem for a lot of baby boomers who grew up in the sixties. If you have a sobering experience to share regarding drug use in your past, share it with your kids when they are old enough to use the information in a positive way. If you've lost friends to drugs, or if your drug use has caused a loss of relationships or a job or self-respect, then talk about that with your kids. Help them to learn from your experience.

If you've never used drugs, then tell your kids how you stood up to peer pressure. Let them know that they can do it too. Be an example and a role model to your kids.

Ronald Reagan closed his televised address on the Campaign Against Drug Abuse (September 14, 1986) with a challenge to all Americans—a challenge I leave with you:

> In this crusade, let us not forget who we are. Drug abuse is a repudiation of everything America is. The destructiveness and human wreckage mock our heritage. . . .
>
> As we mobilize for this national crusade, I'm mindful that drugs are a constant temptation for millions. Please remember this when your courage is tested: You are Americans. You're the product of the freest society mankind has ever known. No one, ever, has the right to destroy your dreams and shatter your life.

THREE STRIKES AND YOU'RE OUT

The problem of crime . . . demands that we seek transformation of our legal system, which overly protects the rights of criminals while it leaves society and the innocent victims of crime without justice.

Ronald Reagan
First State of the Union Address
January 26, 1982

At a little before 11:00 P.M. on a June night in 1992, eighteen-year-old Kimber Reynolds and her friend, Greg Calderon, stepped out of the popular Daily Planet restaurant. They had just finished dessert and coffee. Though it was late in the evening, it was a well-lit, trendy part of town, with lots of coffee shops, restaurants, art galleries, bookstores, and theaters—a Carmel-style arts community in the middle of the central California community of Fresno. There were other people on the sidewalk and behind the big plate glass window of the restaurant. The street seemed safe and calm.

It was anything but.

Kimber had parked her car at the curb, directly in front of the restaurant, in full view of the patrons. Greg let himself into the car on the passenger side. Kimber checked traffic on the one-way street and then walked around the car to the driver's side. As she started to open the car door, she heard the roar of a motorcycle behind her. The cycle seemed to appear out of nowhere. Turning, Kimber found herself pinned against the car door by two men on a stolen motorcycle. One man, armed with a .357 magnum, grabbed for Kimber's purse. She resisted, tugging the purse back.

The man with the gun jammed the muzzle against her ear and shot her. She died some twenty-six hours later at the hospital with her mom and dad at her side.

One of the two men who caused Kimber's death was Joseph Michael Davis, a loser with a rap sheet as long as your arm: drugs, gun violations, burglary, grand theft auto, resisting arrest, and more. He had been in trouble with the law since he was fourteen, had spent more of his adult life in prison than out of it, and was a hard-core methamphetamine user. Witnesses agree that Davis was the triggerman. The other loser was Douglas David Walker, who was out of jail on a temporary release. He had promised to return to jail to finish a sentence for a drug conviction three months earlier, but had never bothered. Like Davis, Walker was a career criminal. His first offense was for selling heroin as an eleven year old.

Within hours of Kimber's death, Kimber's grieving dad—wedding photographer Mike Reynolds—appeared on *The Ray Appleton Show,* a local radio talk show on KMJ 580 AM, a station that also airs my show. Reynolds went to the KMJ studios, located just two blocks from where Kimber was fatally shot. He appeared on live radio to talk about Kimber's life and death and to ask the public for help in bringing her killers to justice. As it turned out, a listener to the show knew the two men on the motorcycle and had heard them brag about the killing. Moved by Mike Reynold's words on the Appleton program, the listener called the police and identified the killers.

The police quickly began closing the net on Davis and Walker, and Davis knew it. When he learned that police had questioned his mother, Davis told her, "Next time you see me, I'll be in a pine box—and I'm gonna take some cops out with me." A short time later, SWAT (Special Weapons and Tactics) officers located Davis at an apartment building. As they were getting in position to arrest him, Davis surprised the officers, flinging open the door of his second-floor apartment and firing. His first shot wounded an officer—then the gun jammed. Davis leaped over the balcony and hunkered down behind the stairs. The officers returned fire, targeting what they could see of the perpetrator through the spaces between the stairs.

At the end of the shoot-out, the wounded officer and all the other officers survived. Davis didn't make it. Ten rounds of pistol fire, plus four shotgun blasts had hit him. They had to pry the gun out of his hand.

About a week later, police spotted Douglas Walker driving a car and arrested him. He pled guilty to being an accessory in Kimber's murder. For his part in Kimber's death, he received a nine-year prison sentence—which, with one day off for every day of good behavior, meant he could be back on the street in four and a half years. Interviewed on ABC's *20/20* after a year in prison, Walker said, "I've only got three and a half years to go. There's nothin' that could stop me from parole." Douglas Walker would be inconvenienced for a few years. Fair payment for helping to snuff out the life of an eighteen-year-old girl?

A lot of people would look at Mike Reynolds and say, "Poor guy. His daughter's a statistic, and he and his wife, Sharon, are crime victims. Well, what can you do?"

But Kimber Reynolds was not just a statistic. And Mike Reynolds is not just a victim. With Kimber as his inspiration, this grieving father devoted himself to making a difference. The very night Kimber died, he made a promise to her that he would do everything in his power to spare other parents what he and his wife were going through and to prevent other young people from being cut down too early as Kimber had been. The day he appeared on the Appleton show on KMJ, Mike Reynolds predicted that his daughter's killers would turn out to be hardened repeat offenders. He was right.

So Mike Reynolds began to talk to people—to legislators, to judges, to police officers, and to the governor of California, Pete Wilson. A month after Kimber's death, he called a select group of community leaders and criminal justice experts to a barbecue in his backyard. Out of that meeting, and other meetings that followed, came a brilliantly simple concept called Three Strikes and You're Out. One of the most powerful features of Three Strikes is that it is proactive, not reactive. Instead of putting people away after they have already taken a life, Three Strikes looks at prior convictions for violent crime and says that *any* felony, violent or not, becomes a trip wire that sends a felon away for life. It gets the would-be killer out of decent society before some innocent person becomes the next victim.

Another concept that became part of Three Strikes is the ratcheting up of punishment for each additional offense or strike. By providing an increasingly stepped-up sentence, Three Strikes would force bad guys to spend more time in prison sooner. Mike Reynolds and his fellow brainstormers also came up with the idea of reducing time off for good behavior, so that repeat offenders would serve a minimum of 80 percent of their sentences before being paroled. As he relates in his book, *Three Strikes and You're Out!—A Promise to Kimber,* the working group came up with a powerful, practical plan for overhauling and strengthening the criminal sentencing process in the state of California. Here are the main features of that plan:

- Double the sentence for a conviction of any felony if there is a previous serious or violent felony conviction.
- Triple the sentence or twenty-five years to life, whichever is greater, for any combination of two prior violent or serious felony convictions coupled with any new felony.
- Probation, a suspended sentence, or commitment to a diversion program as substitute for serving time in prison is prohibited for felons with a least one prior conviction of a serious or violent felony.
- Any felon with at least one prior serious or violent felony conviction must serve any subsequent felony sentence in a state prison (as opposed to a county jail).
- Terms are to be served consecutively, rather than concurrently.
- Maximum allowable time off for good behavior is reduced from 50 percent to 20 percent.
- Juvenile convictions for serious or violent felonies count as prior convictions if the felony was committed when the juvenile was sixteen or seventeen years old.
- When a defendant has at least one prior conviction for a serious or violent felony, the district attorney is required to plead and prove all known prior felony convictions. Prior felony convictions cannot be used as part of a plea bargain.[8]

I don't have space in this book to detail the tortuous process that Mike Reynolds went through to turn the Three Strikes dream into the toughest, most effective anticrime law in America. But I urge you to go to your bookstore or call the publisher at 1-800-497-4909 and order a copy of *Three Strikes and You're Out!—A Promise to Kimber* by Mike Reynolds, Dan Evans, and California Secretary of State Bill Jones. Read the story of the vicious media attacks against Mike Reynolds and Three Strikes, the indifference and outright hostility of liberal legislators in the California statehouse who tried to scuttle Three Strikes, the setbacks, the heartbreaks, the disappointments, and the ultimate triumph. In that book, Mike Reynolds shows you how to grab the political system by the throat and make it respond to the needs of We the People. It's a powerful story, and a practical blueprint for dramatically reducing violent crime. By January of 1997, Three Strikes had become law in twenty-one states besides California, and the concept continues to spread nationwide.

In June of 1996, the California State Supreme Court dealt Three Strikes a setback, giving judges more leeway to disregard prior strikes and to issue more lenient sentences. One of the fundamental concepts of Three Strikes is to eliminate judicial wiggle room, so that even liberal, soft-on-crime judges would be forced to mete out the punishment three-time losers deserve. Still, even though California's Three Strikes law is not as strong today as it was originally intended in all cases, it still applies in most cases by far, and it is still sweeping a lot of bad guys off California streets.[9]

In the first three years of Three Strikes, the law has been used to sentence 15,000 people. Initially, opponents of Three Strikes (mostly trial lawyers and liberal politicians and newspapers) predicted that the cost of enforcing Three Strikes would bankrupt the state. They warned that California would have to build half a dozen new prisons to house the 230,000 felons to be locked up by Three Strikes. Now, if you boil that argument down, what the opponents are saying is that we should save money by leaving bad guys on the street to rape and kill. But as it turns out, the anti-Three-Strikes crowd were wrong all the way around. They didn't count on the fact that Three Strikes would do what it was designed to do: deter crime! In October 1996, California prison officials announced that they were scaling back prison construction plans. Three Strikes had deterred crime to the point where there would only be 181,000 inmates by the year 2000. Two prison construction projects were completely canceled—and hundreds of millions of tax dollars were saved—because under Three Strikes, bad guys were either already locked up, behaving themselves, or fleeing the state.[10]

From the 1960s right up until the enactment of Three Strikes, crime rates in all categories showed a steady, frightening rise. Murder rates nearly tripled from 1965 to 1995; robberies and forcible rapes increased over 500 percent; and aggravated assaults increased over 600 percent. According to a National Crime Victimization survey, nearly 37 million people were injured by criminals from 1975 to 1995. But in the first year of California's Three

Strikes law, crime statistics suddenly did an about-face! The murder rate dropped dramatically—from 4,095 in 1993 to 3,699 in 1994. After three years of Three Strikes, there have been about *2,000 fewer murders* in California than prior murder trends indicated. In other words, 2,000 people are living today who would have been murder statistics if not for Mike Reynolds and Three Strikes. In that same three-year period, from 1994 through 1996, there were also 3,560 fewer rapes, 68,265 fewer robberies, and 33,859 fewer aggravated assaults. That adds up to almost 108,000 fewer victims of violent crime in California over those three years. "That's a 25 percent drop in violent crime per year," says Mike Reynolds. "Compared with 1993 statistics, that's like getting one year crime-free every fourth year!"[11]

What is the economic impact of Three Strikes? Well, what does crime cost us? Aside from the human toll, it's impossible to accurately calculate the dollar cost of crime in our society. Some estimates place the annual cost of crime at around $425 billion a year—a figure that includes everything from home security systems to insurance losses to medical losses to the cost of apprehending, trying, and incarcerating the bad guys. There are even such hidden costs as the loss of tourism dollars, as the state of Florida suffered after a well-publicized spate of car-jackings and murders of foreign tourists. Researchers at UC San Francisco and the National Public Services Research Institute in Landover, Maryland, put the average cost of treating a crime-related injury at $41,000. The cost of *all* crime-related injuries in America totals over $200 billion for medical and psychological expenses and lost productivity.[12] When violent crime is cut, lives are saved—and money is saved. Three Strikes doesn't cost. It pays.

Mike Reynolds is a hero. When victims are wounded, they sit and suffer. When a hero is wounded, he gets up and fights back. Mike Reynolds took his grief and loss and turned it into practical solutions to the crime problem in California and across the nation. He fought back—big time. Californians sleep more soundly and safely tonight, thanks to the courage, determination, and compassion of this American hero.

Before Three Strikes, police officers found they were arresting the same few bad guys over and over again, because a tiny percentage of the population is responsible for the largest percent of the crime. With Three Strikes in place, this tiny percentage of the population disappeared behind bars, and the crime rate dropped like a stone. Three Strikes is one of the most powerful weapons we have ever had against the cancer of crime. And it's only the beginning. There's so much more that you and I can do to defeat crime and to free our Shining City from the shadow of fear.

TO STOP CRIME, REBUILD THE FAMILY

In January 1994, Jesse Jackson hosted the mayors of Atlanta, Detroit, and Pittsburgh on his CNN show. His subject: crime in the city. Jackson began by saying to the mayors, "You have everything you want: a Democratic president, a Democratic House, a Democratic Senate. What do you want from government to deal with the crime question?" The first to respond was Mayor Bill Campbell of Atlanta. "Government's not the issue," Campbell replied. "It's really the breakdown of the family structure that is the critical ingredient propelling these kids into a life of crime." Incredibly, Jesse Jackson and the other mayors completely ignored Campbell's on-target assessment and focused primarily on ways government could spend more money on antipoverty programs, more recreational facilities, and so forth.

Mayor Campbell is right, and neither Jesse Jackson nor the other mayors on that show could see the evidence staring them in the face. People don't commit crimes because they need a place to shoot hoops. Crime is not the result of a lack of government education or a lack of government programs. People turn to crime because of a breakdown in their families. The family is where people are supposed to learn values and virtues—the importance of hard work, discipline, self-respect, respect for others, morality, faith, and family love. When the family breaks down, children have no place to learn these things.

According to research reported by Patrick F. Fagan of the Heritage Foundation, there is a clear link between the breakdown of marriage and the incidence of crime. In *Making America Safer* (edited by Edwin Meese and Robert E. Moffit), Fagan cites the following findings:

- Over the past three decades, the rise in violent crime corresponds to the rise in families abandoned by fathers.
- For every 10 percent increase in the number of children living in single-parent homes we see a 17 percent increase in juvenile crime.
- Neighborhoods high in crime are also highly concentrated with families abandoned by fathers.
- Even in high-crime neighborhoods in the inner city, 90 percent of kids

from stable, intact two-parent homes grow up without becoming involved in crime—despite growing up under the poverty line. Among inner-city families that are unstable and unsafe, only 10 percent grow up without becoming involved in crime.[13]

Liberalism approaches crime from a false premise. Liberals believe that *poverty causes crime* and that if one could eliminate poverty with a government program, crime would disappear. If you believe that economics determines behavior (as liberals do), you will seek only economic solutions to behavior problems, such as big-spending government programs to buy off criminals so they won't commit crimes anymore. We conservatives know that it's not economics but values and character that determine behavior.

It's easy to see why liberals are confused into thinking that poverty causes crime, because crime really does tend to flourish in the poor sections of every American city. But the fact that poverty and crime tend to concentrate in the same parts of town doesn't mean that poverty causes crime. The fact is, crime also tends to flourish in the parts of town where the most federal money is spent—around the housing projects, in places where you find heavy welfare dependency, rent subsidies, food stamps and WIC (supplemental nutrition for Women, Infants, and Children), government-sponsored day care, and on and on. You might as well say that government spending causes crime. (Maybe it does, but I'm not saying that.)

We have to look deeper for the real cause-and-effect linkage between poverty, federal spending, and crime. And here is the root cause of all three of these problems: *a breakdown of values and virtues rooted in a breakdown of the family.* This is not to say that all poor people have rotten values and rotten families—there are many poor people who live honestly, work hard, love their families, but for one reason or another haven't made it in life. We have to be careful not to overgeneralize. But I think it is fair to say that some poor people—and certainly those who are trapped in a multigenerational cycle of dependency on government checks—are poor because they lack the values that enable a person to achieve a measure of success and security in life:

1. Self-discipline
2. Responsibility

3. Work ethic
4. Commitment to education and personal improvement
5. Willingness to defer short-term gains and instant gratification in order to achieve long-term goals

If a person lacks those five ingredients, he or she is virtually destined for a life of poverty. This is the root cause of most poverty in America, and once this fact is understood, it becomes easier to find solutions to the problem.

If a person doesn't have these five ingredients, and if that person does have (a) extreme selfishness, (b) a lack of empathy for others, (c) an attitude of I-am-entitled-to-what-you-have-and-I-have-a-right-to-take-it-from-you, and (d) an attitude of I-want-what-I-want-and-I-want-it-now-and-I-don't-care-who-gets-hurt-or-how-I-get-it, *that person is a criminal*. The career criminals who roam our streets and fill our City with fear are not victims of grinding poverty and social injustice. They are evil, self-centered, unindustrious, irresponsible, pathological, antisocial predators. They became what they are, for the most part, because they never learned decent values and never acquired strong character.

The fact that a criminal may have come from a rotten home does not excuse his criminal behavior, nor does it alter the fact that he must be punished for past crimes and deterred from future crimes. Liberals say we should be compassionate and understanding toward criminals; they say that criminals can't help it that they came from rotten homes and fell into a rotten way of life. But you know what? A lot of people who came from identical or worse family backgrounds managed to avoid becoming criminals. A rotten family background doesn't determine a person's fate. People make choices in response to the rotten things that happen to them in life, and *those choices determine their fate*. We must hold all people responsible and accountable for their choices and behavior.

DEMAND LEGISLATION THAT PUNISHES CRIMINALS AND DEFENDS VICTIMS

Some areas that need to be addressed include legislation at both the federal and state levels, which would:

- Create truth-in-sentencing guidelines to require violent felons to serve at least 80 percent of their sentences. "You have about six percent of the criminals committing about 70 percent of the violent crimes and serving only about a third of their sentences nationwide," says Congressman Bill McCollum (R-Florida). "We've not been keeping these folks locked up."[14] A study in the state of Georgia found that the average prisoner released in 1995 had been sentenced to 5.87 years, but served only 2.33 years—or only 39 percent of the sentence. In 1990, the situation was even worse, with prisoners being turned loose after serving only 26 percent of their sentences. Strict truth-in-sentencing guidelines would force judges to impose well-defined punishment on various offenses, eliminating the capriciousness of judges who are overly lenient or overly harsh.

- Limit the ability of judges to suspend sentences or run sentences concurrently. When a criminal can serve concurrent sentences, it's like getting three or four crimes for the price of one. Why should we give crooks a bargain on criminal activity?
- Defend victims' rights: the right of crime victims to offer audio and video testimony to be kept on file for future hearings; the right to full restitution; the right to protection from intimidation or threat by the offender; the right to be notified of court proceedings; the right to be consulted in plea bargains; the right to be in court during trials concerning crimes against them; the right to make a statement during sentencing proceedings; the right to be notified if offenders are released or if they escape from custody.
- Make certain classes of heinous federal crimes eligible for the death penalty, including death for drug trafficking kingpins.
- Bloc-grant crime prevention funds to cities and counties so they can use it to fight crime as they see best—not with strings attached by Washington lawmakers and bureaucrats.
- End federally ordered early releases from prison as a solution to overcrowding. Violent felons should never, ever, EVER be unleashed on an innocent public simply to meet some arbitrary quota. Other solutions to overcrowding must be found, such as contracting with prisons operated by private-sector companies, converting closed military barracks into prisons, or paying other states with surplus prison space to house overflow population.
- Limit death-row appeals, many of which are frivolous.
- Limit the rights of prisoners to sue over prison conditions—a time-wasting, money-wasting practice that ties up our courts and prisons

with flimsy complaints from bad guys with too much time on their hands.

- Reinstate the idea that prisons are to be no-frills, no-fun detention centers where felons work productively. We must stop making prisons places where the dregs of our society enjoy free HBO, free weight rooms, and better law libraries than most universities. It's time that prisons look like prisons once again.
- Require that local communities be notified when sex offenders, murderers, and kidnappers are released in their area.

The success of Three Strikes in California has already proved that tough laws and severe punishment reduce crime. The issue of crime and punishment should no longer be a matter of debate between the right and the left. It's time for liberals and moderates to admit the truth about crime: To curb it, punish it. As Ronald Reagan observed in a speech on August 1, 1973, "The crime problem has indeed become a matter of widespread concern, even among people of different philosophies. Today's hard-liner on law and order is yesterday's liberal who was mugged last night."

LAW AND ORDER— AND NO FEAR

[In America], as nowhere in the world, we are established to provide the ultimate in individual freedom consistent with law and order.

Ronald Reagan
Eureka College Library Dedication Speech
September 28, 1967

An acquaintance of mine who has traveled all over Asia, including several trips to Singapore, tells me that a person can drop a wallet on any street in Singapore, come back two days later, and find it right where he left it, completely undisturbed. It's hard to believe, but he swears it's no exaggeration. When you compare crime statistics in Los Angeles with crime statistics in Singapore, it is easy to believe it's true. See Figure 4.1.

Figure 4.1. Crime Statistics in Los Angeles and Singapore

	Los Angeles	Singapore
Population	3,400,000	2,800,000
Murders in 1993	1,100	58
Rapes in 1993	1,855	80
Robberies in 1993	39,227	1,008
Car thefts in 1993	65,541	3,162

Though Singapore has a population almost as large as LA's, it has about one-twentieth as much crime. What this comparison represents is not merely two different cultures, but two starkly different attitudes toward the problem of crime. The Republic of Singapore (an island city-state located off the southern tip of the Malay Peninsula) views the primary role of government as one of protecting the safety of its citizens and the tranquillity of its society. The government of Singapore uses its authority to aggressively punish criminal behavior. The government of the United States, on the other hand, sees its role as one of protecting the rights of accused criminals and finding excuses for not punishing criminal behavior. While the U.S. government ignores its constitutional mandate to "establish justice" and "insure domestic tranquility," Singapore carries out that mandate, and the results can be seen in the crime statistics.

I'm sure you recall the controversy over the 1994 sentencing of American teenage delinquent Michael Fay to three strokes of a rattan cane, plus two months in prison, for vandalism, mischief, and dishonest retention of stolen property. A number of media critics in America responded to the sentence, calling the justice system in Singapore "barbaric." President Clinton termed the punishment "excessive." Many American commentators and politicians tried to bully the Singapore government, demanding that the country bend its laws and go easy on poor Mikey. It's interesting to note that none of these critics called for an end to *all* caning in Singapore—they just didn't want some Third World country whupping the delinquent derrierre of an American brat!

Prime Minister Goh Chok Tong of Singapore responded to American criticism with some well-aimed advice: "We deal severely with criminals and antisocial behavior. We have seen that in such cases, to be kind to the individual offender is to be cruel to the whole society—and to the individual. Strict punishment deters those who have been punished from repeating the offense." Singapore's crime statistics prove the policy works. A few months before the Michael Fay incident even occurred, Singaporean member of Parliament Koo Tsai Kee correctly diagnosed the ills of our own society:

> There is a tendency, particularly in the West, to ask society to carry an individual's sin, whether it be assault, drug-taking, vandalism, murder or mere teenage pregnancy. If an individual commits a crime, society is asked to share the blame. There is no demand for individual accountability. There is no right or wrong. This is misplaced compassion.[15]

To those cultural chauvinists who called Singapore "barbaric," let me ask you this: Which is the more barbaric place to live—a city ruled by fear or a city ruled by law? A city that punishes criminals or a city whose law-abiding citizens hide behind iron bars? In Singapore, a person can walk anywhere at night without fear. In America, people look over their shoulders and avoid certain parts of town, even in broad daylight. You tell me: Which is the civilized nation and which is barbaric? Which looks more like a Shining City?

Understand, I don't advocate flogging criminals with rattan canes. We don't need to go that far in order to restore justice and tranquillity to America, and to make her truly a Shining City on a Hill. We simply need to take the commonsense steps that we've examined in this chapter to reform our criminal justice system, at the same time restoring and empowering the American family.

In all the clamor and debate over the caning of Michael Fay, almost everyone seems to have missed what I think is the most important factor in the low Singaporean crime rate: strong moral values. In a much-needed sermon to America, Prime Minister Tong offers this moral advice: "Don't destroy traditional politeness and deference taught to children, avoid misguided compassion, and never remove that spur that makes people work and pay for themselves, or undermine self-control, discipline, and responsibility. And always hold the man responsible for the child he has fathered."[16]

Prime Minister Tong is talking about values. He's talking about family. He's talking about responsibility. When we, as an American society, make a collective decision to restore these lost virtues of our American heritage, we will begin once again to establish justice and ensure domestic tranquillity in our Shining City on a Hill.

PART TWO

THE CORNER
OF FAITH
AND CHARITY

The second cornerstone
of the City on a Hill is the
Civic and Religious
sector

CHAPTER FIVE

A
CITY
OF FAITH

AN ANGEL
ON HIS SHOULDER

I was raised to believe that God has a plan for everyone and that seemingly random twists of fate are all a part of His plan. My mother—a small woman with auburn hair and a sense of optimism that ran as deep as the cosmos—told me that everything in life happened for a purpose. She said all things were part of God's Plan, even the most disheartening setbacks, and in the end, everything worked out for the best. If something went wrong, she said, you didn't let it get you down: You stepped away from it, stepped over it, and moved on. Later on, she added, something good will happen and you'll find yourself thinking, "If I hadn't had that problem back then, then this better thing that did happen wouldn't have happened to me."

Ronald Reagan
From *An American Life*

Whatever happens now, I owe my life to God and will try to serve him in every way I can.

Ronald Reagan
Diary entry written after being
released from the hospital following
the 1981 assassination attempt

Return with me to March 30, 1981, the day my father was shot. On his own two feet, he walked through the triple glass doors of the emergency room at George Washington University Hospital. At that moment, no one knew he had been shot. Even he didn't know. He thought his Secret Service agent, Jerry Parr, had broken his ribs by jumping on him in the car. "I can't seem to catch my breath," he said as the nurses rushed to help him. Then his knees buckled and he staggered to one knee. Efficiently—but undoubtedly shocked to see the Leader of the Free World collapsing in their ER—the hospital staff carried Ronald Reagan into the trauma center.

Dr. Benjamin Aaron, chief of cardiothoracic surgery at the hospital, thought Dad was having a heart attack. He took Dad's blood pressure—only to find there was *no* blood pressure. Instantly, they shredded Dad's blue pinstripe suit—and that's when they found the entry wound under his left arm. Dr. Aaron said it looked like a buttonhole.

The medical team immediately administered oxygen, IV fluids, and type-O Rh-negative blood, the first pint of what would add up to nearly a gallon of transfusions, half the body's blood supply. The doctors worried because they couldn't control the internal bleeding, and his left lung had collapsed. The X rays showed the bullet lodged about a quarter of an inch from Dad's heart.

Dr. Aaron and the rest of the surgical team met with Dad and Nancy, explaining that they wanted to perform exploratory surgery to remove the bullet. Dad and Nancy agreed. As the doctors were about to scrub for surgery, Dad joked to one of them, "Please tell me you're a Republican." One of the surgeons, said to be a confirmed Democrat, replied, "Today, Mr. President, we're *all* Republicans."

So Dad was wheeled into surgery, and the doctors opened him up and began probing for the bullet. The procedure dragged through one hour, then two, then into a third hour. The surgeons couldn't find the bullet. It was frustrating for them, because the X ray indicated where the bullet *should* have been, but it didn't seem to be there. As time went on, the doctors grew concerned that the longer Dad remained under anesthetic, the harder his recovery would be. They discussed leaving the bullet in him. This is certainly not uncommon with gunshot victims, although there was concern that the bullet might move into an artery. It was a tough call, and the tide of opinion in the operating room was swinging in favor of leaving the bullet and simply getting Dad stabilized.

Just as the doctors were on the verge of closing up, the surgeon found the slug, flattened to about the size and shape of a dime. Once found, it was quickly removed and the operation was brought to a happy close.

Sometime later, in the recovery room, Dad awoke from the anesthesia. He was groggy and weak, but aware of his surroundings. He saw figures, gowned in white, moving around him. He couldn't speak, because of the tube down his throat, so he motioned for something to write on. One of the nurses handed him a pad of pink paper and a pen. In a weak hand, he scrawled, "I'm alive, aren't I?" Nancy still has that piece of paper among her personal treasures.

Dad used that pad to kid with the nurses. When one of them asked how he was feeling, he wrote (quoting a sickbed line by W. C. Fields), "All in all, I'd rather be in Philadelphia."

At that point, no one but the doctors knew how close America came to losing Ronald Reagan. It frightens me to think what would have happened had that bullet not stopped a quarter of an inch from Dad's heart. The Reagan family would have lost so much, but the world would have lost even more: the optimism of the 1980s, America's return to pride and prosperity, and the end of global communism. All of that potential was compressed into the tiny space between a madman's bullet and my father's heart.

I didn't know it yet, but a miracle had taken place in those hours.

I arrived at my Sherman Oaks home to find reporters and cameras thronging the neighborhood. A lot of my feelings toward the press were confirmed during the brief walk between my car and my back door, when I was pelted with some of the stupidest questions I ever heard in my life. Once inside, I became a prisoner in my own house. Neither Colleen nor I could go outside because reporters hovered out there like a swarm of killer bees.

Our friends Don and Dottie Price came over to help us keep our sanity. Don took Cameron for a walk and, since he was still in his suit and tie from work, the newspaper photographers figured he was a Secret Service agent. And that's how he was identified when the picture of Don walking Cameron appeared in all the papers the next morning.

All I wanted at that moment was to hop a plane to Washington, but the word came back through the Secret Service that everything was okay; my father wasn't in any danger (right!), and the family shouldn't be seen rushing to his side lest the country take it as a sign that things were really bad.

Well, things *were* really bad, for crying out loud! But I didn't have a clue *how* bad.

After a while, the lead agent on our security detail, Cliff Baranowski, came and said, "Listen, Mike, they're rustling up a plane for you. It'll take off at six tonight. You'll get into Washington quite late, stay overnight in the White House, and tomorrow you'll go to the hospital to see the president." He said it in crisp, businesslike tones, like Joe Friday on *Dragnet*.

"Okay," I said. "Fine."

"One more thing," Cliff added. "When you get on the plane, they'll give you a blanket, earplugs, and a box lunch."

"You're kidding."

"No, I'm not kidding," said Cliff. "The only plane we could get is a C-130 transport. Frankly, it's not a very comfortable airplane, so you need to dress warmly."

Inside the plane, I quickly found out what the blanket, earplugs, and box lunch were for. The C-130 was a big, hollow hulk without a galley for food preparation—and without any insulation. When the heater was on, it was 400 degrees in that plane; when the heater shut off, it was instantly *minus*-400. The scream of the engines coming through the aluminum airplane skin jarred the bones and rattled the teeth.

We took off from a private terminal at LAX. It was a terrible flight—not only noisy and uncomfortable, but miserable with worry for Dad. Also on the flight were Colleen and Cameron, Maureen and her fiancé, Dennis Revell, Patti, and a few Secret Service agents. Ron, who was with the Joffrey Ballet at the time, took a plane from Nebraska and arrived before we did.

The person most visibly affected by the assassination attempt was Patti. We were all profoundly affected, of course, but I spent a lot of time with her during the trip to Washington and back, because she was absolutely broken. Patti had never been happy about Dad being president, and to have this happen just three months into his presidency reinforced all her negative feelings about politics.

Remember I said that a miracle took place in those first few hours that my father was in the hospital? There were many fragile links in the chain of events that preserved Ronald Reagan's life: Agent Parr's prompt decision to take Dad to the hospital, the explosive-tipped bullet that stopped short of the heart and failed to explode, the discovery of the bullet when doctors had nearly given up, and on and on. If just one of those links had been broken, we would have lost our dad and the world would have lost a great man.

Cardinal Terence Cooke of New York expressed it well when he visited Dad during his recovery and told him, "Mr. President, you surely have an angel sitting on your shoulder."

The chain of events that spared Ronald Reagan's life had a profound effect on the faith of all of us in the Reagan family—most of all, perhaps, for Patti. She was the one who struggled the most with Dad, with his conservative politics, with his public life as president, and now with his wounding by a would-be assassin. Sometime later, Patti was discussing the incident with a friend who is a hospital nurse. When Patti mentioned the white-clad people Dad saw when he awoke from the anesthesia, the woman asked, "Are you sure your dad said the people wore *white*?"

"Absolutely," said Patti. "He was definite about that."

"That's odd," said her friend. "No one in a recovery room or intensive care wears white. They all wear green scrubs."

Patti was shaken. She quickly called Nancy and told her about the conversation with the nurse. "You know," said Nancy, "in all that happened that day, I didn't even think of that—but you're right, all the hospital personnel *were* wearing green, not white." So who were the white-gowned figures Dad saw in the recovery?

Could they have been . . . *angels*?

Patti and Nancy aren't the only ones who think so.

ONE NATION UNDER GOD

Without God, there is no virtue, because there's no prompting of the conscience. Without God, we're mired in the material, that flat world that tells us only what the senses perceive. Without God, there is a coarsening of the society. And without God, democracy will not and cannot long endure. If we ever forget that we're one nation under God, then we will be a nation gone under.

Ronald Reagan
Speech, Ecumenical Prayer Breakfast
Republican National Convention
Dallas, Texas, August 23, 1984

The real crisis we face today is a spiritual one. At root, it is a test of moral will and faith.

Ronald Reagan
Speech before the annual convention of the
National Association of Evangelicals
Orlando, Florida, March 8, 1983

It is only natural that Ronald Reagan would find himself surrounded by angels in a time of crisis. He has always been a man of quiet but profound faith. As far back as I can remember, Dad and God have always been on good speaking terms. To Dad, God is not some remote Cosmic Authority; rather, God is a good and constant friend. In his autobiography, *An American Life,* Dad talked about the spiritual foundation he received as a boy, primarily from his mother, Nelle:

> Nelle assumed responsibility for the spiritual preparation of my brother and me. She first took us to Sunday school, then, when we were older, to the main services, but always said she'd leave it up to us to decide whether we wanted to actually join the church. At twelve, I made my decision and was baptized as a member of the Disciples of Christ. . . .
>
> I have always prayed a lot; in those days [the Great Depression], I prayed things would get better for our country, for our family, and for Dixon [Dad's hometown in Illinois]. I even prayed before football games. . . . I didn't pray to win—I didn't expect God to take sides—but I prayed no one would be injured; we'd all do our best and have no regrets no matter how the game came out.
>
> But I was afraid to reveal this to my older and more sophisticated teammates. Then, to my amazement, everyone in the room said that they prayed—and to my surprise, they all said they prayed along the same lines that I did.
>
> That was the last time I was ever reluctant to admit I prayed.[1]

Dad's early spiritual foundation shaped his life, his worldview, and even his political beliefs. When he was a boy, schoolchildren were taught the truth about how their nation began and the principles of faith that America was founded upon. So there was no contradiction between Ronald Reagan's inner life of faith and his view of America's heritage as "one nation under God." His faith in God was seamlessly welded to his faith in America as a Shining City on a Hill.

Ronald Reagan, like most Americans of his generation, clearly understood that America was built on the firm foundation of a rich, moral Judeo-

Christian heritage. Faith in God is central to America's history and the American philosophy of government. The idea that America is a purely secular nation or that the First Amendment requires the complete exclusion of religion from public life is a heresy that has only arisen in the last few decades of this century. People can only adopt such a view by being ignorant or dishonest about our history and our founding documents, which are steeped in Judeo-Christian principles.

The Puritans and the Pilgrims who came to the New World in the 1600s left England in order to be free to worship God according to their own conscience. As my father was fond of recalling, it was the great Puritan leader John Winthrop, the first governor of the Massachusetts colony, who reminded his fellow Puritans to maintain their faith in God. Why? Because the Lord Himself had sent them to the New World to be a light before the nations—"a Shining City upon a Hill."

Ronald Reagan talked about Winthrop and his vision of a Shining City when he rededicated the newly refurbished Statue of Liberty during the Statue's centennial celebration, July 3, 1986. Standing alongside Nancy, Lee Iacocca, and President and Madame Mitterrand of France, and shaded by the great copper-clad lady Dad often called "the other woman in my life," Dad described his own belief in the divinely appointed purpose of the United States of America. "Call it mysticism if you will," he said, "but I have always believed there was some divine providence that placed this great land here between the two great oceans, to be found by a special kind of people from every corner of the world, who had a special love for freedom and a special courage that enabled them to leave their own land, leave their friends and their countrymen, and come to this new and strange land to build a new world of peace and freedom and hope."

America was no accident of history in Ronald Reagan's mind. It was placed here by the hand of God to be a Shining City, illuminating the world. That is what the early founders of America believed as well. William Penn, the English Quaker founder of the colony of Pennsylvania, warned, "If we will not be governed by God, we must be governed by tyrants." Tragically, his warning may be on the way to fulfillment in our time.

The very first Contract with America was not written by Newt Gingrich in 1994, but by Thomas Jefferson in 1776. That contract was the Declaration of Independence, and it proclaimed that man is master of the government, not government the master of man. The basis of this bold new concept was nothing less than a belief in God, the Source of all our rights.

"We hold these truths to be self-evident," it reads, "that all men are created equal, that they are endowed by their Creator with certain unalienable rights, that among these are life, liberty and the pursuit of happiness."

In his *Notes on the State of Virginia*, Jefferson—the third president of the United States—wrote these lines, which read like a commentary upon the core concept of the Declaration: "God, who gave us life, gave us liberty. And can the liberties of a nation be thought secure when we have removed their only firm basis, a conviction in the minds of the people that these liberties are a gift of God? That they are not to be violated but with His wrath? Indeed, I tremble for my country when I reflect that God is just; that His justice cannot sleep forever."

If involving God in government is unconstitutional, then the first and worst offender is the father of our country, George Washington. In his inaugural address of 1789, he told the nation, "The propitious smiles of Heaven can never be expected on a nation that disregards the eternal rules of order and right which Heaven itself has ordained." And James Madison—one of the chief framers of our Constitution and the fourth president of the United States—agreed. "Before any man can be considered as a member of civil society, he must be considered a subject of the Governor of the Universe," wrote Madison. "We have staked the future of all of our political institutions upon the capacity of each and all of us to govern ourselves, to control ourselves, to sustain ourselves according to the Ten Commandments of God."

John Adams, second president of the United States and one of the framers of our Constitution, warned in 1798, "Our Constitution was made only for a moral and religious people. It is wholly inadequate for the government of any other."

And what about Thomas Paine, that rabble-rousing Englishman whose fifty-page pamphlet *Common Sense* (published January 10, 1776) had such a profound influence on both the American and French Revolutions? If Tom were alive and kicking today, he'd *really* be kicking to see what has become of his beloved America! And I firmly believe he'd probably be sitting behind a microphone, blasting the liberals as a radio talk show host! And what was Thomas Paine's commonsense view of religion in public life? "The cause of America is in a great measure the cause of all mankind," he wrote. "Where, say some, is the King of America? I'll tell you, friend: He reigns above."

What I call "The Corner of Faith and Charity" has always been one of the main intersections in our Shining City on a Hill. If our founding fathers could see how we have shut Judeo-Christian faith and morality out of American public life, they'd think we had lost our minds—and our souls. And they would be right. The principles of the Bible are the foundation of our government. Those who designed our government and wrote our Constitution were well acquainted with Proverbs 29:2, which tells us, "When the righteous are in authority, the people rejoice; /But when a wicked man rules, the people groan." In fact, our system of government is based upon the model found in another Old Testament passage, Isaiah 33:22. (See Figure 5.1.)

Figure 5.1. Old Testament System of Government

Branch of Government		Isaiah 33:22
The Judicial Branch	➔	For the LORD is our Judge,
The Legislative Branch	➔	The LORD is our Lawgiver,
The Executive Branch	➔	The LORD is our King;
		He will save us.

At the time America declared her independence, each of the thirteen colonies had its own constitution, and most of those state constitutions had a written requirement that those who served in public office had to be people of faith. This passage from the Delaware Constitution, adopted in 1776, was typical:

Everyone appointed to public office must say: "I do profess faith in God the Father, and in the Lord Jesus Christ His only Son, and in the Holy Ghost, one God and blessed forevermore; and I do acknowledge the Holy Scriptures of the Old and New Testaments to be given by divine inspiration."

Clearly, the founding fathers and the framers of our Constitution never dreamed that the First Amendment—our guarantee of religious freedom—would ever be stood on its head and turned into a weapon to suppress religion! America is not a theocracy, nor will we ever permit the establishment of a state religion—but neither is America a secular nation. The founding fathers saw no contradiction whatsoever in the idea of America as a nonsectarian, pluralistic, yet godly nation.

THE MEDICINE
OF FORGIVENESS

This is the real task before us: to reassert our commitment as a nation to a law higher than our own, to renew our spiritual strength. Only by building a wall of such spiritual resolve can we, as a free people, hope to protect our own heritage and make it someday the birthright of all men.

Ronald Reagan
Speech before the
Conservative Political Action Conference
Washington, D.C., March 20, 1981

Ronald Reagan spoke the words quoted above just ten days before a bullet came within a quarter of an inch of ending his life. As it turned out, the same spiritual strength and resolve he urged America to rediscover would become the strength he relied on to recover from his wounds. None of us in the Reagan family knew what to expect as that cold, noisy C-130 military cargo plane descended toward Washington. Would Dad be conscious when we saw him? Would he seem weak and helpless? Even at seventy, he was the strongest man we knew, and none of us had ever seen him sick or wounded before. How would this event affect his presidency? Would he even be able to serve out his term? Doubts and questions churned inside us as the plane settled onto the tarmac, long past midnight.

Colleen and I spent the night in the Lincoln Bedroom. We got up the next morning and, over breakfast, we discussed what we were going to do that day. Nancy Reynolds, the First Lady's press secretary, told us that Ron and Patti were already at the hospital, and we wouldn't be able to see Dad until later. That didn't set well with Maureen and me. Being Nancy's stepchildren, we often felt treated as—well, as stepchildren. But I decided to make good use of the time by paying a visit to the other men who had been wounded that day—Jim Brady, Agent McCarthy, and Officer Delahanty.

After breakfast, Colleen and I got into one of the old armor-plated Cadillac limousines that the White House used at that time (Maureen and Dennis got into another limousine) and we started out. The Secret Service agents were edgy because at that point they didn't know if Hinckley had acted alone or if he was part of a larger conspiracy. They worried about other attempts on the family. As we drove down Pennsylvania Avenue, I noticed that the bulletproof window next to me was going down all by itself. So I leaned forward, tapped Agent Baranowski on the shoulder and calmly said, "Cliff, should this window be going down?" Cliff Baranowski turned around, saw the open window, and literally turned *white*! He lunged over the backrest of the front seat, gripped the top of the window glass with both hands, and tried to manually pull the window up again.

I watched as Cliff struggled and cussed that window. Obviously, the White House limousine fleet was falling apart like everything else left over from the Carter administration. I figured that if we could just get Dad back on his feet again, all those things that were falling apart—the economy, the military, the national morale, the windows in the White House limousines—would soon be good as new again. And I was right.

Officer Delahanty was at a different hospital from Dad and the others, and we visited him first. Then we headed for George Washington University Hospital. We arrived as Ron and Patti were coming out; they had just been with Dad. We visited Agent McCarthy, and he predicted he would be the first one out of the hospital (he was right). Then we visited Jim Brady.

It tore my heart to see Sarah Brady hovering over her gravely wounded husband, pleading with him to live, practically pouring her own spirit and vitality into his limp body. Sarah Brady pulled Jim Brady through those critical weeks after he was shot. Because of her, Jim Brady is alive today.

Next, we went to a holding area to wait. We waited. And we waited some more. Nancy was in the room with Dad, and though I knew Dad would need a lot of support from Nancy to get better, I was getting impatient. Why was it taking so long for the doctors to let us see him? Finally, one of the Secret Service agents came and I thought, *Great, now we can go in.* Instead, the agent said, "The doctors don't feel the president is strong enough to see the rest of the family right now. You can come back in twenty-four hours."

We were all stunned. "That's stupid!" I said in my usual diplomatic manner. "Let me talk to the doctor!"

"Sorry, the doctor's not available right now."

Maureen and I were fuming. Even then, after having come all that way to visit our father in the hospital, we were being treated like stepchildren. Maureen turned to me and said, "Michael, you've got to be my bird dog.

You've got to sniff out a way to get us into Dad's room." She knew I could con my way into anywhere.

"Leave it to me," I said. I walked out of the holding area and poked around until I found a door to another holding room. The door was unlocked, so I barged right in and found myself face-to-face with one of Dad's doctors. I said, "What's this I hear about you wanting to keep me and my sister from seeing our dad?"

He stuttered and stammered, and I knew we were in. Soon, Maureen, Dennis, Colleen, and I were all ushered into the room. The drapes were fastened shut for security reasons, so there was no sunlight. For some reason, the room was very hot. I could tell Dad had some pain, and he seemed weakened and tired from the ordeal, but he was alert and easy to talk to. As we were chatting, he deadpanned, "Michael, if you're ever shot, make sure you're not wearing a new suit."

I hadn't really been planning to get shot, new suit or no new suit. So I said, "Excuse me?"

He grinned. "You know, that was a brand-new suit I was wearing yesterday. First time I ever wore it. Michael, do you know what happens when they bring you into the emergency room of the hospital? They don't go to you and say, 'Please remove your suit, Mr. President.' No, they take a pair of scissors and cut your clothes right off of you! The last time I saw that suit, it was sitting in a corner of the emergency room, completely shredded."

"I can see how that would be upsetting, Dad," I replied. "Of course, there is something to be said for the fact that they saved your life."

"Oh, I'm not complaining," he said. "The doctors and nurses here are great. But I sure did like that suit. You know, I hear the parents of the young fella who shot me live in Denver. The father's in the oil business, I think."

"Yeah," I said. "I read that in the paper."

"Well," he continued, "I think the least they could do is buy me a new suit."

"Dad, I think they owe you that much."

The assassination attempt affected my father's spiritual life in two important and seemingly contradictory ways. On the one hand, it denied him one of his greatest pleasures in life—spending time with God's people in God's house, worshiping his Lord. He's never gotten over the memory of his longtime friend, Jim Brady, writhing on the ground with his forehead in a pool of blood. Dad always blamed himself for that. It hurt him deeply to know that three other men had taken bullets intended for him, and he never again wanted to put innocent bystanders in harm's way. He worried about some other would-be assassin coming into the church and killing or wounding people who had come to worship. Dad was also conscious of the fact that when he was sitting in the pew, many other people would be so distracted by his presence, they wouldn't be able to concentrate on the music or the message. As much as he enjoyed being in church on the Lord's Day, he reluctantly avoided attending church for the next eight years.

On the other hand, the assassination attempt prompted him to make a profound commitment, which he mentioned to me shortly after the shooting. "Michael," he said, "I've thought a lot about the events of that day, and how close I came to losing my life. Not only would my earthly life have been over, but also everything I wanted to do for the American people would have ended right then and there. I look at all the things that could have gone wrong that day—yet God controlled every circumstance. I believe He spared me for a purpose. Michael, I want you to know I've made a decision to recommit the rest of my life, and the rest of my presidency, to God."

One of the evidences of that commitment was the way he responded to the young man who shot him. Dad never expressed any bitterness toward John Hinckley. In fact, all of us in the Reagan family are convinced that one of the factors that sped Dad's recovery was his commitment to living out his Christian faith. If there is one central theme of Christianity, it is forgiveness—God's forgiveness of sinful human beings because of the sacrifice of Jesus Christ upon the cross, and our forgiveness of one another. The principle is found in such passages as Ephesians 4:32: "And be kind to one another, tenderhearted, forgiving one another, just as God in Christ forgave you."

Dad would be the first to say that Hinckley should be held accountable for his actions. Forgiveness without accountability is just the indulgence of evil. But he also said his recovery was linked to his ability to release all resentment toward the troubled young gunman. Resentment, he said, is a poison that works against the healing process. Forgiveness is a medicine.

Ronald Reagan committed his life and his presidency to God, and I think the evidence of history demonstrates that he was faithful to that commitment throughout his eight years in office. Near the end of his second term, he went to the United Nations Building in New York and gave a final address to that organization. Thanks to Ronald Reagan's strong leadership, the U.S. and the Soviet Union had just reached an agreement to dramatically reduce their stockpiles of nuclear weapons, so it was a time of real hope and optimism for the entire world. Near the end of the speech he gave on September 26, 1988, he remarked, "When we grow weary of the world and its troubles, when our faith in humanity falters, it is then that we must seek comfort and refreshment of spirit in a deeper source of wisdom, one greater than ourselves." That was not only a statement of my father's faith in God, but of the way he conducted his presidency and the way he lives his life.

THE POWER OF PRAYER

You know, in one of the conflicts that was going on through-out the past year, when views were held deeply on both sides of the debate, I recall talking to one senator who came into my office. We both deeply believed what it was we were espousing, but we were on opposite sides. And when we fin-ished talking, as he rose, he said, "I'm going out of here and do some praying." And I said, "Well, if you get a busy signal, it's me there ahead of you."

Ronald Reagan
Annual National Prayer Breakfast
Washington, D.C., February 4, 1982

Prayer has always been an integral part of Ronald Reagan's life, and the prayers of others were especially important to him after he was felled by a bullet in Washington, D.C. "It's a remarkable feeling to know that people are praying for you and for your strength," he wrote in his book *Speaking My Mind*. "I know firsthand. I felt those prayers when I was recovering from that bullet."[2]

Prayer and worship are clearly important values in American life as well. "More than half the American people," observes historian Paul Johnson, "still attend a place of worship over a weekend, an index of religious practice unequaled anywhere in the world." According to surveys cited by the Heritage Foundation, 94 percent of blacks, 87 percent of whites, 91 percent of women, and 85 percent of men claim to pray on a regular basis. Amazingly, even among the 13 percent of the population who list themselves as agnostic or atheist, some 20 percent pray daily! (To whom, I wonder?)

These same surveys found that people who practice their religious faith by attending church are more likely to be married, less likely to be divorced or single, and express a higher level of satisfaction in their lives. Women who practice their religion achieve greater sexual satisfaction in marriage than moderately religious or nonreligious women do. Urban poor church-goers are more likely to move out of poverty than nonchurchgoers and less likely to fall into such social problems as drug abuse, crime, divorce, out-of-wedlock births, and suicide. One researcher, Richard B. Freeman of the National Bureau of Economic Research, observed:

> [Church attendance] is associated with substantial differences in the behavior of [black male youths from poverty-stricken inner-city neighborhoods] and thus in their chances to "escape" from inner city poverty. It affects allocation of time, school-going, work activity and the frequency of socially deviant activity. . . . It is important to recognize that our analysis has identified an important set of variables that separate successful from unsuccessful young persons in the inner city.[3]

Other studies among poor inner-city black and Hispanic middle-school children showed that children with low church attendance exhibited more pessimism about the future, while students who attended church at least once a week demonstrated optimism, better relationships with parents, serious and realistic goals in life, and an ability to see the world as a friendly environment for their achievement rather than a hostile place in which they would likely fail. Students with higher church attendance were less likely to view racism as an obstacle in the way of reaching their goals and more likely to feel a sense of control over their own destinies.

Churchgoing and prayer were found to improve physical health, increase longevity, hasten recovery from illness and injury, and reduce the incidence of deadly diseases. In short, people who practice their faith live longer. Researchers at Johns Hopkins University School of Public Health found that cardiovascular disease—a leading killer of the aged—is significantly less among people who have regularly attended church throughout their lives. Mortality rates for other diseases, such as cirrhosis of the liver, arteriosclerosis, certain cancers, and emphysema, are also markedly lower among those who attend church regularly. Blood pressure is lowered an average of 5mm of pressure by regular church attendance.

Perhaps the most startling findings in the Heritage Foundation report are the results of a 1982 study by cardiologist Robert B. Byrd at the UC San Francisco Medical School. He studied the effects of prayer on people with illnesses. In random-sample, double-blind tests, he found that recovery rates were better for heart surgery patients who were prayed for than patients who were not prayed for. None of the patients were told that they were being prayed for, and none of the doctors and nurses knew which patients were being prayed for and which were not. The people who prayed had no contact with the patients. Those who received prayer had markedly fewer cardiopulmonary arrests and post-op congestive heart failures. They also had a lower incidence of pneumonia and needed fewer antibiotics than the group receiving no prayer.

My father had a similar experience. Shortly after becoming governor of California, he was diagnosed with an ulcer. For over a year, he watched his diet, downed untold quantities of Maalox, and prayed daily for healing—but no healing came. In fact, the pain in his stomach got worse as time went on and the problems of being governor weighed on him. Then one morning, he got up, went to the medicine cabinet, reached for his usual dose of Maalox to start the day—and a thought occurred to him: *I don't need this stuff anymore.* So he decided to forego the Maalox and see what happened.

He went to his Sacramento office and started his workday. He soon noticed that the ache in his stomach was gone. One of his first appointments for the day was with a businessman from the LA area. They talked for a while about the man's concerns, and as he was about to leave, the man turned to my father and said, "Governor, I just want you to know that I'm part of a group of people who meet every day and pray for you."

"Well," said Dad, "I sure can use it—and I put a lot of stock in the power of prayer. Thank you—and please thank the others for me."

The afternoon of the same day, Dad met with another businessman. Again, at the end of their meeting, this man said he was part of a group that met daily to pray for Dad.

A few days later, Dad went to his doctor for his regular checkup—and the doctor was stunned to find that there was no sign of an ulcer. Dad was healed. Believe what you want, but he knew it was the power of prayer.

Clearly, there is no force in America that can claim to have the positive influence on our lives and our society that faith in God does. Those who have tried to lock religion out of our schools, our political institutions, and our public institutions have done America a great disservice.

It is sobering to remember the words of John Winthrop in 1630. He predicted that America would be a place of blessing and influence throughout the world: "We shall be as a City upon a Hill. The eyes of all people are upon us." But he issued a warning: "If we shall deal falsely with our God in this work we have undertaken and so cause Him to withdraw His present help from us, we shall be made a story and a byword through all the world." Will we continue to be the Shining City upon a Hill that John Winthrop and Ronald Reagan envisioned? Or will we instead serve as an example of the destruction that comes upon a society when it deals falsely with God?

That's the decision we make today.

"GOD WILL HOLD YOU TO ACCOUNT"

A state is nothing more than a reflection of its citizens; the more decent the citizens, the more decent the state. If you practice a religion, whether you're Catholic, Protestant, Jewish, or guided by some other faith, then your private life will be influenced by a sense of moral obligation, and so too, will your public life. One affects the other. The churches of America do not exist by the grace of the state; the churches of America are not mere citizens of the state. The churches of America exist apart; they have their own vantage point; their own authority. Religion is its own realm; it makes its own claims.

We establish no religion in this country, nor will we ever. We command no worship. We mandate no belief. But we poison our society when we remove its theological underpinnings. We court corruption when we leave it bereft of belief. All are free to believe or not believe; all are free to practice a faith or not. But those who believe must be free to speak of and act on their belief, to apply moral teaching to public questions.

Ronald Reagan
Speech, Ecumenical Prayer Breakfast
Republican National Convention
Dallas, Texas, August 23, 1984

On Christmas Eve 1996, President Bill Clinton and his family attended an evening service at Washington's National Cathedral. As people filed up the aisle to receive Communion, some would stop at the railing near where President Clinton sat and offer him Christmas greetings. One man who stopped and spoke to the president was Reverend Robert Schenck, general secretary of the National Clergy Council. He said, "God will hold you to account, Mr. President." He spoke politely and softly, but his words seemed to strike Bill Clinton like a bolt of lightning from heaven.

Reverend Schenck's words referred to Bill Clinton's veto of the partial-birth abortion ban, which had been passed by huge bipartisan margins in both houses of Congress. Just a few weeks earlier, the House had overridden the president's veto—but the Senate later sustained that veto by a single vote. Infuriated at being challenged, even in such a respectful, polite way, the president ordered his Secret Service agents to roust Reverend Schenck. As the choir sang "What Child Is This," agents of the Secret Service held Reverend Schenck, reached into his jacket, lifted his wallet, and began rifling through it. Spectators watched the ugly scene as Reverend Schenck was detained and treated like a criminal outside the Cathedral for some fifteen minutes.

An eyewitness to these proceedings, Steve Myers, editor of the online *Exegesis Update*, said, "If the President feels threatened by God's Word, it is not because his life is under threat, but because his Eternal Life is under threat, and that is beyond the jurisdiction even of the Secret Service." Ronald Reagan would never have felt threatened by those eight politely spoken words, "God will hold you to account, Mr. President." He already held himself accountable before God, and his conscience was clear.

Ronald Reagan proclaimed the truth. Bill Clinton can't face the truth. So—like some tyrant from the Old Testament, ordering his servants to toss one of God's uppity prophets in a dungeon—Bill Clinton sent his bodyguards to silence a man of God. That's *wrong*. And it's typical of what has been going wrong in America for a long time.

Many people have a mistaken notion that the First Amendment is about separation of church and state. Check it out. You won't find that phrase in the First Amendment, or anywhere else in the Constitution. The First Amendment states quite simply:

Congress shall make no law respecting an establishment of religion, or prohibiting the free exercise thereof; or abridging the freedom of speech, or of the press; or the right of the people peaceably to assemble, and to petition the government for a redress of grievances.

That's the whole amendment right there. Reverend Schenck had a constitutional right to say what he said, to exercise his religion and freedom of speech, and to petition the leader of his government for redress of a most horrible grievance.

All of us, as people of faith, have not only a constitutional right but also a *moral obligation* to do what Reverend Schenck did. We have a duty to do whatever we can to influence our government toward a more godly and moral path. We are morally bound to confront our government and call it to account whenever it violates our moral and spiritual sensibilities. And if suctioning a near-born baby's brains out of her skull when she's all of three inches from being fully born doesn't violate our moral and spiritual sensibilities, then I don't know what will!

Jesus called his people to be *salt* and *light*. Salt is a preservative. Light is illumination. People of faith preserve and illuminate society by being bold, outspoken, and active in practicing their faith. Christianity is not a private matter. Jesus taught his followers to be very public about their faith. If we, as people of faith, do not project our faith in the public arena—in politics, in the schools, in the marketplace, and in the neighborhood—then we are disobedient to our faith.

The First Amendment was never written to protect government from being influenced by religion. It was written to keep government from establishing or suppressing religion. The First Amendment protects the church from government interference, not the other way around. At some point in recent history, people stopped reading the First Amendment and began substituting their own cockeyed interpretation of it: "The First Amendment allows you to practice your religion in private, but not out in the open where the rest of us might be bothered. Keep your religion behind closed doors. It doesn't belong out in public."

Puh-leeeze! To say a person has religious freedom only in private is the same as saying we have no religious freedom at all. Folks behind the Iron Curtain, living under the hammer and sickle, had that much religious freedom: Believe what you want, but keep it to yourself. That's not freedom—and that's not what the First Amendment says.

The First Amendment guarantees the "free exercise" of religion. It guarantees you the right to walk right up to the president of the United States and say, "God will hold you to account, Mr. President." This is not the Soviet Union under Stalin. This is not Hitler's Germany. This is America, for crying out loud! This country was founded for the precise reason that we, as Americans, will not put up with kings! We have always demanded—and will continue to demand—our God-given right to talk back to our leaders, to tell them they're wrong, and to hold their feet to the fire until their soles (or their souls) sizzle.

GOD IS NOT A DIRTY WORD

Freedom prospers when religion is vibrant and the rule of law under God is acknowledged. When our Founding Fathers passed the First Amendment, they sought to protect churches from government interference. They never intended to construct a wall of hostility between government and the concept of religious belief itself. The evidence of this permeates our history and our government. The Declaration of Independence mentions the Supreme Being no less than four times. "In God We Trust" is engraved on our coinage. The Supreme Court opens its proceedings with a religious invocation. And the members of Congress open their sessions with a prayer. I just happen to believe the schoolchildren of the United States are entitled to the same privileges as Supreme Court justices and congressmen.

Ronald Reagan
Speech before the annual convention of the
National Association of Evangelicals
Orlando, Florida, March 8, 1983

Students in a Dickson County, Tennessee, middle school were given an assignment to write a research paper on a topic they felt strongly about. Some kids wrote about politics. Others wrote about the environment. Some wrote about reincarnation and magic. Ninth-grader Brittney Settle wrote about the life of Jesus Christ. She got her paper back with a big red zero across the top. "It's not appropriate to write a paper on personal religious beliefs in a public school," her teacher explained. "Find another topic and write another paper."

When Brittney's parents took her case to the principal, they expected a reasonable response. After all, the First Amendment guarantees their daughter both the right to free exercise of her religion and the right to free speech. They figured that, even though this teacher didn't understand their daughter's rights, the principal would clarify the policy and everything would be okay. To their astonishment, the principal backed the teacher. When Brittney's parents went to the school board, the school board backed the principal. When Brittney's parents took the case to court, the court backed the school board. In November 1995, Brittney's parents petitioned the United States Supreme Court—but the high court refused to hear the case, allowing the lower court rulings against Brittney to stand.

For Brittney Settle, the First Amendment didn't exist.

A seventeen-year-old Atlanta student named Scott McDaniel handed a note to a fellow student in the hallway between classes. Nothing wrong with that. No violation of school rules. But the assistant principal demanded to see the note. Scott's friend shrugged and handed the note over. The assistant principal examined the note—an invitation to attend an off-campus meeting of the Fellowship of Christian Athletes. It would have been better for Scott if it had been an invitation to a satanist club or a dope-smoking party. The assistant principal threatened to suspend Scott for (*gasp!*) "possession of Christian materials."

Like a lot of her classmates at Sam Houston Elementary School in Texas, nine-year-old Audrey Schwab won an award for jogging five miles—a paper certificate in the shape of a jogging shoe. All the kids who won the award were invited to decorate their paper jogging shoes, which would be displayed in the hallway. Other kids decorated their jogging shoes with slogans like SAVE THE WHALES or TOO COOL or CAN'T TOUCH THIS. Audrey decorated hers with the message JESUS LOVES US. Her jogging award was not displayed with the rest because, in the words of school officials, her message was "inappropriate for a public school."

God is not a dirty word, but kids in today's public schools are taught to think so. Our children are educated in an atmosphere of moral sterility and complete church-state alienation. The message this sends to our kids is that morality is meaningless and faith is irrelevant to real life. This is an abuse of the minds and souls of our children.

The U.S. Supreme Court kicked organized prayer out of the public schools in 1962 with its decision in *Engle v. Vitale*. Does that mean that God has been kicked out of school as well? According to legions of overzealous, out-of-control teachers, principals, and school boards, reinforced by the irreligious extremists of the American Civil Liberties Union and the People for the American Way, God is bad for kids!

Ronald Reagan crusaded against this mindless assault on our kids' First Amendment rights long before he was president and throughout his political career. "Where were we when God was expelled from the classroom?" he asked in a speech at an Eisenhower College fund-raiser on October 14, 1969. He continually marveled at the inverted logic of antiprayer court rulings. "Sometimes, I can't help but feel the First Amendment is being turned on its head," he said in a 1984 speech. "Ask yourselves: Can it really be true that the First Amendment can permit Nazis and Ku Klux Klansmen to march on public property, advocate the extermination of people of the Jewish faith and the subjugation of blacks, while the same amendment forbids our children from saying a prayer in school?"

Let's be clear on this: The First Amendment does not ban God from school. It does not in any way limit the right of schoolchildren to exercise their faith in school. On the contrary, it specifically bars the government from infringing a child's religious expression in any way! "Congress shall make no law respecting an establishment of religion, or prohibiting the free exercise thereof; or abridging the freedom of speech. . . ." Can you find anything in those words that would bar Brittney Settle from writing a paper on the life of Jesus? Or prevent Scott McDaniel from inviting a buddy to an off-campus meeting of Christian athletes? Or keep Audrey Schwab from sharing a message of Jesus' love with her classmates?

If the founding fathers who wrote and ratified that amendment were here today, they'd start a war all over again because of the mockery we have made of our constitutional rights. As Thomas Paine once said, "As to religion, I hold it to be the indispensable duty of government to protect all conscientious professors thereof"—including Brittney, Scott, and Audrey—"and I know of no other business which government hath to do therewith." Kids have an absolute, irrevocable right to express their faith in the public schools, as long as they are not disruptive about it. That's fact. Any teacher, school administrator, state official, or black-robed judge who says otherwise is dead wrong.

But what about atheist kids, you ask? What about other kids at school who might be offended by the statement Jesus loves us on a paper jogging shoe? Doesn't the First Amendment protect them from having to hear about Jesus? Nope. If you think so, show it to me in the amendment. If you are so concerned that an atheist or agnostic kid might get his feelings hurt by the words *Jesus loves us,* let me ask you this: Where is your concern for Audrey's feelings?

Listen, the First Amendment is about freedom *of* religion, not freedom *from* religion. Being an atheist, an agnostic, or a Neo-Orthodox Belly-Button Worshiper doesn't give you the right to squelch anyone else's freedoms. The First Amendment defends the robust, active practice of religion. It doesn't protect anyone from having his or her poor little sensitive feelings hurt—least of all by something as essential to American life as the free exercise of religion.

We all get our feelings hurt; we all get offended from time to time. Atheists may be offended by my religious expression or that of my kids—but so what? I'm offended by a lot of stuff that comes from the left—lies from the Clinton White House, slanted news reporting, liberal marches on Washington, history revision about the Reagan 1980s—but I don't file a lawsuit over it or try to shut down the First Amendment rights of other people. I deal with it, I get over it, I turn the channel, I move on. Same with religious expression in school.

People who don't want to tolerate the religious expression of others need to get over it. There's always something in life that is offensive or that causes discomfort. It's time to grow up. It's time to learn to get along with others.

We need to make the public schools faith-friendly once more. There is a saying that "nature abhors a vacuum." When a vacuum is created, there is a natural tendency for something to rush in and fill it. If you don't believe me, get a shovel and try digging a hole in the surface of a swimming pool. The instant you scoop out a shovelful of water, the hole disappears and water rushes in and seeks its own level. Nature abhors a vacuum.

In the same way, human nature abhors a moral vacuum. If you try to raise children in a godless, morals-free, values-neutral environment, something will rush into the souls of those kids, filling up the space where faith, morality, and values should be. And whatever rushes into the souls of those kids will be something too terrible to contemplate.

The children in our schools deserve to learn that Abraham Lincoln's second inaugural address—which is so brief that the entire text is engraved in marble on the Lincoln Memorial—contains no less than twelve references to God. They deserve to hear that the source of their freedoms, as clearly stated in the Declaration of Independence, is not a benevolent government but the fact that their Creator has endowed them with certain inalienable rights. They deserve to learn that without God as the source of our rights, the idea that we call America cannot be explained or understood. America is not a secular nation. It never has been. If it ever truly becomes a secular nation—as it appears to be headed toward becoming right now—then we will have to change the name, because it will no longer be America.

Look at how we stand truth and logic on their heads in this country: Flag-burning is sacred speech. Graffiti-tagging is sacred speech. *Hustler* magazine is sacred speech. The only kind of speech that's *not* protected as sacred in America? Speech about God!

So what's the solution? Well, there are a number of Republicans in the House—including Speaker Newt Gingrich and Illinois representative Henry Hyde—who believe the answer is a constitutional amendment to require tolerance of religion in public education and public life. If people want to do that, I don't have a big problem with it. But I don't think it's really going to solve anything. After all, we have a First Amendment that is clearly, elegantly, simply written, and its meaning is unmistakable.

I would rather see us enforce the amendment we've got than pass another amendment that will simply be ignored, twisted, and stood on its head. There's nothing wrong with the First Amendment; it's just fine the way it is. The only problem is that we don't obey it. Instead of amending and adjusting our Constitution to fit the insanity of our society, why don't we just restore our society to sanity? Or does that make too much sense?

We are one nation under God. Let's act like it. Here are some practical suggestions for restoring faith—and sanity—to America:

Elect leaders who will appoint and confirm judges who affirm the role of faith in public life. Presidents appoint federal judges, and senators confirm them. So it is crucially important that we have people in office who understand the historic and constitutional roles of faith in American public life. Republicans tend to appoint such judges, and Republican legislators (plus a few conservative "blue dog" Democrats) tend to confirm them—something to think about when you go into that voting booth.

Raise your kids to understand that the Constitution guarantees them religious freedom—including the freedom to express their faith on school grounds, during school hours, as long as they are not disruptive. If your kids want to write a paper on the life of Jesus or pray in the lunchroom or ask God's help before a big test or write *Jesus loves us* on a paper jogging shoe, support them and encourage them in that. Read the First Amendment with them and tell them that no one in the school or in American society can take that right away. Teach them to stand up and be bold for their faith and for the Constitution. If other kids in your community are taking a stand in their school for their faith, support them in any way you can.

Focus on spiritual growth and moral development for yourself and your kids. There was a time in America when people used to focus on improving the *soul*. Now they are obsessed with gratifying the *self*. Let me tell you, the *self* is a mighty poor substitute for the *soul*. So help your kids build their souls. Read the Bible and pray together as a family. Let your children see you praying and seeking God's help in various situations. Attend your house of worship regularly. Get involved in a Bible study. Encourage your children to be involved in church- and even school-based Bible studies and prayer groups. Send your kids to Christian camps—and take the entire family to a family camp.

Get involved in a spiritually based group where you can ask others in the group to pray for you and hold you accountable. Make a decision to always tell the truth, even in the smallest matters, even if it costs you. Make a decision to honor your promises, especially your covenant of fidelity in marriage. Take your ethical decision making off the sliding scale of everybody does it, and make all decisions on the basis of this-is-what's-right-and-that-is-what's-wrong.

Most important of all, explore the depths of your relationship with God on a daily, intimate basis. Spend regular time with him in prayer—not only talking to him, but also listening to him. Listen for God's voice speaking to you from his Word and in the stillness of your own spirit. Be open with others—especially your children—about the insights and strength to be gained from a daily walk with God. That's the kind of example our kids need to see. That's the kind of example Ronald Reagan set for me—and for the nation.

On February 4, 1982, a little less than a year after the assassination attempt, he spoke before the National Prayer Breakfast in Washington, D.C., and said these words, which make a fitting closing for this chapter:

> Those of you who were here last year might remember that I shared a story by an unknown author, a story of a dream he had. He had dreamt, as you recall, that he walked down the beach beside the Lord. And as they walked, above him in the sky was reflected each experience of his life. And then reaching the end of the beach, he looked back and saw the two sets of footprints extending down the way, but suddenly noticed that every once in a while there was only one set of footprints. And each time, they were opposite a reflection in the sky of a time of great trial and suffering in his life. And he turned to the Lord in surprise and said, "You promised that if I walked with You, You would always be by my side. Why did You desert me in my times of need?" And the Lord said, "My beloved child, I wouldn't desert you when you needed Me. When you see only one set of footprints, it was then that I carried you."
>
> Well, when I told that story last year, I said I knew, having only been here in this position for a few weeks, that there would be many times for me in the days ahead when there would be only one set of footprints and I would need to be carried, and if I didn't believe that I would be, I wouldn't have the courage to do what I was doing.
>
> Shortly thereafter, there came a moment when, without doubt, I was carried. . . . Well, God is with us. We need only to believe. The psalmist says, "Weeping may endure for a night, but joy cometh in the morning."
>
> Speaking for Nancy and myself, we thank you for your faith and for all your prayers on our behalf. And it is true that we can sense and feel that power.
>
> I've always believed that we were, each of us, put here for a reason, that there is a plan, somehow a divine plan for all of us. I know now that whatever days are left to me belong to Him.

Ronald Reagan knew that his life was part of a larger plan—an eternal plan that wove together the actions of individuals and the destinies of great nations. You and I are part of that same plan, and we are put here for the same reason—to serve God and to influence some little piece of the world for him. As Ronald Reagan did after the assassination attempt in 1981, let us dedicate whatever days are left to us to God, and let us do everything in our power to turn our nation back to him.

CHAPTER SIX

A CITY

OF HOPE

AND CHARITY

THE FAILURE
OF FEDERAL COMPASSION

*The size of the federal budget is not an appropriate barome-
ter of social conscience or charitable concern.*

Ronald Reagan
Address, National Alliance of Business
October 5, 1981

I remember many Saturday chats during my boyhood, riding alongside
my dad in the front seat of his red station wagon. As we'd drive up the coast
to his Malibu ranch, I'd ask question after question, trying to figure out how
the world works. One conversation in particular made a big impression on
me.

"Dad," I asked, watching the coastal scenery whip by, "you make a lot of
money in the movies, don't you?"

"Well," he replied, "I guess the acting trade has been pretty good to me,
Michael. Why do you ask?"

"I was just wondering," I said, shrugging.

Then Dad frowned that clench-jawed frown of his—you know the one I
mean. "Of course," he said, "I don't get to keep very much of the money I
earn."

"What do you mean, Dad?" I asked. "Why don't you get to keep it?"

"The government takes most of it."

" *Most* of it?" I asked. "You mean more than *half?*" I couldn't believe that the government would be so unfair as to take over *half* of Dad's money away from him.

He laughed explosively. "I'll say more than half!" he said. "Son, when I get a paycheck, the government sometimes takes as much as *91 percent* of it!"

Ninety-one percent! I added it up in my fourth-grade mind and realized that meant my dad only got to keep nine cents on the dollar. What a gyp! "Dad, that's nuts!"

He chuckled. "I agree with you there, Michael."

"Well, what does the government do with all that money?"

"Oh, the government does some good things with it—and some not so good. A lot of that money goes to pay the soldiers and buy the tanks and planes to defend our country. And some of it goes to build highways, like the one we're driving on right now. And an awful lot of it goes to something called welfare."

"Welfare?" I asked. "What's welfare?"

"Well, every now and then, people get down on their luck, so they need a helping hand. And there are people who are disabled in some way and can't make their own living. So the government helps these people. That's all very good. But there are also a lot of people who could work, but choose not to, and the government pays them too."

"But that's wrong," I said. "If people are able to work, they shouldn't get money for doing *nothing!*"

"That's right, Michael," he said. "It doesn't make sense to you and me, but that's the way the government does things. In fact, the government not only pays you not to work, but when you add up all the benefits you can collect from Uncle Sam, you find out that the government pays you more for doing nothing than you can make working at a lot of jobs. So in a way, the government is keeping people from working by making laziness pay off."

Dad knew. He had seen the principle in action for years. Back in the early 1930s, after FDR was inaugurated, Ronald Reagan's father, Jack—who was one of the few Democrats in mostly Republican Dixon—was appointed to oversee federal relief programs in the Dixon area. My dad, who was in college at the time, would drop by Jack Reagan's office after classes so they could go home together, and he would see all these men he knew, fathers of his classmates, waiting in line at Jack's office for a government handout. He saw the despair and, yes, the *shame* in those faces. These were proud men, and the Depression had robbed them of their dignity and their manhood.

So Jack Reagan went around the county, asking farmers and storekeepers if they could use an able-bodied man or two. Then he'd go back to his government office and hand out jobs to those who had been unemployed the longest. He knew that those proud men wanted work, not handouts. And at first, the men were glad to get a job, any job. In time, however, when Jack would parcel out jobs, there were no takers. The men in line would just shuffle their feet and look at the floor. Finally, one of the men explained. "Jack," he said, "the last time you found me a temporary job, the relief office took my family off welfare. I can't do that to my family again."

That experience had a powerful influence on Ronald Reagan's thinking about the whole issue of social welfare and so-called safety nets. He knew that government programs were administered bureaucratically, without compassion or efficiency. He knew that the welfare state is a drag on the American economy and the American family. It forces middle-class taxpayers to support not only the truly needy, but also those who simply *refuse* to take responsibility for themselves and their families. Because welfare benefits terminate if the father stays in the home, government programs create an incentive to destroy families—a form of federally sponsored child abuse. Where, Ronald Reagan asked, is the compassion in that?

For most people, the goal of reforming and privatizing the welfare system is a fairly new idea. To Ronald Reagan, it has been a lifelong passion. When he became governor of California—a state with more people on the welfare rolls than any other state in the Union—Ronald Reagan finally had a chance to do something about the welfare problem. After his two successful terms in Sacramento, and while campaigning against Gerald Ford for the Republican presidential nomination in 1976, he contrasted the federal welfare mess with his accomplishments in California:

> The truth is, Washington has taken over functions that don't truly belong to it. . . . Voices that are raised now and then urging a federalization of welfare don't realize that the failure of welfare is due to federal interference. Washington doesn't even know how many people are on welfare—how many cheaters are getting more than one check. It only knows how many checks it is sending out. Its own rules keep it from finding out how many are getting more than one check.

Well, California had a welfare problem. Sixteen percent of all welfare recipients in the country were drawing their checks in our state. We were sending welfare checks to families who decided to live abroad. One family was receiving its check in Russia. Our caseload was increasing by 40,000 people a month. Well, after a few years of trying to control this runaway program and being frustrated by bureaucrats here in California and in Washington, we turned again to a citizens' task force. The result was the most comprehensive welfare reform ever attempted. And in less than three years we reduced the rolls by more than 300,000 people, saved the taxpayers two billion dollars, and increased the grants to the truly deserving needy by an average of 43 percent. We also carried out a successful experiment which I believe is an answer to much of the welfare problem in the nation. We put able-bodied welfare recipients to work at useful community projects in return for their welfare grants.

Throughout his political career, Ronald Reagan preached the belief that if there was ever such a thing as a good welfare program, its number one goal should be to put itself out of business. Welfare programs ought to solve the problem of poverty, not perpetuate it. No government welfare program in American history has ever worked that way. Instead, the welfare state has steadily grown bigger and bigger, like a balloon being inflated to the point of bursting. Back in 1948, social welfare programs comprised less than 10 percent of federal spending; by the 1970s, welfare spending climbed to over 50 percent of federal spending; by 1980, it reached nearly 62 percent.

As federal social spending climbed, economic growth began to lag. From 1947 to 1951, federal spending consumed only 15 percent of gross domestic product (GDP), and the GDP was growing at an annual rate of 4.2 percent. From 1952 to 1974, Uncle Sam spent 19 percent of the GDP, and economic growth slowed to around 3.3 percent. Since 1975, Washington has never spent less than 22 percent of the GDP, and economic growth has slowed to 2.5 percent.

Economists agree that there is a point where the cost of the welfare state exacts such a toll on the economy that the economy can no longer sustain the weight. Economists Richard Vedder and Lowell Galloway of the congressional Joint Economic Committee place the optimum level of federal spending at 17.6 percent of the GDP—and Washington hasn't spent that small a percentage since 1965! As of 1996, Washington has been spending about 21 percent of the GDP on maintaining the welfare state, which means government is about one-fifth larger than it can afford to be. The result of our binge of welfare spending is that we have lost hundreds of billions of dollars of economic output. That means jobs lost, opportunities vanished, the American dream denied to millions of hardworking people. Lowell Galloway estimates that every dollar of welfare cuts would expand the U.S. economy by $1.38, and that every $100 billion in welfare spending cuts would add $895 to the median income of the American family.[1]

But how do we go about achieving long-overdue reductions in the welfare state? Federal approaches such as the Welfare Reform Act of 1996 and state reforms such as workfare (shifting welfare recipients from welfare rolls to state-subsidized private-sector jobs) are steps in the right direction. But they are *baby* steps. It's very late for America, and we can't afford to make gradual, incremental changes in the way we approach the social crisis in America.

The welfare state wastes money by the billions, that's for sure—but money is the *least* important resource wasted by government welfare. What's worse is the waste of lives, the waste of families, the waste of children growing up in conditions of dependency and poverty. Welfare perpetuates not only economic poverty, but also a poverty of values. We must act now to save those human souls trapped in a social and moral underclass. True compassion demands that we quit cheating them with government checks and that we start pointing them in the direction of hope, opportunity, and self-respect.

Throughout his two terms as president, Ronald Reagan tried to implement real, lasting solutions to the burgeoning problem of welfare dependency in America, but facing a Democrat-controlled Congress and lacking the power of a line-item veto, it was uphill sledding. In his second inaugural address, January 21, 1985, the fortieth president of the United States told the nation "a growing economy and support from family and community offer our best chance for a society where compassion is a way of life. . . ."

In other words, Ronald Reagan wanted to move the question of how to solve social problems out of Washington and over to what I call the Corner of Faith and Charity. That corner was once one of the busiest intersections in our Shining City on a Hill. But the Corner of Faith and Charity has become rather rundown and lifeless since the federal government got into the compassion business. If we truly want to make a caring and (above all!) lasting difference in the lives of our fellow Americans who are infirm, disadvantaged, or just down on their luck, we need to stop sending them downtown to the City Square. We need to send them to a place where people truly care. There's a lot of help available at the Corner of Faith and

Charity—and we can do more to make sure that there is always help for those who truly need it.

We have spent five trillion dollars since LBJ unleashed his War on Poverty—and let me tell you, folks, we have lost that war! We have more poverty, more crime, more drug addiction, more shattered lives, and more broken families today than at any other time in our history. The welfare state does not work. It should not merely be reformed. It should be shut down. Period.

PRIVATIZING THE COMPASSION BUSINESS

We also believe in the integrity, decency and sound good sense of grassroots Americans. . . . Our private sector initiatives task force is seeking out successful community models of school, church, business, union, foundation, and civic programs that help community needs. Such groups are almost invariably far more efficient than government in running social programs.

Ronald Reagan
First State of the Union Address
January 26, 1982

In her book *What I Saw at the Revolution: A Political Life in the Reagan Era,* Peggy Noonan makes an observation that captures the character and spirit of Ronald Reagan. She writes:

> Once Anne Higgins [Dad's chief of correspondence] asked [President Reagan] to call the Rossow family of Connecticut to congratulate them on their fine family. At the time Mr. and Mrs. Rossow had fourteen children, most adopted and many handicapped. The president not only called but, typically, asked to speak to everyone in the family. . . . He not only spoke to them, he invited them to visit. A few weeks later two vans drove up and deposited the sixteen Rossows at 1600 Pennsylvania Avenue. . . . This happened all the time in Reagan's White House. . . .
> Ronald Reagan was utterly egalitarian. He never thought he was stooping to these people, he didn't think he was better. . . . He even deferred to his secretary, writing his letters in longhand, neatly printing out the

entire name and address on the top of the page so she wouldn't have to look it up. Sometimes he didn't have the zip code, and he'd be apologetic and ask if she could please look it up if she has a minute.[2]

That's my dad. That is so *utterly* Ronald Reagan. He loves people. He never felt superior to anyone, even while he was the Leader of the Free World. And he genuinely enjoys getting to know grassroots folks who are making a difference in the world—one human life at a time. That's the way we solve our problems as Americans; that's the way we meet the needs of the disabled; that's the way we meet the needs of the poor; that's the way we help people who are hurting. Ronald Reagan believed that compassion should wear a human face.

We conservatives believe in lopping back the overgrown welfare state. But simply shrinking government is not enough to restore Ronald Reagan's dream of the Shining City on a Hill. At the same time we are dismantling the welfare state, we must aggressively rebuild our compassion industry and our opportunity society. We must empower our religious and civic sector to rise to the challenge of doing what government can no longer afford to do, and has never done well. We must make sure the engine of our economy is humming so that when people leave the welfare rolls, they can quickly land on a payroll.

If we attempt to shrink the role of government without expanding the role of the religious and civic sector—and the family and business sectors too—then two disastrous results will follow: (1) There will be a vacuum in society where government social programs used to be. People who have been enmeshed in the government safety net for decades or even generations will suddenly find themselves in free fall. And that will produce the next result: (2) People will revolt. The image of needy and disabled men, women, and children being cast out of government programs and into the street will be played and replayed by the liberal media and liberal politicians—and the voters will demand a return to paternalistic big government. The new Reagan revolution will be over—and the Shining City on a Hill will just be a dream that never was.

As Congressman George Radanovich observes in his "Blueprint to Renew Society": "The American people will not allow us to redefine the role of government unless they are satisfied other institutions in this country will assume their rightful roles." The American people elected the Republicans of the 104th Congress and the 105th Congress because they knew that government is too big, too controlling, and too expensive. The people knew the Republicans wanted to cut big government and make it smaller again, and they saw it as a good goal. But when the Republicans got down to specifics—like modest reductions in the growth of such programs as school lunches, Medicare, and Social Security—the liberals in the Congress and the media successfully demagogued the issue, painting conservatives as evil villains who wanted to starve children and old people. It was a ridiculous charge, but it was made so loudly and repetitiously by attack ads on TV that the lie wormed its way into the public consciousness. People who voted Republican in 1994 began to wonder if maybe these Republicans weren't moving too fast after all.

The Republicans, meanwhile, kept chanting, "Smaller government, smaller government! Dismantle the Department of Education! Cut food stamps! Cut welfare!" They didn't take time to make sure the people understood *why* they wanted to shrink government. They didn't make the case that cutting the Department of Education would make education stronger by decentralizing and defederalizing it. They didn't adequately make the case that welfare harms families and society. They didn't assure the public that there would be jobs for the unemployed and help for the truly needy after welfare reform took place. So people got nervous about the Republican agenda, and public support for the Republican agenda softened. Republicans lost the PR battle and came off looking like a bunch of evil Scrooges.

So how do we accomplish our goal? How do we make sure the American people will support our effort to shrink the federal government? In order to rebuild our Shining City on a Hill, we have to revitalize the Corner of Faith and Charity. We have to empower our civic and religious charities to repair the damage done by decades of misplaced welfare state "compassion." Following are some workable strategies for accomplishing these goals.

GET OUT THE TRUTH ABOUT WELFARE AND CHARITIES

The truth is that welfare is a failure and private sector charities are a success. The liberal argument goes something like this: "America's social problems are so big that only big government can handle them. Private sector charities aren't up to the job." Wrong! Fact is, the past few decades of failure have proved that government isn't up to the job. As Robert Sirico, president of the Acton Institute, observes, "The public has been taxed $5 trillion on means-tested welfare assistance for thirty years. The poverty rate is roughly the same, illegitimacy has zoomed 400 percent, and experience suggests the underclass is less socialized into the mainstream than ever."[3] Do we want this same government to preside over the *next* thirty years of social decay—or are we finally ready for a change?

Liberals point out that government, at all levels, spends about $950 billion every year on welfare programs—that's nearly a *trillion* bucks, folks! Private and religious charities (not counting churches) currently spend about $360 billion per year—less than half what the government spends. Therefore, according to flawed liberal logic, private and religious charities could never afford to take over the work of the welfare state. But here's where that line of reasoning breaks down.

Do you know how much money it would take to raise every poor family and individual above the poverty line? It's nothing like a trillion dollars! Fact is, it would only take *one-tenth* of the local, state, and federal welfare budget for a single year—a mere $100 billion—to raise the income of all poor people above the poverty line. That's less than a third of the $360 billion that passes through private and religious charities every year.[4] Obviously, these charities do more with that money than simply raise people out of poverty. The point is that adequate resources are available in the private sector. Our religious and civic charities not only can handle the job, but they are our *only hope* of solving the problem.

Unlike private and religious charities, the welfare bureaucracy is unbelievably inefficient. Out of every welfare dollar spent, less than thirty-five cents actually reaches a welfare recipient.[5] And no one knows how many of those recipients are truly needy in the first place! As Jennifer Marshall, welfare policy analyst for Gary Bauer's Family Research Council, observes,

> Every year, welfare consumes more tax dollars without any incentives to cut costs or monitor results. In the words of Indianapolis Mayor Steve Goldsmith, "The federal government offers the best deal in town: The more you spend, the more you get. Don't worry about results." The national average spending for government-subsidized homeless shelters is $22 per person per day. By contrast, Sister Connie Driscoll operates St. Martin de Porres House of Hope, a homeless shelter in Chicago, at an average cost of $6.73 per person per day. Sister Connie receives no government funding. But she does get results. The House of Hope has the most impressive

success rate in Chicago. Only 6 percent of its residents find themselves on the street again.[6]

Because the private sector is so much more efficient than the welfare state, civic and religious charities can accomplish far more than the government on a fraction of the money now being taxed and spent by Uncle Sam. Religious and civic charities generally hold aid recipients accountable for making changes in their lives so that they will not remain in a condition of dependency. The welfare state manages poverty as a chronic condition; private sector charities try to cure the problem.

The welfare state also places a heavy tax burden on hardworking individuals and businesses, which undermines economic growth and produces more poverty. Welfare puts a drag on the economy. This hurts America's ability to create jobs and opportunities while reducing disposable income to fund charitable giving.

George Bush talked about a "kinder, gentler America" and proceeded to increase social spending, which increased class friction. Only by shifting the welfare burden from government to the private sector can we truly make America a "kinder, gentler" nation. Most hardworking taxpayers know the feeling of standing in a checkout line behind a couple buying groceries with food stamps, thinking, *I'm paying for my groceries—and theirs too. They're able-bodied. They could work. Why are they on food stamps?* Well, maybe there's a very good reason why they're on food stamps—but then again, maybe not. The point is, when we put private and religious charities in charge of America's antipoverty programs, we can know that if people are receiving assistance, odds are they genuinely deserve it—and that knowledge alone will help reduce the level of resentment and anger in our society.

TO INCREASE CHARITABLE GIVING, CUT TAXES

Tax cuts free wage earners from having to work two or three jobs just to make ends meet, and that means people have more free time for volunteer work. History shows that volunteerism and charitable giving rise and fall with changes in government policy. When government gets bigger, raises taxes, and expands its role into the realm of charity and social action, people give less money and volunteer less time.

Charitable giving increased steadily from the early 1940s through 1964.

Then it began to decline, even though total wealth in America continued to increase. What happened in 1964 that changed people's minds and hearts about giving to charity? That was the year Lyndon Johnson unveiled his massive Great Society social welfare program! Charitable giving did not begin to rise again until 1981—the first year of the (*ahem!*) Reagan administration—and it continued to rise throughout the kind, gentle, charitable Reagan 1980s. From 1981 to 1989, charitable giving rose 5.1 percent per year, adjusted for inflation (the average rate of increase from 1955 through 1980 was only 3.3 percent). During the Reagan 1980s, charitable giving rose by 56 percent (adjusted for inflation) to $121 billion in constant 1990 dollars. In fact, Americans increased their charitable giving by substantially more than they increased purchases of consumer goods.[7]

Times were tough in 1981—the American economy was still in the throes of its Jimmy Carter hangover. But Ronald Reagan spoke frequently and compellingly about the need to reduce social spending and increase volunteerism in America, and Americans eagerly responded. Between 1984 and 1989, the Gallup polling organization reported that the number of Americans involved in charitable volunteer work rose astoundingly, from 34 percent in 1984 to 50 percent in 1989.[8] "The volunteer spirit is still alive and well in America," Ronald Reagan announced in his first State of the Union address—and he was right.

TAX CREDITS AND SUPERDEDUCTIONS

The government should offer taxpayers dollar-for-dollar tax credits or "superdeductions" for charitable giving. This is the ideal yes-yes solution to the question of how to shift the burden of social programs from the welfare state to the compassionate private sector. Under the present system, when you make a charitable donation, you can only take a deduction that reduces your taxable gross income. But under the system I'm proposing, you could take a dollar *right off the top of your tax bill* for every dollar you donate to a qualified private or religious charity. By doing so, you shift those dollars directly from the welfare state and into private sector programs, where the money is used more effectively, more efficiently, and more compassionately. This plan would enable private and religious charities to compete with— and ultimately replace—the welfare state.

Another advantage of this plan is that it would allow taxpayers to "vote with their dollars" for the kinds of programs they want to support. Instead of being forced to support programs they dislike or distrust or which offend their values, taxpayers could fund the programs they feel give the most bang for the buck. Liberal taxpayers could support liberal programs, and conservative taxpayers could support conservative programs. Catholic donors could give to Catholic charities, Protestant donors to Protestant charities, Jewish donors to Jewish charities, and atheists can do whatever they want. This plan gives the taxpayers a greater say over the way charitable funds are spent and creates a powerful system of accountability. Much of this money would be spent right in the communities where it is donated so that the people providing the money could see with their own eyes if it is being well spent or not.

This plan would be fairer to taxpayers than the present system, which gives wealthy donors an unfair advantage over middle-class taxpayers who do not always itemize deductions. Generous donors who do not itemize are, in effect, penalized for their generosity. They give to good causes but receive no tax break. Under the new tax credit system, *all* taxpayers—rich, middle-class, and not-quite-middle-class—could take a tax credit right off the top of their tax bill, whether they itemize or not.

Another variation on the dollar-for-dollar plan would be the "superdeduction," an extra enticement to generosity. Under the superdeduction plan, taxpayers would receive a tax credit that is, say, 10 percent or 20 percent *larger* than their donation. If you give a dollar to charity, you get to take $1.10 or $1.20 off your taxes, up to a certain limit. As private sector charities grow, the welfare state could be phased out gradually until it is out of business completely. Instead of having compassion extorted out of your hide by the big stick of the IRS, you could afford to give to support civic and religious charities out of combined motives of love for your neighbor and economic self-interest. If the government were to give a charitable superdeduction for being generous, greed wouldn't pay!

RESPECT FOR RELIGIOUS CHARITIES

Our government must learn to overcome decades of bias against cooperating with religious institutions. Because of a misreading of the original intent of the First Amendment, our government has been treating faith-based charities and social action organizations with distrust and even hostility.

Case in point: During the early 1990s, the state of Texas, through its

Commission of Alcohol and Drug Abuse, tried to shut down faith-based drug rehab programs such as Victory Outreach and Teen Challenge because they used faith and morality to cure drug abuse instead of doctors and psychologists—despite the fact that these faith-based programs showed a much higher cure rate than the secular programs! Both Victory Outreach and Teen Challenge were able to show 70 percent cure rates or better for their 100 percent privately funded programs. Government programs, by contrast, are many times more expensive (in taxpayer dollars!) and produce a less than 10 percent cure rate. How do the faith-based programs do it? Victory Outreach founder Freddie Garcia explains, "We believe that sin is the reason why people take drugs. . . . We believe that the drug addict is a slave to sin, not to drugs. We believe that drug addiction is a spiritual problem, and that Jesus Christ is the solution."[9]

The state of Texas refused to allow these programs to operate unless they completely changed their approach from a faith model to a medical model. They would have to hire psychiatrists, counselors, and social workers, and they would have to embrace the medical notion that addiction is a disease. In other words, they would have to function exactly like all the government-sanctioned programs that were only getting less than 10 percent cure rates. Despite high cure rates and zero taxpayer cost, the state of Texas was on the verge of shutting these successful programs down.

Then Texas governor George W. Bush stepped in. In May 1996, he established a government task force to study ways that the state of Texas and faith-based community action programs could work together to solve problems, ranging from poverty to drug abuse to crime. The seventeen-member task force included Freddie Garcia of Victory Outreach and J. Herbert Meppelink of Teen Challenge. The goal of the task force, according to Governor Bush's order, was "to identify ways that Texas can create an environment where faith-based organizations will flourish and meet the needs of people in crisis with focused and effective aid."[10]

The new approach Texas is taking toward faith-based private charities must become a model for the entire nation. Fortunately, our national leadership is beginning to take notice. "Freddie Garcia has achieved results that are almost unheard of," says Newt Gingrich, Speaker of the House of Representatives. "All too often the bureaucracy has tried to put folks like Freddie out of business because they don't have a Ph.D. or they don't fill out the paperwork right. [But] they run very inexpensive neighborhood programs that feel more comfortable to people on the street."[11]

Our American tradition of lending a hand in time of need is based on our American tradition of faith. Throughout our history, Jewish, Catholic, and Protestant Americans have obeyed the Great Commandment of both Testaments to " 'love the LORD your God with all your heart, with all your soul, with all your strength, and with all your mind,' and 'your neighbor as yourself.' "[12]

Religious charities don't want tax money or any other kind of help from the government. They just want to be left alone to carry out their ministry. Unfortunately, observes Robert L. Woodson Sr., president of the National Center for Neighborhood Enterprise, religious charities are continually bedeviled by government bureaucrats and regulators who "insist you've got to be certified by the state and comply with rules, like having a 36-inch door rather than a 34-inch door. . . . The government officials cling to their regulations, and kids who might be rescued are sleeping in crack houses or under bridges."[13]

Newt Gingrich—who, like fellow Georgian Jimmy Carter is intensely involved in the faith-based antipoverty program Habitat for Humanity—says that America needs to return to what works. And what works, he says, is faith in God. "We need to get back to one-on-one missionary work," Newt explains. "We are in the business of changing and saving people, not maintaining them in their decay. If you don't start with a faith-based approach, then you haven't started anything."[14]

The source of all of America's social problems—poverty, broken families, child abuse, child neglect, crime, abortion, teen pregnancy, drug abuse, and on and on—is *not* a lack of funding or a lack of government programs. It is a lack of spiritual and moral strength in our people—the very essence of what faith-based programs offer. The good news that religious charities proclaim to our society is that when people live in dependence on God, they don't need to live in dependence on the welfare state.

The record shows that when genuine compassion is unleashed in our society, it comes much more from the faith-based right than from the state-based left. *The American Enterprise* magazine reports that religious conservatives—who are so often maligned by liberals as "narrow-minded" and "mean-spirited"—are the most generous, openhearted segment of the American population. In fact, religious conservatives are more than twice as likely as the general population to donate time to charities, and they give more than twice as big a percentage of their income to charitable causes.[15]

REVIVE THE SPIRIT OF VOLUNTEERISM

Bill Clinton muddied the concept of true volunteerism with his big-government AmeriCorps program, which slid through the liberal 103rd Congress. According to the congressional General Accounting Office, AmeriCorps "volunteers" receive a pay-plus-benefits package totaling $26,700 per volunteer for ten months' work, which would work out to almost $32,000 for twelve months. The package includes pay, a complete health plan, and a $4,725 college scholarship. That's not volunteerism. That's a very well paid entry-level job! (The Clinton administration originally sold the plan with a $17,600 per "volunteer" price tag—about 40 percent less than the reality.)

I'm not saying AmeriCorps didn't do some good things. Those federally paid "volunteers" cleaned up beaches and riverbanks, planted some 200,000 trees, cleaned up a lot of neighborhoods, filled out countless reams of government paperwork, and changed an untold number of lightbulbs. Of course, the original idea of AmeriCorps was to provide an army of paid "volunteers" to work alongside private charitable organizations to improve the lives of needy Americans. The reality is that over a quarter of all AmeriCorps "volunteers" ended up working in federal, state, or local governmental agencies, where they became simply entry-level government bureaucrats, not charitable volunteers.

In theory, section 132(a)(3) of the National and Community Service Trust Act of 1993 (the charter document of AmeriCorps) is supposed to prevent "volunteers" from being "used to perform service that provides a direct benefit to any . . . partisan political organization"—but that's not the way it worked in practice. In Denver, AmeriCorps "volunteers" were supposed to help improve the lives of people in poorer neighborhoods. But instead they were used to walk precincts and distribute political attack literature against city councilman Hiawatha Davis. And in San Francisco, many AmeriCorps "volunteers" were used in an all-out assault against Three Strikes and You're Out anticrime legislation.

In a February 28, 1993, op-ed piece in the *New York Times,* Bill Clinton promised that AmeriCorps would not be yet another liberal big-government social program: "While the Federal Government will provide the seed money for national service, we are determined that the participants—the individuals who serve and the groups that sponsor their service—will guide the process. Spending tens of millions of tax dollars to build a massive bureaucracy would be self-defeating." That's what Bill Clinton *said.* But what he *did* was to build yet another massive, self-defeating federal bureaucracy, spending *hundreds* of millions of tax dollars! The General Accounting Office's audit of AmeriCorps books in the first year found that 88 percent of its funding came from the taxpayers.[16]

We can't afford any more big-government "volunteer" programs. They destroy the spirit of true volunteerism in America. They prop up and enlarge the wasteful and bureaucratic welfare state. By offering benefits and scholarships, they compete with the military, making it harder for the armed forces to attract quality recruits. They are easily misused for political gain by the left. And they just cost too much.

As someone once said, "Bad charity drives out good." Welfare state charity is the worst form of charity in the world. We can no longer afford to look at social problems and say, "That's government's job." It's our job. It's our ministry. It's our calling as people of faith, compassion, and responsibility. The era of the New Deal and the Great Society must end. Now. It's time to begin a *new* era—the Era of Compassion.

When Ronald Reagan spoke to the National Prayer Breakfast in Washington, February 4, 1982, he made precisely this point with one of his favorite New Testament stories:

> Remember the parable of the Good Samaritan? He crossed the road, knelt down, and bound up the wounds of the beaten traveler, the Pilgrim, and then carried him into the nearest town. He didn't just hurry on by into town and then look up a caseworker and tell him there was a fellow back out on the road that looked like he might need help.
>
> Isn't it time for us to get personally involved, for our churches and synagogues to restore our spirit of neighbor caring for neighbor? . . . We should be doing God's work on earth. We'll never find every answer, solve every problem, or heal every wound, but we can do a lot if we walk together down that one path that we know provides real hope.

EMPHASIZE PERSONAL RESPONSIBILITY

As Americans, we must emphasize personal responsibility; we must hold people accountable for their own lives and the welfare of their own families. From our political leaders to plain folks in the Neighborhood, we must all begin speaking the language of individual responsibility, moral autonomy, and human dignity. We have to stop treating able-bodied, able-minded (but values-impaired) people as victims. In order for us to be a stable, self-governing society, we must demand that every American shoulder the responsibilities that go with freedom. As Lord Acton once observed, "Liberty is not the freedom to do what you *wish;* it is the freedom to do what you *ought.*"

The patron saint of liberalism, John Fitzgerald Kennedy, put it another way: "Ask not what your country can do for you; ask what you can do for your country." You often hear liberals invoke the name of JFK—but when was the last time you heard any liberal leader recite those famous words? Today's liberals only talk about what government can do for you, what liberal politicians can give you. Since JFK's time, liberals have figured out that you can't buy votes and power with personal responsibility—only with government giveaways.

If the left wishes to abdicate the virtues that made America great—such as hard work and individual responsibility—so be it. We on the right will extol those virtues. We will trumpet the words of Lord Acton and John F. Kennedy and Ronald Reagan. We will make sure today's young generation grows up hearing the truth that genuine freedom always entails personal responsibility—not the freedom to do what we *wish,* but the freedom to do what we *ought.*

REAL COMPASSION

Is there really any doubt at all about what will happen if we let them win this November? Is there any doubt that they will raise our taxes? That they will send inflation into orbit again? That they will make government bigger than ever? And deficits even worse? Raise unemployment? . . . And they'll do all that in the name of compassion. It's what they've done to America in the past. But if we do our job right, they won't be able to do it again.

Ronald Reagan
Acceptance Speech
Republican National Convention
Dallas, Texas, August 23, 1984

Before going to Washington as president, Dad liked to visit the city as citizen Reagan, enjoying the tourist's-eye view of the city's historic buildings and monuments. His favorite stop on the gawker's tour was always the Lincoln Memorial. A few weeks after his inauguration, on February 5, 1981, he greeted teenage members of the U.S. Senate Youth Program during a ceremony in the White House Rose Garden. During his informal remarks, he encouraged this group of young Americans to do what he had often done—tour the city and view the historic sites of America's capital.

Then he asked them, "Have you been to the Lincoln Memorial yet? Let me tell you something I learned the first time I visited there. I found out that if you stand on one side of that great statue of Abraham Lincoln and look up at his face, you can see the compassion of Lincoln etched into his features. Then, if you walk around to the other side—and the sculptor must have intended this—you can see the strength of the man. You get a different view of Lincoln's character, depending on which side of the statue you view. Strength—and compassion."

You may have noticed, as you've been reading through this chapter, that one word occurs again and again: *compassion*. We all know it's easy to talk about compassion. Many people talk that talk. But Ronald Reagan walked that walk. He made a genuine, lasting difference in the way people live their lives.

Dr. Marvin Olasky knows a thing or two about compassion. He is the cofounder of the Center for Effective Compassion and the author of a book called *The Tragedy of American Compassion*. On December 13, 1995, Dr. Olasky gave a talk at the Family Research Council's "World Without Welfare" symposium in Washington. One of the things he talked about was the real meaning of *compassion:*

> The literal meaning of *compassion* is not just writing a check, but having personal involvement with the needy—"suffering with them." That's what "compassion" means: suffering with people, not just giving to them. The poverty-fighters of old knew that welfare doesn't mean passing a bill, but helping a person to *fare well*. These are some simple, elementary things that our legislators seem to have forgotten.
>
> The older generation knew that people should be challenged. When an able-bodied man came to a homeless shelter, for example, he often was asked to chop wood for an hour or two. Or maybe whitewash the wall of a building. That way he could provide part of his own support and also help

those unable to chop. They knew. They demonstrated through those work tests that even the most run-down person is not just a taker. He can also be a giver. They knew that everyone is made in God's image and is capable of helping. Why have so many people forgotten that?

To listen to a lot of liberals today, you'd think they invented the idea of compassion. They think they trademarked it, copyrighted it; and they sure won't let anyone lay claim to it but themselves. "Certainly conservatives couldn't have compassion! How could they? Conservatives are mean! Conservatives are selfish! Conservatives give tax breaks to the rich and hate the poor and starve little children and kick little puppies! Mean, evil, nasssssty conservatives!" You've heard that song before.

Ronald Reagan had to listen to that tired old song throughout his political career. During the 1980 campaign, Jimmy Carter several times insinuated that Ronald Reagan was a hard-hearted racist. "You'll determine," Carter told a Chicago audience on October 6, 1980, "whether or not America will be unified or, if I lose this election, whether Americans might be separated, black from white, Jew from Christian, North from South." These idiotic charges continued throughout the Reagan presidency, right up to this assessment at the end of his presidency by the then-governor of New York: "At his worst," grumbled Mario Cuomo, "Ronald Reagan made the denial of compassion respectable."

We listened to that tired old song through the long, hot budget debate of 1995 and 1996, when liberals in the Congress, the media, and the unions attacked the Republican Contract with America as "something Ebenezer Scrooge would have dreamed up" and the "Contract *on* America." The Republican Speaker of the House became "The Gringrinch Who Stole Christmas."

In a Christmas 1994 broadcast on British television, Jesse Jackson railed against conservatives, calling us racists, saying, "In South Africa the status quo was called racism. We rebelled against it. In Germany it was called fascism. Now in Britain and the U.S., it is called conservatism." And just a few days earlier, at a meeting with the *Chicago Sun-Times* editorial board, Jackson had made the outrageous claim that "the Christian Coalition was a strong force in [Nazi] Germany. It laid down a suitable, scientific, theological rationale for the tragedy in Germany. The Christian Coalition was very much in evidence there." This, even though the Christian Coalition did not even exist until 1989! (Many people don't realize that Christian Coalition founder Pat Robertson was active in the civil rights movement of the 1960s and campaigned for the desegregation of churches.)

Even though conservatives are the most antitotalitarian, antibigotry people on the planet, even though conservatives are the ones who are constantly warning against state power and too-big, too-powerful government, we are continually being compared to Nazis and slave-owners of the Old South. To the closed liberal mind, the word *conservative* is synonymous with "racist, bigot, antipoor, antichildren, anticompassion." Ronald Reagan certainly had to deal with those stupid charges throughout his career, even though he was raised from infancy to care about his fellow man, and to be completely color-blind where race is concerned. In his book *An American Life*, he recalled:

> My parents constantly drummed into me the importance of judging people as *individuals*. There was no more grievous sin at our household than a racial slur or other evidence of religious or racial intolerance. A lot of it, I think, was because my dad had learned what discrimination was like firsthand. He'd grown up in an era when some stores still had signs at their door saying, NO DOGS OR IRISHMEN ALLOWED.
>
> When my brother and I were growing up, there were still ugly tumors of racial bigotry in much of America, including the corner of Illinois where we lived. At our one local movie theater, blacks and whites had to sit apart—the blacks in the balcony. My mother and father urged my brother and me to bring home our black playmates, to consider them equals, and to respect the religious views of our friends, whatever they were. My brother's best friend was black, and when they went to the movies, Neil sat with him in the balcony. My mother always taught us: "Treat thy neighbor as you would want your neighbor to treat you," and "Judge everyone by how they act, not what they are."
>
> Once my father checked into a hotel during a shoe-selling trip and a clerk told him: "You'll like it here, Mr. Reagan, we don't permit a Jew in the place."
>
> My father, who told us the story later, said he looked at the clerk angrily and picked up his suitcase and left. "I'm a Catholic," he said. "If it's come to the point where you won't take Jews, then some day you won't take *me* either."
>
> Because it was the only hotel in town, he spent the night in his car during a winter blizzard and I think it may have led to his first heart attack.[17]

I was brought up exactly the same way—and frankly, I'm tired of being slandered and caricatured simply because I'm a conservative. I have liberal friends, and liberals listen to my radio show. There are liberals reading this book. I know that not all liberals are pompous, self-righteous, elitist demagogues like Bill and Hillary, Tom Daschle, and Dick Gephardt. There are many Americans who, while liberal, are not so shallow as to truly believe that all conservatives are greedy villains bent on starving children, killing old people, and raping the environment.

If you are one of these thoughtful, fair-minded liberals, I want to say a special word to you. Even though you and I come from different political perspectives, I want us to reach across this political gulf that separates us, and I want us to learn to understand each other.

Most of all, I hope that whenever you hear people demonizing and mindlessly attacking conservatives, as has happened so much over the past few years, you will speak up—not to defend Ronald Reagan or Michael Reagan or the Republicans, but simply to speak up for the truth. Tell them, "Look, I don't agree with conservatives, but let's be real. These people are not monsters. They're family people; they're Americans. They want what's best for America's children and America's future. They just differ from us in how to get there."

Please stand up for the truth. That's all I ask.

Let me tell you some truth you may have never heard before—the truth about the history of the Republican Party. The fact is, the Republican Party has *always* been the party of genuine compassion.

The founder of the GOP was a disaffected, antislavery Democrat named Alvan E. Bovay, who met with other abolitionists in a Congregational church in Ripon, Wisconsin. The two guiding principles of the newly founded Republican Party were the right to own land and the right of all men to be free. The first Republican candidate for president was explorer-environmentalist John C. Fremont, who campaigned in 1856 on a freedom platform—"Free soil, free labor, free speech, free men, Fremont." He lost the election, but four years later the Republicans captured the White House; their standard-bearer's name was Abraham Lincoln.

Opposing slavery was risky in those days. Republican Senator Charles Sumner of Massachusetts was beaten unconscious on the floor of the United States Senate by cane-wielding Democratic Representative Preston S. Brooks. It took Sumner three years to recover from the beating, but he returned to the Senate and continued to speak out against slavery. His fellow

Republicans in the Congress passed the 13th Amendment to the Constitution, which outlawed slavery, and passed federal legislation that extended full civil rights to blacks. At the same time, the Republican president, Abraham Lincoln, issued the Emancipation Proclamation. More in sorrow than in anger, Lincoln took this nation into the horrors of war in order to expunge the horrors of slavery. After the Civil War, Republicans passed the Civil Rights Act of 1866, recognizing former slaves as full U.S. citizens.

In 1869, the Republicans elected the first black American to Congress (the first black Democrat was not elected until 1935). In 1870, Republicans passed the Fifteenth Amendment, guaranteeing voting rights regardless of race, creed, or previous condition of servitude. Two years later, Republicans passed federal laws requiring equal pay for equal work by women employees of the government.

When the Republicans recaptured the White House, the Eisenhower administration worked hard for civil rights. In 1954, President Eisenhower sent the National Guard to enforce the Supreme Court's *Brown v. Board of Education* decision, which declared "separate but equal" schools unconstitutional. Eisenhower also integrated the armed forces, appointed the first Civil Rights Commission, and created the Civil Rights Division of the Justice Department. He called for and signed the Civil Rights Act of 1957.

Democrats filibustered against the Civil Rights Act of 1964—and Republicans ended the filibuster so the bill could be brought to a vote and signed into law. The longest peacetime economic expansion in U.S. history occurred under Ronald Reagan and George Bush, creating 20.7 million new jobs. During that same period, communism collapsed and the winds of freedom swept across Europe and parts of Asia.

Republicans have good reason to be proud of their tradition of compassion and their dedication to making the world a better place for all people. Neighbors helping neighbors has always been the American way. As a people, we are still willing to look out for one another, but we are completely out of patience with the failed and destructive welfare state. The revolution begins today—a revolution of genuine, effective compassion for people who are truly in need.

When I think of the job that needs to be done, I think of Marcella, a bright third grader in a California public school. One day not long ago, Marcella's class went to the school library where Jeanie, the librarian, read to the children from the Dr. Seuss book *The Cat in the Hat*. After reading to the class, Jeanie invited the kids to take a book from the shelves and spend the next half hour reading. All the kids did so except Marcella.

Jeanie knew a little about Marcella's background. She was the child of a welfare mom with a drug problem and her father was in prison. Twice, Child Protective Services had taken Marcella and her brother out of the home because of neglect. Each time, they were returned after a few weeks in foster care.

Jeanie sat down beside Marcella, who sat alone in the corner. "Wouldn't you like to find a nice, happy book to read?" asked Jeanie.

"I don't want to read a happy book," said Marcella, turning away. "I never have any nice days."[18]

You tell me: What has the welfare state ever done for Marcella? I can't help believing that if America would trade in the failed welfare state for a genuinely compassionate society, kids like Marcella could be saved. Instead of receiving only a check and some food stamps, her mother could receive a message of hope and faith from people who really care, from people who can make a difference in their lives. If we start now, we may yet be in time to save Marcella, so that she can enjoy reading books—and have some nice days.

We conservatives are unwilling to maintain an uncaring status quo for another thirty years. We want to lick the problem. Conservatives don't believe we must resign ourselves to a future with a growing, permanent, dependent underclass. The brigades of the new Reagan revolution are committed to putting every able-bodied, able-minded American to work at the task of building the Shining City on a Hill. We will build it with individual responsibility, the restoration of two-parent families, and an abiding faith in God.

Candidate Ronald Reagan had a vision for America that he shared with the nation at the conclusion of the John Anderson–Ronald Reagan presidential debate, September 21, 1980. I can't think of a more fitting way to close this chapter than with his vision of America's past—and her shining future:

> I've always believed that this land was placed here between the two great oceans by some divine plan—that it was placed here to be found by a special kind of people—people who had a special love for freedom. . . .
> We came from a hundred different corners of the earth. We spoke a multitude of tongues. We landed on this eastern shore and then went out over the mountains and the prairies and the deserts and the far western

mountains to the Pacific, building cities and towns and farms, and schools and churches. If wind, water, or fire destroyed them, we built them again. And in so doing, at the same time, we built a new breed of human called an American—a proud, an independent, and a most compassionate individual.

Two hundred years ago, Tom Paine, when the thirteen tiny colonies were trying to become a nation, said, "We have it in our power to begin the world over again." Today, we're confronted with the horrendous problems that we've discussed here tonight. And some people in high positions of leadership tell us that the answer is to retreat—that the best is over—that we must cut back—that we must share in an ever-increasing scarcity. . . .

Well, we, the living Americans, have gone through four wars. We've gone through a Great Depression in our lifetime that literally was worldwide and almost brought us to our knees. But we came through all of those things and we achieved new heights and new greatness. . . . For two hundred years, we've lived in the future, believing that tomorrow would be better than today, and today would be better than yesterday. I still believe that. I'm not running for the presidency because I believe I can solve the problems we've discussed tonight. I believe the people of this country can; and, together, we can begin the world over again. We can meet our destiny—a destiny to build a land here that will be, for all mankind, a Shining City on a Hill.

I think we ought to get at it.

PART THREE

MAIN STREET

The third cornerstone
of the City on a Hill is
Business

CHAPTER SEVEN

A

THRIVING

CITY

THE EDUCATION
OF RONALD REAGAN

Government's view of the economy could be summed up in a few short phrases: If it moves, tax it. If it keeps moving, regulate it. And if it stops moving, subsidize it.

Ronald Reagan
Remarks to the White House
Conference on Small Business
August 15, 1986

Dad was a good actor. Not a great actor, but very good.

The really *great* actor in our family was Mom. If you haven't done so already, you should definitely catch Jane Wyman's Oscar-winning performance in *Johnny Belinda* as well as her Oscar-nominated performances in *Magnificent Obsession*, *The Blue Veil*, and *The Yearling*. If Dad had gotten the kind of roles he wanted, I think he might have been a great actor too. He certainly turned in a career performance as dashing Drake ("Where's the rest of me?!") McHugh in *King's Row* (1942). And his supporting role as George "The Gipper" Gipp in *Knute Rockne, All American* (1940) will always be remembered as well.

But for the most part, Dad was cast as the romantic lead in lightweight pictures. He was perfectly cast in such roles, of course, and he carried them off well in such comedies as *John Loves Mary, The Hasty Heart, The Girl from Jones Beach,* and, yes, *Bedtime for Bonzo.* He made a lot of entertaining movies, but the limited range of roles he was offered at Warner Brothers always frustrated him. In the end, he resigned himself to the fact that he had become (by his own overly harsh description) "the Errol Flynn of the B movies." Perhaps if he had gotten the roles and enjoyed the career he *really* wanted in Hollywood, he never would have gone into politics. Hollywood's loss was America's gain.

Ronald Reagan's movie career actually prepared him for his political life, not just in honing his communication skills but, even more important, in shaping his beliefs and his values. In the previous chapter, I mentioned the talks Dad and I had while driving up to the ranch and the outrage I felt when I learned that the government took as much as 91 percent of his earnings in taxes. Here's a little more background on Ronald Reagan's early experience of having his bank account plundered by Uncle Sam, and how that experience shaped his later views.

In 1941, right after Dad finished filming *King's Row,* he joined the army. His uncorrected vision wasn't good enough for overseas service, so he remained stateside, at first as a liaison officer loading troop convoys and then working for Army Air Force Intelligence at "Fort Roach" (the old Hal Roach Studios in Culver City, which the War Department commandeered to make training films). Before he went into the army, however, his agent, Lew Wasserman, negotiated a seven-year contract for him worth $1 million (that was when a million bucks was a lot of money). So Dad made a lot of money once the war was over and he returned to making movies for Warner Brothers. But it also put him in the 82 to 91 percent tax bracket.

"You could only make four films," Dad once explained, "and then you were in the top tax bracket. In those days, the studio didn't say, 'We want this picture done *well.*' They said, 'We want this picture done *Friday.*' So an actor could easily do more than four films a year—but why bother? You're better off financially if you make your four pictures, then take off for the country."

What was happening to Ronald Reagan during those years—though he didn't realize it at the time—was that he was getting an education in something that didn't have a name yet: *supply-side economics*—or, as it later came to be known, *Reaganomics.* He was learning that when you tax an activity, you discourage that activity. The more you tax it, the more you discourage it. Tax it enough, the activity stops. The same principle that applies at the micro-level to one Hollywood actor making movies also applies at the macro-level to an entire economy. It was the beginning of Ronald Reagan's belief that America was overtaxed, and that if taxes could be cut, the engine of prosperity would roar, lifting the fortunes and hopes of everyone in society, both great and small.

Ronald Reagan understood that Main Street—America's business district and one of the four cornerstones of the Shining City on a Hill—thrives in an atmosphere of freedom and grinds to a halt in an atmosphere of oppressive taxation and regulation. During the 1980s, he brought Main Street America out of the economic calamity of the Carter years and into a golden era of prosperity. And Main Street responded by generating jobs, benefits, goods, services, and opportunities for all Americans. The Reagan 1980s were good for business and good for everybody. If we would only rediscover the lessons of that era, the coming millennium could be even better.

TAX CUTS
AND INCREASED REVENUE

We're accused of having a secret. Well, if we have, it is that we're going to keep the mighty engine of this nation revved up. And that means a future of sustained economic growth without inflation that's going to create for our children and grandchildren a prosperity that finally will last.

Ronald Reagan
Acceptance Speech
Republican National Convention
Dallas, Texas, August 23, 1984

Picture a swank D.C. restaurant, the Two Continents, located in the Washington Hotel directly across from the Treasury Building. It's December 1974, and the weather is bitterly cold. Inside, sitting over cocktails, are three men: Jude Wanniski, an editorial-page writer for the *Wall Street Journal*, Dick Cheney, President Ford's White House chief of staff (he will later be George Bush's secretary of defense and oversee Operation Desert Storm), and a portly, thirtyish, highly animated young economist named Arthur B. Laffer.

"Look, Cheney," says Laffer, "the idea is so simple, it's child's play! If I could just show you—Well, here, let me draw you a graph." And Laffer takes a pen from his pocket and spreads out a napkin in front of him.

"Art! Wait! Don't do that!" Wanniski protests.

Laffer looks up in annoyance. "What's the matter?"

"That's a linen napkin," says Wanniski, taking a yellow legal pad from his briefcase and passing it across the table. "Use this pad. I don't mind buying the drinks, but I'm not buying linen napkins for you to doodle on."

Laffer snatches the legal pad and hurriedly draws a simple parabolic curve, sketches in a few lines and arrows, scrawls a few words here and there, then shoves it across the table. "See?"

Cheney and Wanniski look at the drawing. Then at Laffer. Then at the drawing again. What Cheney and Wanniski see on the legal pad looks something like Figure 7.1.

Figure 7.1. The Laffer Curve

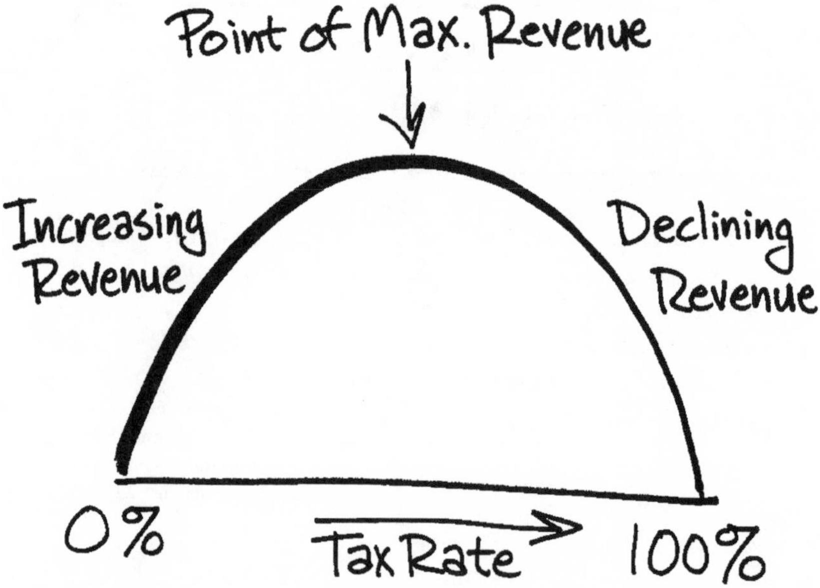

"Like I said," Laffer explains, "the concept is child's play. It's so simple, so obvious, that all those brainy Keynesian economists completely miss it! At the left-hand side of the scale you have a tax rate of 0 percent. How much revenue does the government collect in taxes with a 0 percent tax rate? Zero dollars! As you move toward the right-hand side of the scale, the revenue rises to a certain point—the point of maximum revenue—then it begins to decline once more. By the time you get to the right-hand side of the scale and a 100 percent tax rate, you are again collecting zero dollars in revenue. Why? Because when government confiscates all income through taxation, there are no longer any incentives for taxpayers to work and produce wealth."

"Arthur," Wanniski says excitedly, "this is sheer genius! The principle is not new, of course, but—"

"Exactly," adds Cheney, leaning back and stroking his chin. "We've all seen it happen: Government raises taxes in order to bring in more revenue—but instead, revenues stay flat. People change their behavior to avoid paying the higher taxes. So we end up with higher tax rates—but no more revenue to the treasury than we had before."

"And this curve shows precisely why," says Wanniski. "This is a wonderful teaching device, Art! When did you come up with this?"

Laffer spreads his hands. "Why—just now. It occurred to me as we were talking."

Wanniski picks up the legal pad. "Do you mind if I keep this, Art? I'd like to write about this curve of yours in the *Journal*—giving you full credit for the idea, of course."

Laffer looks at Wanniski, then at Cheney, then at Wanniski again. And a grin spreads across his face.

I invented the dialogue, but that's pretty much how the Laffer Curve was born. True to his word, Jude Wanniski began trumpeting the Laffer Curve in the pages of the *Wall Street Journal*. Wanniski not only coined the term *Laffer Curve*, but also coined the name of the economic theory the curve represented: *supply-side economics*. He became a zealot, a missionary, a fanatic for the concept of cutting taxes to spur economic growth. Soon—thanks to Wanniski and his editor, Robert Bartley—the editorial pages of the *WSJ* were filled with the economic gospel of lower taxes and increased growth, as prophesied by such supply-siders as Paul Craig Roberts III, Martin Anderson, and Norman B. Ture (all of whom later worked in the Reagan administration).

One person who was paying close attention to the *WSJ* editorials was a retired actor and former California state governor named Ronald Reagan. Throughout his career, he had also studied such free-market economists as Murray Weidenbaum, Milton Friedman, George Gilder, and Friedrich

Hayek. From the mid 1970s through the 1980s, his closest advisors included Alan Greenspan and Arthur Burns. A lot of people forget that Ronald Reagan himself majored in economics and sociology when he was in college and that his fascination with economics goes back well before his acting career.

Ronald Reagan understood the workings of a sound economy. And he knew what it was like to be whacked by the blunt end of a *stupid* economic policy. He had paid 91 percent tax rates, and he knew what confiscatory taxes did to a taxpayer's productivity. When he made up his mind to run for president, he didn't just want to get *elected* president. He wanted to change American society for the better. And he knew exactly what he was going to do once he got in office.

In October 1976, after he ran for and lost the presidential nomination to Gerald Ford, and while Ford and Jimmy Carter were engaged in a heated run for the White House, Dad wrote a newspaper column that was syndicated nationwide. It was called "Tax Cuts and Increased Revenue," and it read in part:

> Warren Harding did it. John Kennedy did it. But Jimmy Carter and President Ford aren't talking about it. The "it" that Harding and Kennedy had in common was to cut the income tax. In both cases, federal revenues went up instead of down. . . . The presidential candidates would do us all a service if they would discuss the pros and cons of the concept. Since the idea worked under both Democratic and Republican administrations before, who's to say it couldn't work again?[1]

Ronald Reagan had the evidence on his side when he wrote those words. Before the Kennedy tax cuts were enacted, the U.S. economy was plodding along at an annual growth rate of 2 percent a year, about the same as it has been doing lately under Bill Clinton. Soon after the cuts went into effect, the growth rate of the economy tripled to 6 percent in 1964, and the economy continued to grow at around 5 percent a year throughout the remainder of the 1960s. Ronald Reagan knew it had happened before, and he believed it could happen again. He had ideas, he had convictions, and he had a grasp of what needed to be done to rescue America from its economic doldrums. The views of the supply-siders squared perfectly with his experience in the motion picture business. The Laffer Curve resonated in his soul. Ronald Reagan regarded taxes the way a mongoose regards a venomous snake.

He didn't get a chance to show what he could do in 1976. He had to wait out the Blunder Years of the Carter administration in order to show what supply-side economics could achieve, which is probably just as well. The four years of Jimmy Carter provided a vivid counterpoint to the astoundingly successful eight years of Ronald Reagan and supply-side Reaganomics.

WHERE DO DEFICITS COME FROM?

A major reason I was elected president was because the American economy had become a basket case. Here we were, a country bursting with economic promise, and yet our political leadership had gone out of its way to frustrate America's natural economic strength. It made no sense. My attitude had always been—let the people flourish.

With the help of some Democratic "boll weevils" in Congress, we enacted the largest tax and budget cuts in history. Later we would enact the most extensive reform ever of the tax code. In the process, we cut inflation, interest rates, and unemployment. The consequence is that we have enjoyed the longest peacetime economic expansion in our nation's history.

Ronald Reagan
Speaking My Mind: Selected Speeches
(New York: Simon & Schuster, 1989, pp. 74-75)

In assessing Ronald Reagan's accomplishments in strengthening Main Street, the Business district of the Shining City on a Hill, it's important to understand what he was up against. He inherited an economic crisis that had actually begun during the Nixon-Ford years, and was magnified by the mismanagement of Jimmy Carter. Inflation had reached 13.5 percent and the prime rate stood at 21.5 percent by 1980. Unemployment and poverty were rising, income was falling, production was stagnant, and the stock market was on the brink of collapse. The American people had lost their optimism and hope for the future. A mind-set had settled over America— and around the world—that there could be no brighter tomorrow, no end to inflation, no creation of new wealth, no avoidance of worldwide depression and that there could be only the sharing of an ever-increasing scarcity. Only one voice dared to express optimism for the future: the voice of Ronald Reagan. His program for restoring the American Dream was simple but profound:

- Slash taxes.
- Slash domestic spending.
- Slash oppressive regulations on business.

He knew it wouldn't be easy to get his agenda through the Congress. The Democrats controlled both the House and the Senate. Every budget he sent to Congress was declared DOA—dead on arrival—by the Democratic leadership on Capitol Hill. So Ronald Reagan couldn't initiate the kind of far-reaching, fundamental reforms he would have liked. He never got the deep budget cuts he wanted. During his first term, he was only able to jawbone the Congress into slowing the rate of growth in real spending (that is, spending adjusted for inflation) from the Carter era's 5 percent annual increase to a 3.7 percent increase. Yet even his most modest budget-snipping proposals were routinely greeted with howls of protest from the tax-and-spend side of the aisle.

Ronald Reagan thought he had a deal with the Democrats to cut federal spending back in 1982 when he signed TEFRA (Tax Equity and Fiscal Responsibility Act) into law. TEFRA was supposed to fix what critics considered to be the "overgenerous" aspects of the 1981 ERTA (Economic Recovery and Tax Act), a package of much-needed tax cuts for individuals and corporations that Ronald Reagan rammed through the 97th Congress. He didn't like TEFRA, because it took back about a third of the tax cuts that the American people had gained under ERTA, but he reluctantly agreed to sign it in exchange for a promise that the Democrat-controlled Congress would cut three dollars in federal spending for every one dollar of tax increase under TEFRA. Before it was over, Dad learned a hard but valuable lesson: He found out that he could trust but verify when dealing with the Soviets, but that he must verify, period, when dealing with liberal Democrats in the Congress. Trust is right out the window with that bunch. Ronald Reagan gave the Democrats the tax increase they wanted; fifteen years later, he's *still* waiting for those spending cuts!

Though he never got the spending cuts he was promised, Ronald Reagan was able to completely overhaul the tax system in the 1980s. Passed in August 1981, the Economic Recovery and Tax Act cut individual marginal tax rates across the board and gave the business community expanded investment tax credits and depreciation deductions. In fact, ERTA was the most massive and far-reaching tax overhaul in history. It became the engine that kept the economy strong and stable throughout the next fifteen years, in spite of three massive tax hikes that followed—in 1982 under Reagan (TEFRA), in 1990 under Bush, and in 1993 under Clinton.

Before ERTA, top marginal tax rates were a sky-high 70 percent; from 1981 to 1986, Ronald Reagan cut the top rates all the way down to 28 percent. ERTA (and its follow-up, the Tax Reform Act of 1986) created such a low baseline of tax rates that even the huge Bush and Clinton tax hikes were unable to drag the economy to a standstill. The 1990 tax bill signed by George Bush helped produce the recession that led to his defeat in the 1992 election—yet the economy was resilient enough to bounce back even before he left office. Clinton's 1993 tax hike[2] caused some economic indicators to lag, but overall, the Clinton economy continued to chug along very nicely on the fumes of Reaganomics, allowing Clinton to be easily reelected in 1996. Because Ronald Reagan set the tax rates so low in 1981 and 1986, Bill Clinton was only able to muscle the effective top marginal rate up to 39.6 percent—far less than the 70 percent top rate under Jimmy Carter. Imagine what Clinton might have done if there had been no Ronald Reagan, and if Clinton (who once said he never met a tax he didn't like) had been able to *start* with a 70 percent baseline—and began hiking taxes from there!

There are a lot of myths about the 1980s and Reaganomics—the myth that Ronald Reagan's tax cuts exploded the deficit or that the rich didn't pay their fair share under Reagan. The fact is, the deficit did grow during the 1980s, but not because tax cuts reduced federal revenue. After Ronald Reagan cut taxes, tax revenue exploded—from $599 billion in 1981 to $991 billion in 1989. Even adjusted for inflation, revenue grew by 20 percent from 1981 to 1989—from $767 billion to $916 billion (in constant 1987 dollars). Figure 7.2 shows the revenue figures, as published in *Budget of the United States Government,* Historical Tables, Fiscal Year 1993, Table 1.3, p. 17.

Figure 7.2. Annual Federal Revenues, 1980–1989

(Totals in billions of dollars)

Fiscal Year	Total Revenue (not adjusted for inflation)	Total in FY 1987 Dollars (adjusted)	Total as a Percentage of the Gross Domestic Product
1980	$517.1	$728.1	19.6%
1981	599.3	766.6	20.2%
1982	617.8	738.2	19.8%
1983	600.6	674.3	18.1%
1984	666.5	730.4	18.0%
1985	734.1	776.6	18.5%
1986	769.1	790.0	18.2%
1987	854.1	854.0	19.2%
1988	909.0	877.3	18.9%
1989	990.7	916.2	19.2%

The significant net tax cuts of ERTA actually took effect on January 1, 1983. You'll notice that from 1983, when the economic effects of the Reagan tax cuts kick in through the end of the Reagan presidency, revenue goes steadily *up*. If tax cuts caused deficits, as liberal politicians and media critics claim, revenue should go *down*. Anyone who tells you the Reagan tax cuts caused the deficits of the 1980s is either ignorant—or lying to you. America isn't going broke because we're not taxed enough; America is going broke because politicians spend too much.

Although federal debt continued to pile up during the Reagan years, the annual deficits actually were getting smaller after 1986. Look at the numbers, as published in *Budget of the United States Government,* p. 17, and shown in Figure 7.3.

Figure 7.3. Annual Federal Deficit, 1980–1989

(Totals in Billions of Dollars)

Fiscal Year	Total Revenue (not adjusted for inflation)	Total in FY 1987 Dollars (adjusted)	Total as a Percentage of the Gross Domestic Product
1980	$73.8	$104.0	2.8%
1981	79.0	101.0	2.7%
1982	128.0	152.9	4.1%
1983	207.8	236.8	6.3%
1984	185.4	203.2	5.0%
1985	212.3	224.6	5.4%
1986	221.2	227.3	5.2%

Fiscal Year	Total Revenue (not adjusted for inflation)	Total in FY 1987 Dollars (adjusted)	Total as a Percentage of the Gross Domestic Product
1987	149.8	149.8	3.4%
1988	155.2	149.8	3.2%
1989	152.5	141.0	2.9%

Notice especially how the deficit drops in adjusted-for-inflation dollars and as a percentage of the GNP after the 1986 Tax Reform Act, which dropped top marginal rates to 28 percent. Continuing on through the Bush years, the same table shows that the steadily shrinking Reagan deficits suddenly begin to balloon once more when George Bush breaks his read-my-lips pledge and signs the 1990 tax increase. See Figure 7.4.

Figure 7.4. Annual Federal Deficit, 1990–1993

(Totals in Billions of Dollars)

Fiscal Year	Total Deficits (not adjusted for inflation)	Total in FY 1987 Dollars (adjusted)	Total as a Percentage of the Gross Domestic Product
1990	$221.4	$196.2	4.0%
1991	269.5	228.6	4.8%
1992	290.4	238.1	4.9%
1993	254.7	202.7	4.0%

If George Bush had continued the Reagan policy of low taxes coupled with spending cuts, the deficit could have been eliminated entirely, and Bush would now be looking back on the extraordinary accomplishments of his *second* term. That's not just my assessment. That's the conclusion reached by the bipartisan Congressional Budget Office in January 1989. The CBO projected a steadily falling deficit, assuming the rules of the game were not changed. Unfortunately, both Bush and Clinton decided to change the rules. The economy slowed its growth, taxpayers began hiding their earnings, and the deficit grew.

Despite Ronald Reagan's calls for spending cuts, and despite Democratic promises to Ronald Reagan during the TEFRA negotiations, federal spending *more than doubled* during the Reagan years, from $590.9 billion in 1980 to $1.25 trillion in 1990. Adjusted for inflation, that's a 33.4 percent increase in spending. When spending increases 33 percent while revenue increases 20 percent, it is clearly spending—not tax cuts—that is to blame for the deficits. What if Congress had kept its promise to Ronald Reagan? What if we had achieved real cuts in federal spending at the same time the Reagan tax cuts were bringing more revenue into the U.S. Treasury? For one thing, we would all be more prosperous today. For another, America would be climbing out of debt instead of free-falling toward bankruptcy and a day of fiscal reckoning. If we want to see a return to the kind of widespread, roaring prosperity that America enjoyed in the 1980s—plus a reduction in the deficit leading to an actual paydown of the debt—we must cut taxes and cut spending.

In 1980, Jimmy Carter's last year in office, the IRS received just 4,414 individual tax returns listing adjusted gross income of a million dollars or more. In 1987, that number rose to 34,944. Critics of Ronald Reagan might think this is just more proof of the charge that the rich got richer and the poor got poorer under Reagan, but that's not so. All income classes benefited under Reaganomics because the entire economy improved—not just one segment of the economy. Figure 7.5 shows how real, adjusted-for-inflation household incomes rose from 1983 to 1989.

Figure 7.5. **Household Income, 1983–1989**

Highest 20 percent of households:	up 18.8 percent
Second-highest 20 percent of households:	up 11.6 percent
Middle 20 percent of households:	up 10.7 percent
Second-lowest 20 percent of households:	up 10.1 percent
Lowest 20 percent of households:	up 12.2 percent

And because this is America, the land of the American Dream of upward mobility, there was dramatic movement of people from the lower income levels to the higher income levels. A Treasury Department study found that of those wage earners who were in the bottom 20 percent of income in 1979, an amazing 85.8 percent had climbed to the next or higher income level by 1988. In fact, 65 percent had moved up two levels or more under Reaganomics! Even Isabel Sawhill and Mark Condon of the liberal Urban Institute had to admit that "when one follows individuals instead of statistical groups defined by income, one finds that, on average, the rich got a little richer and the poor got much richer."[3]

The Reagan tax cuts produced the longest peacetime economic boom in U.S. history (ninety-two straight months of growth without recession, November 1982 to July 1990). The economy grew at an average rate of 3.5 percent from 1983 through 1990, as compared with an average rate of 1.6 percent from 1973 to 1982.

The Reagan 1980s created 18.6 million new jobs (1980 to 1990), and expanded civilian payrolls by nearly 20 percent. Contrary to the repeated claims of the left, most of these were good jobs. About 82 percent were in well-paid, skilled occupations, and only 12 percent were low-paid, "burger-flipping" occupations. (Under Carter, 42 percent of new jobs were low-paid, low-skilled jobs, and the number of well-paid, skilled positions actually declined 10 percent.) Nearly a quarter of those newly created jobs went to African-Americans. Unemployment, which stood at 7.1 percent when Ronald Reagan took office, fell to 5.3 percent by the time he left office.

Reaganomics boosted family incomes at all levels. Median family income, adjusted for inflation, fell 10 percent from 1978 to 1982 but rose 11.3 percent from 1983 to 1989, after Reaganomics began to kick in. The American standard of living (expressed as disposable income) increased 18 percent (adjusted for inflation) from 1982 to 1990.

At first glance, all the statistics I've just cited would seem to be only about how well families did in the Neighborhood during the 1980s, not how well Main Street fared. But these statistics also give us a good snapshot of how Main Street was doing. If the families in the Neighborhood were doing well, it was because the wage earners in the Neighborhood had good, well-paying jobs to go to down on Main Street. If Main Street does well, so does the Neighborhood. The economic health of the Neighborhood is a good indirect indicator of the vitality on Main Street.

But there are also some direct indicators as well. The United States under Ronald Reagan experienced a healthy surge in manufacturing. Output rose by 38 percent in real inflation-adjusted dollars from 1980 to 1989, and manufacturing productivity rose nearly 42 percent from 1980 to 1990.

Thanks to Ronald Reagan, America in the 1980s became the wealthiest society the world has ever known. An economy that was on the ropes and nearing total collapse was brought back to full health and vigor. Even after the Bush and Clinton tax hikes, our standard of living is still the highest in the world—higher than Germany's by about 25 percent and higher than Japan's by about 40 percent—because of what Ronald Reagan accomplished in eight years as president. It didn't happen by accident. The statistics prove it.[4] Ronald Reagan did exactly what he set out to do, exactly what he said a president should do when he wrote his October 1976 newspaper column,

"Tax Cuts and Increased Revenue." His plan worked—far beyond what even he expected. And it can work again.

America must return to what works. And what works is Reaganomics.

RESTORING TAX SANITY

Republicans believe every day is the 4th of July, but Democrats believe every day is April 15.

Ronald Reagan
Observation made on
more than one occasion

Our opponents are openly committed to increasing our tax burden. We are committed to stopping them, and we will. . . . They would place higher and higher taxes on small businesses, on family farms, and on other working families so that government may once again grow at the people's expense. You know, we could say they spend money like drunken sailors, but that would be unfair to drunken sailors. . . . It would be unfair, because the sailors are spending their own money.

Our tax policies are and will remain prowork, progrowth, and profamily. We intend to simplify the entire tax system—to make taxes more fair, easier to understand, and most important, to bring the tax rates of every American further down, not up. Now, if we bring them down far enough, growth will continue strong; the underground economy will shrink; the world will beat a path to our door; and no one will be able to hold America back—

And the future will be ours.

Ronald Reagan
Acceptance Speech
Republican National Convention
Dallas, Texas, August 23, 1984

One of the earliest tax protestors in history was a spunky young lady named Godiva.

Now, you probably thought Lady Godiva was only famous for her equestrian skills, especially bareback riding. You may have even thought she was just a legend. But no, Lady Godiva was an actual Englishwoman who lived between A.D. 1040 and A.D. 1080 in Coventry, England. Her husband was Leofric, the Earl of Mercia, and together they founded the Benedictine monastery in Coventry.

English historian Roger of Wendover recorded that, in the year 1057, seventeen-year-old Lady Godiva became outraged when she discovered the enormous tax rates her husband, the Earl of Mercia, had levied on the people of Coventry. She pleaded with him to cut the people's taxes, but Leofric told her to mind her own business. She coaxed and cajoled, but still he refused. She stamped her foot and held her breath until she turned blue. And finally, just to get his bride off his back, the Earl said, "Enough, already! You want to know when I'm going to cut taxes? I'll tell you! The day you ride naked on horseback through the Town Square, that's when!" He thought he had laid the matter to rest. He never imagined Lady Godiva would take him up on it!

The very next day she went into the stable, shed her clothes, and hopped aboard the nearest nag. Strategically arranging her long tresses for the sake of modesty, she nudged the horse toward the Town Square. After her ride through town, she returned home and found her husband at the front door, looking rather shaken.

"Well?" she asked. "I kept my side of the bargain."

True to his word, Leofric cut the taxes.

That's one way to get the job done, but I don't recommend it. You could get arrested!

We need a drastic overhaul of our tax structure every bit as much as the good people of Coventry needed one. It's not just that the tax *rates* are too high. The sheer *complexity* of the tax code is causing the rest of us to lose our shirts! According to the Tax Foundation, our tax system imposes $192 billion in annual compliance costs on families and businesses. The IRS calculates that Americans annually spend 5.4 billion hours on their tax returns—more than all the man-hours used to build all the cars produced in America in a year. The direct and indirect costs of the tax system are by far the largest budget item of every American family and every American business. The average family pays more in taxes than for food, clothing, shelter, and transportation *combined*.

Our tax system is so hopelessly complicated and flawed, there's no point trying to fix it. The only sensible solution is to scrap it and start fresh. Following are some tax reform ideas we must implement *now*.

ENACT THE FLAT TAX

This is not rocket science, folks. We now have a tax system that punishes hard work and achievement, penalizes thrift and investment, and is a hundred times more complicated than anything NASA ever had to launch. The solution is to create a tax system that fits on a postcard—and that's what a flat tax does. Unlike the multitiered, discriminatory progressive tax, a flat tax features a single low rate for everybody. That's what makes it flat.

The beauty of the plan is its simplicity: There would no longer be preferences and loopholes, and there would be much less of an incentive to cheat. The current tax code is so complicated that even the IRS can't understand it, and the complexity of the system triggers wasteful audits and intimidating confrontations between the IRS and taxpayers. The flat tax would dramatically reduce both taxpayer fraud and IRS abuses. The rules would be so simple that the only items the IRS might question are a taxpayer's income and number of dependents.

A flat tax would boost the economy in a number of ways. For example, it would encourage economic growth and capital formation by eliminating double taxation of savings and investment. All income would be treated equally and taxed only once. The flat tax could be structured in such a way that taxpayers could take a mortgage interest deduction, which is good for the construction and real estate industries. The flat tax could also allow a superdeduction for charitable contributions (see Chapter 6) that would benefit our religious and civic charities. John S. Barry, policy analyst for the Heritage Foundation, adds:

> The flat tax, by increasing economic growth and removing 24 million Americans from the federal income tax rolls, itself serves as a charitable program. All Americans, especially those at lower income levels, will realize more economic opportunities and lower taxes. The flat tax will give individuals the freedom to make their own decisions on how to spend their own money without fear of being penalized through the federal income tax structure. These benefits will do more for individual Americans than any nonprofit organization—and certainly more than any federal government program—ever can.[5]

By boosting incentives for people to start new businesses, to work hard, and to save, the flat tax will generate higher employment, greater productivity, and higher wages. A flat tax would also:

- Replace 600-odd IRS forms with a postcard-size form. (Actually, there would be one postcard for individuals and a somewhat different postcard for businesses.)
- Take power out of the hands of politicians and social engineers who use the tax code to control our behavior and spending patterns.
- Increase the creation of wealth. (According to Harvard economist Dale Jorgenson, implementation of a flat tax would instantly create a trillion dollars of new wealth.)
- Spur faster economic growth.

Reliable estimates project that a flat tax would add about 1 percent of additional economic expansion per year to the economy, as opposed to the present progressive tax system. What would an additional 1 percent of growth mean? According to Congressman David Dreier (R-California), it would mean 200,000 new small businesses created over the next four years, 6 million new jobs created over the next eight years, and $700 billion more in tax revenue over the next eight years (enough to balance the budget without spending cuts and enough to keep Social Security solvent for the next three decades). That's not a bad down payment on our Shining City, not bad at all.

One of the common misunderstandings about the flat tax is the fear that it would unfairly shift the burden of taxation from the rich to the middle class and poor. The fact is, the flat tax would provide a massive tax benefit to the poor and middle class. All taxpayers would be allowed to completely exempt a base amount of income from taxation. The Dick Armey–Richard Shelby plan, for example, would only require a family of four to pay taxes on income over $33,300. Any income up to that amount is tax-free. Many middle-class families paying thousands of dollars of tax under the current system would pay nothing, zero, nada under the Armey-Shelby flat tax.

One particularly attractive by-product of the flat tax is that it would finally depoliticize the IRS. No longer could politicians use the IRS as a tool to reward friends, punish enemies, and dispense political favors—a practice that probably goes back to FDR, but which has been refined into an art form by the Clinton administration. According to articles published in the *Wall*

Street Journal (October 22, 1996) and the *Washington Times* (January 20, 1997),[6] the Clinton White House appears to have sent audit-happy IRS agents to harass conservative groups such as the Christian Coalition, the Heritage Foundation, the National Rifle Association, Citizens Against Government Waste, the Freedom Alliance, and the Western Journalism Center. Reporters have been unable to find any liberal groups that have been similarly targeted.[7]

The Western Journalism Center is one of the leading organizations investigating Clinton scandals, such as the murky death of Vince Foster. WJC executive director Joseph Farah noted that the IRS was much more interested in WJC's investigation of the Foster matter than it was in WJC's accounting and bookkeeping practices. When WJC's accountant questioned the direction of the probe, the IRS field agent replied, "Look, this is a political case, and it's going to be decided at the national level." It should surprise no one that at the time all of these IRS probes of conservative groups were launched, the head of the IRS was Margaret Milner Richardson, a Clinton campaign operative and longtime close friend of first lady Hillary Rodham Clinton. The flat tax would make it impossible for politicians like the Clintons to use the IRS for vindictive political purposes.

Beware of liberal attempts to distort the plain, simple meaning of the term *flat tax*. Dick Gephardt, the House Democratic leader from Missouri, floated a scheme that he had the brass to label a flat tax,—yet his plan contained five tax brackets, plus increased taxes on families earning under $40,000 a year, and a capital gains tax increase. Despite what Gephardt and Co. would have you believe, a flat tax has one rate and no brackets. If it has brackets, it's not flat—simple as that.

ELIMINATE THE CAPITAL GAINS TAX

One of the most damaging taxes to the economy of Main Street—and to family budgets across America—is the capital gains tax. It depresses investment, ties up assets, and prevents capital from being moved through the economy to encourage growth. The liberal charge that a capital gains tax cut would only benefit the rich just won't wash. While upper-income taxpayers would benefit from a capital gains rate cut, the middle class—people who own homes and invest in taxable investments such as mutual funds—would also receive much-needed tax relief. Many people are shelving assets they would sell if not for the confiscatory capital gains tax. Cutting the rate would put billions of dollars of assets into circulation, which would cause more capital gains revenue to flow into the Treasury.

The best solution would be to simply treat capital gains as you would any other income under a flat tax—just pay the same rate on your capital gains as you do on your paycheck. The value of assets should be indexed for inflation, so that people only have to pay taxes on real gains, not on inflation. For example, if you bought a house in 1970 for $20,000 and sell it in the year 2000 for $220,000, you shouldn't have to pay a capital gains tax on the entire $200,000 difference, because most of that is not a real profit—it's only compound inflation.

ELIMINATE ESTATE TAXES

The government taxes you when you earn the money—then, when you die, it taxes you again. The estate tax is a foolish, unfair tax that hurts American business and American families, destroys jobs, and reduces America's economic output. Repeal of the estate tax would produce an enormous benefit to the economy—around $11 billion a year in extra economic output, according to economist William W. Beach of the Heritage Foundation.

The heaviest estate tax burden falls on small businesses—particularly family-owned enterprises, minority businesses, and family farms. The estate tax forces business owners to take extraordinary defensive measures against their own government—major life insurance purchases, ownership restructuring, gifting of stock, and so forth—in order to protect their businesses from liquidation to pay estate taxes when the owner dies. If there were no estate tax, these maneuvers would be totally unnecessary.

Perhaps the most senseless aspect of the estate tax is that it raises a depressingly small amount of revenue for the enormous amount of suffering it causes. According to Beach, the unified gift and estate tax raised only $14.7 billion in 1995, yet the cost of complex tax avoidance schemes totaled many times that figure. What's even more tragic, the estate tax is counterproductive. If it were repealed, the revenue generated by extra growth in the economy would more than compensate for the paltry amount of revenue this destructive tax takes in.[8]

ADOPT DYNAMIC RATHER THAN STATIC SCORING

The government bases its tax policy on the assumption that the behavior of individual and corporate taxpayers is *static,* that people do not change the way they work, operate businesses, invest, or save according to changes in the tax law. The fact is, most of us order our lives around the tax code. We don't make a move without calling our accountant and asking, "If I do X, what's gonna happen to me on April 15?"

The opposite of static scoring is dynamic scoring, and dynamic scoring is a fundamental law of supply-side Reaganomics. Ronald Reagan knew that when he cut taxes, people would change their behavior, become more productive, start more businesses, and create more jobs. That's human nature. Ronald Reagan was right, and Reaganomics succeeded because dynamic scoring takes into account the way people actually respond to changes in the tax code.

When liberals claim that the Reagan tax cuts increased the deficit, they are appealing to the fact that most people think in static rather than dynamic terms. Superficially, it seems to make sense: If you cut taxes, revenue has to go down, right? Wrong. If you cut taxes, people spend more, invest more, start new businesses, hire more employees, and create more wealth. The economy expands and revenue goes up. That's the Laffer Curve. That's the cold, hard, indisputable evidence of the 1980s.

When government entities such as the Congressional Budget Office, the Joint Committee on Taxation, or the Office of Management and Budget make economic and budget forecasts based on static scoring, they actually erect a bias in favor of higher taxes. That's why George Bush and Bill Clinton sought to raise taxes to close the deficit; that's why George Bush used to campaign in the primaries against Ronald Reagan, calling the Reagan tax cut plan "voodoo economics." Bush was a static thinker. Dynamic scoring looks like voodoo to those who have a static mind-set. But to those who understand how human nature and human economies truly work, dynamic scoring merely states the obvious: People are not stupid. When taxes go up, people look for ways to avoid paying them.

History shows that static scoring always leads to major errors in economic forecasting. For example, in 1986, when the capital gains tax was hiked from 20 percent to 28 percent, the Congressional Budget Office (CBO) predicted taxable capital gains would top $225 billion by 1989; the actual number in 1989: $150 billion. That same year, 1986, CBO forecast that increased corporate rates in the 1986 Tax Reform Act would raise corporate tax revenue from $89 billion in 1986 to $101 billion in 1987; instead, corporations shifted from equity financing to debt financing in order to avoid taxes—and corporate tax revenue *dropped* to $84 billion. In January 1990, CBO predicted taxable capital gains would reach $269 billion the following year; actual 1991 figure: $108 billion.[9]

BLOCK FUTURE TAX HIKES

We know from sad experience that what government gives, government has a tendency to take away. Under Ronald Reagan, government gave us long-overdue tax cuts. Under George Bush and Bill Clinton, tax rates began leapfrogging upward again. Once we have a flat tax with reasonable rates, what's to stop some later Congress and president from raising taxes again to finance liberal vote-buying schemes? We need to begin now to make it difficult (in fact, well nigh impossible) for future politicians to raise taxes. One way to do that would be to make a constitutional amendment requiring a two-thirds supermajority of both houses in order to raise taxes. This would make a tax hike possible in the event of a genuine emergency. If, for some reason, higher taxes were truly needed to save the country, certainly two-thirds of the Congress would recognize the need. Odds are, however, that a flat tax with low rates will provide all the money government truly needs to carry out its constitutional duties.

DEMAND ACROSS-THE-BOARD, NOT "TARGETED," TAX CUTS

The only tax cuts Bill Clinton is (reluctantly) willing to support are so-called "targeted" tax cuts. A targeted tax cut is a gift that the government gives to one group of Americans to the exclusion of others. It is designed to accomplish some political objective, usually fostering class envy by favoring a lower economic class while maintaining punishing tax rates on the upper economic classes. Targeted tax cuts may be a slick way to buy votes, but they do not produce economic growth, nor are they designed to. Clinton has proposed tax cuts that target small businesses, minority entrepreneurs, and parents with kids in college. But those tax cuts leave ordinary middle-class wage earners high and dry. That's not what America is all about.

Targeted tax cuts are a form of discrimination and preferential treatment. Vice President Al Gore called it exactly right during the 1996 campaign when he attacked Bob Dole's 15 percent tax cut as "indiscriminate." That's the whole idea. Tax cuts should not discriminate—they should be fair, nonpreferential, and across the board. Just as a rising tide lifts all boats, tax cuts should lift the entire economy and promote greater individual freedom. Bill Clinton, Al Gore, and other liberal Democrats want to use the tax code to pick some in our economy as winners, others as losers. They want to use the tax code to dictate our economic behavior.

DEFEND SMALL BUSINESS AND REDUCE FEDERAL REGULATIONS

In announcing his Economic Recovery Plan on April 28, 1981, Ronald Reagan said, "Let us not overlook the fact that the small, independent businessman or -woman creates more than 80 percent of all the new jobs and employs more than half of our total workforce. Our across-the-board cut in tax rates for a three-year period will give them much of the incentive and promise of stability they need to go forward with expansion plans calling for additional employees." Ronald Reagan appreciated both the importance and the difficulties of small business in America. He had a warm spot in his heart for the small businessman or -woman in America because of an experience that was very close to his heart. Ronald Reagan's father, Jack, was a small businessman, and as a young man, Ronald Reagan watched helplessly while the relentless steamroller of the Great Depression crushed his father's dream of owning his own shoe store.

One Christmas Eve, as the family gathered to celebrate, there was a knock at the door. Jack opened the door to find a postman with a special-delivery letter. Jack's face brightened. The letter was from the shoe company that he worked for. *What a surprise,* he thought. *A Christmas bonus!* Jack's wife and sons, Ronald and Neil, watched in anticipation as Jack tore open the envelope and withdrew a piece of blue paper. He read it—then slumped into a chair. "Well, that's quite a Christmas present," he said in a hoarse whisper. "The company just laid me off."

After Christmas, Jack Reagan found a job running a shoe outlet in

Springfield, two hundred miles from Dixon. He had to leave his family to work there. Once, during football season, Ronald Reagan was in Springfield with the team, so he stopped by his father's store to say hello. He recalled the shock of seeing the place where his father worked:

> His store was a grim, tiny hole-in-the-wall. Although he'd cleaned it up, there wasn't much anybody could have done with the store. There were garish orange advertisements promoting cut-rate shoes plastered on the windows, and the sole piece of furniture was a small wooden bench with iron arm-rests where his customers were fitted.
>
> When I saw the store I thought of the hours he'd spent when we were boys talking about the grand shoe store he dreamed of opening one day. . . . I looked away, not wanting him to see the tears welling up in my eyes.[10]

Ronald Reagan always had a soft spot in his heart for entrepreneurs and small business owners—people with big dreams, people who often faced huge odds and obstacles in the struggle to make their dreams come true. Most important of all, he was aware of the fact that all too many of the problems of small businesspeople are caused by government. "We invented the assembly line and mass production," he said in his televised address on the economy, February 5, 1981, "but punitive tax policies and excessive and unnecessary regulations . . . have stifled our ability to update plant and equipment. When capital investment is made, it's too often for some unproductive alterations demanded by government to meet various of its regulations."

As in the 1980s, small businesses still create 80 percent of all new jobs in this country. But unfortunately, 15 percent of those businesses fail within the first year of opening their doors. The two main reasons small businesses fail, according to David Birch of the research firm Cognetics, Inc., are taxes and regulations. In other words, *government is the problem.* Economist Thomas D. Hopkins pegs the direct cost of compliance with federal regulations at about $677 billion in 1996, and that doesn't even begin to calculate such indirect costs as lost productivity. Businesses with 20 to 500 employees shell out an average of $5,298 per worker just to comply with government edicts, and the cost is even higher for firms with fewer than 20 employees (about 90 percent of all U.S. firms), around $5,532 per worker.

Government regulations are, in fact, the hidden killer of most failed businesses. Many entrepreneurs fail to take the cost of federal regulations into account when they start their operations. Only when it's too late do they discover (as Tax Foundation economist Arthur Hall reports) that small corporations pay over $7 in compliance costs for every $1 of income tax they pay. In 1996, over 600 new federal rules took effect, and over 700 new federal rules were adopted in 1996 to take effect in 1997.[11]

CUT SPENDING

Deficits and spiraling debt have become a way of life in America. Our nation is in hock for around 5.5 trillion bucks, or more than $20,000 for every man, woman, and child in America. According to the National Taxpayers Union, a child born today can expect to pay an average of over $100,000 in extra taxes *just to pay the interest* on the debt incurred during his or her first eighteen years of life![12] The federal debt has been climbing year after year for three decades, during Democratic administrations and Congresses and during Republican administrations and Congresses. This is not a Democrat-versus-Republican thing. This is a commonsense thing. A day of reckoning is coming unless we act now.

A balanced budget was the elusive dream of Ronald Reagan. "Our aim," he said in his Oval Office address to the nation on the economy (February 5, 1981), "is to increase our national wealth so all will have more, not just redistribute what we already have, which is just a sharing of scarcity. We can begin to reward hard work and risk-taking by forcing this government to live within its means." Seven years, eleven months, and fifteen days later, Ronald Reagan again went before a TV camera in the Oval Office, this time for his farewell address to the nation at the conclusion of his presidency. In the course of that speech, he said, "I've been asked if I have any regrets. Well, I do: the deficit."

Dad hated leaving office with that part of his job undone. Years before, as governor, he had performed an absolute miracle in saving the state of California from bankruptcy, and he regretted not having the power to do the same as president of the United States. In his autobiography, he described the shock that awaited him when he was first elected governor:

> I learned that things were even worse for California than I'd thought they were during the campaign. Through accounting sleight of hand, the previous administration [of Democratic governor Pat Brown] had con-

cealed the fact that the state government was *broke*. . . . [state director of finance] Caspar Weinberger . . . came to me and said, "The state's spending over a million dollars a day more than it's taking in and it's been doing that for a year."

The Democrats in Sacramento had known about the mounting deficit for almost a year, but had concealed it by altering bookkeeping procedures that pushed the deficit into the subsequent fiscal year; then, they had gone on spending as extravagantly as always, while avoiding the embarrassment of an election-year tax increase.

Now suddenly the state faced its worst financial crisis since the Depression, and it was up to me, as the new governor, to end it.[13]

Let me tell you what Ronald Reagan did over the next eight years as governor of California: Not only did he manage to bring the state's budget back into balance, not only did he completely reform the out-of-control welfare system in the state, not only did he cut taxes, but he also gave the taxpayers of California *four tax rebates totaling $5 billion!* Let me tell you, that drove the liberal Democrats in Sacramento *nuts!* On one occasion, the Democratic leader of the state senate barged into Dad's office, shouting, "Giving that money back to the people is an unnecessary expenditure of public funds!" But unlike the liberal Democrats, Ronald Reagan figured it was the people's money to begin with.

To understand the size and scope of his accomplishment as governor, it helps to realize that, had California been a nation, it would have been the seventh ranking economic power in the world. So why was he able to balance the budget of California, but unable to balance the budget of the number one economic power in the world, the United States of America? The answer is simple: As governor, he had more power. As governor, he had the line-item veto—and he used it 943 times against a Democrat-controlled statehouse to keep spending in line, and his line-item veto was never overridden once. As president, he had no power to keep Congress from spending. Previous presidents, from Washington to Nixon could simply impound funds and refuse to spend money appropriated by Congress, but Congress took that power away from the presidency in the ill-named Budget Reform Act of 1974. It wasn't until the Republican 104th Congress passed the line-item veto that this power was finally restored to the presidency (and a *Democratic* occupant of the presidency, no less!).

If Ronald Reagan had possessed the line-item veto as president, the success story of the 1980s would have been even more astounding than it was, because he would have achieved his dream of tax cuts *plus* real spending cuts. He would have been able to bring America into the black, just as he brought the state of California back to solvency as governor. Ronald Reagan knew that tax cuts are only half the story. The Shining City on a Hill can't be built with tax cuts alone. To complete the job, the budget must also be cut and the national debt paid down. That takes political will and conviction—commodities that are in short supply these days.

You might be thinking, *But hasn't the deficit been reduced under Bill Clinton?* Absolutely. The week before the 1996 election, Clinton announced that the deficit for FY 1996 was $107.3 billion, and he was quick to point out that the actual 1996 deficit was $57 billion less than his budget had originally projected. The reason, according to Bill Clinton: His economic plan, including the 1993 tax increase, was working even better than expected!

The fact is, Bill Clinton's economic plan has done little to reduce the deficit, despite his claims. Every single budget Bill Clinton submitted to the Congress has raised, not cut, spending. It is important to note, however, that the $57 billion in additional deficit reduction that Clinton took credit for is almost exactly equal to the $56 billion in spending cuts the Republican 104th Congress sliced out of Clinton's budget during negotiations with the White House! Republicans cut the deficit—and Bill Clinton took the credit. Other factors that brought down the deficit during Clinton's watch include the end of the savings and loan crisis; defense downsizing initiated by President Bush after the end of the Cold War; and the growth of tax revenues after the end of the 1991 recession. A few brave Democrats are honest enough to admit the truth about deficit reduction in the Clinton era. As former Democratic congressman Tim Penny said, "In reality, Clinton's 1993 five-year budget plan had little to do with the steep drop in the deficit for 1996."[14]

Bill Clinton can't point to a single feature of his budget plan that would produce a lower deficit—except higher taxes. And Clinton's tax hikes have hurt the economy. Economic growth averaged 1.3 percent in 1995 and 2.5 percent over his first term—the slowest expansion in over a century, according to the congressional Joint Economic Committee. Credit card loan delinquencies have zoomed upward under Clinton—the highest since the American Bankers Association began tracking them in 1974—and bankruptcy filings topped the one million mark for the first time in U.S. history in 1996. Wages, adjusted for inflation, have fallen under Clinton (women have experienced a 2.2 percent drop). Clearly, deficit reduction has not been a by-product of a stronger economy.

Clinton raised taxes on the Social Security benefits of senior citizens; he raised gasoline taxes; and he raised taxes on the incomes of American families. Ronald Reagan once said that the way you cure the extravagant spending of government is the same way you cure the extravagance of children: "By simply reducing their allowance." But did Bill Clinton cut government's allowance? Nope. He cut *ours*!

We can't just cut taxes. We can't just cut spending. We must cut taxes and spending *together*.

THE GOLDEN AGE

Our task is far from over. Our friends in the other party will never forgive us for our success, and are doing everything in their power to rewrite history. Listening to the liberals, you'd think that the 1980s were the worst period since the Great Depression, filled with suffering and despair. I don't know about you, but I'm getting awfully tired of the whining voices from the [Clinton] White House these days. They're claiming there was a decade of greed and neglect, but you and I know better than that. We were there.

Ronald Reagan
Republican National Committee Annual Gala
February 3, 1994

In 1992, while running for president, Bill Clinton called the Reagan 1980s "a gilded age of greed and selfishness, of irresponsibility and excess." And Hillary Clinton, in her remarks at the 1993 University of Michigan commencement, said, "Throughout the 1980s, we heard too much about individual gain, about the ethos of selfishness and greed."[15] I think we can learn a lot about selfishness and greed from the Clintons.

After all, it was in 1986, the height of the greedy, rotten 1980s, that the then-governor of Arkansas claimed deductions of $2 a pair for used underwear that he donated to charity, plus $1.50 for his used socks.[16] Here I've been (literally!) sitting on a gold mine in tax dodges, and I've just been tossing my skivvies in the trash when the elastic gets too loose.

And then there's Hillary. Back on October 12, 1981—during the first year of Ronald Reagan's presidency—Hillary wrote her Whitewater chum, Jim McDougal, saying, "If Reaganomics works at all, Whitewater could become the western hemisphere's Mecca."[17] Well, she was half right—Reaganomics does work, but there was no Mecca in Whitewater. Of course, it could just be that she didn't really understand Reaganomics. The way Reaganomics works, everybody gets to keep more of what they *earn;* the way Whitewater works, a few people get to keep whatever they can *grab.* (For example, Bill and Hillary grabbed a 50 percent share in the Whitewater development by only putting up 10 percent of the cash.)

Just to keep things in perspective, we need to remember that it was in 1978—three years *before* Ronald Reagan went to Washington to launch the "gilded age of greed and selfishness"—that Hillary made a boodle in cattle futures, parlaying a $1,000 investment into roughly $100,000, making a $99,541 profit in just ten months. Dow-Jones finance columnist Caroline Baum and commodities speculator Victor Niederhoffer examined the transaction, looking for evidence of illegalities. They found:

- Hillary's annual return was more than 80 times higher than the performance achieved by top speculator George Soros in his best year.
- A totally novice investor, Hillary traded in the biggest bull market in history. But instead of betting with the market, she traded primarily from the short side. In other words, in a market of wildly rising prices, she bet *against* rising prices—and still managed to score a 10,000 percent return on her investment in ten months. The odds against achieving such a feat by honest, legal means are, according to Baum and Niederhoffer, "about the same as those of finding the Dead Sea Scrolls on the steps of the State House in Little Rock."
- Hillary attempted to suppress the evidence of her cattle futures transactions. She fought the appointment of a special prosecutor to investigate her financial dealings. She lied about where the money came from, originally claiming it was a gift from her parents until the Clintons' 1978 and 1979 tax returns were released, showing the source of her windfall. She lied about how the transactions were conducted, originally claiming she placed her own trades after researching cattle futures in the *Wall Street Journal.* After changing her story several times, she

finally admitted that Tyson Foods attorney Jim Blair placed most of her trades. As often happens with crucial Clinton documents, the written confirmations on her two most profitable trades are missing.

- It is irrational to believe that the Clintons would have risked everything in the volatile futures market. Bill earned about $25,000 as the Arkansas state attorney general, while Hillary brought less than $15,000 a year as a Little Rock law firm partner. Both owed student loans and bought furniture on credit. Hillary's open position in the futures market often topped a million dollars—which means that a move in the market of as little as 2 to 5 percent could have completely wiped out the Clintons without warning. The only rational explanation for this behavior is that Hillary knew there was never any risk. The risk would be eliminated if, for example, her broker purchased a large number of futures for various clients, but without placing those futures in any specific client's account until he knew how they had performed. Winning futures were parked in Hillary's account, and losers were dumped into other accounts. This practice is called "fraud," "bribery," and "money laundering."

- At the time Hillary entered into the cattle futures scheme, Bill was up in the polls by 30 points and had a virtual lock on the governor's mansion. Jim Blair, outside counsel for Tyson, helped the governor's wife turn a nest egg into some serious cash. Hillary's broker was Robert "Red" Bone, a former Tyson exec who was later convicted for commodities-trading violations and fined a quarter of a million dollars. What did Blair, Bone, and Tyson Foods want in return for Hillary's windfall (not to mention the generous campaign contributions and free rides on Tyson corporate planes that the Clintons enjoyed)? We know that Tyson received millions in tax breaks from the state of Arkansas while Bill was governor and that regulations were relaxed, which allowed Tyson chicken farms and processing plants to foul the rivers of Arkansas with untreated animal wastes. So there is an appearance here that Tyson Foods certainly got its money's worth—and then some.[18]

Baum and Niederhoffer conclude that, taking all the indicators into account, Hillary's cattle futures transactions score 98 out of 100. This means that, in their minds, the transactions were almost certainly illegitimate. "After extensive research," they concluded, "we have satisfied ourselves that Mrs. Clinton was neither naive nor lucky nor particularly talented as a trader. . . . Mrs. Clinton's representation of the events fifteen years later is highly improbable."[19]

So what do you think of Hillary's incredible good fortune in the cattle futures market? Was it a miracle? Or was it out-and-out dishonest greed?

The tale of greed and selfishness goes on and on. For example, there's the story of the systematic looting of Jim McDougal's Madison Guaranty Savings, which cost American taxpayers well over $73 million. Despite a conflict of interest, which Hillary hid from federal regulators (she had previously represented Madison), she was hired to represent the federal government *against* Madison, and in that capacity she "negotiated" a $1 million fine. Of that million, $600,000 went to Seth Ward (the father-in-law of Hillary's friend and law partner, Web Hubbell), and Hillary collected $400,000 in legal fees. The government got zip.

Another example: In 1993, Hillary Clinton made a series of speeches and public statements in which she loudly attacked the pharmaceutical industry. At the same time, her personal investment portfolio—which was supposed to have been placed in a blind trust but wasn't—was heavily invested in pharmaceutical stocks through a firm called Value Partners I. Because of her attacks on pharmaceutical profits, the price of drug company stocks went down, and Hillary made $275,000 selling short[20] in pharmaceutical stocks—what would normally be called *insider trading,* the very epitome of greed, selfishness, and illegality. At the time of his death, Vince Foster was handling the matter of placing Hillary's investments in a blind trust—seven months late.

Now, there's a very important point to all this that goes beyond mere Clinton bashing. People toss around words like *greed* and *selfishness* without thinking about what those words mean. Remember, after Hillary engaged in all those grubby, greedy, sleazy, and almost certainly *illegal* transactions, grabbing hundreds of thousands of dollars in dirty money she was not entitled to and didn't earn, she and Bill were lecturing you and me about the "greed" and "selfishness" of the 1980s. Imagine a porn queen stepping into a church pulpit and preaching about virtue and modesty. Imagine a serial arsonist dressing up as Smokey Bear and lecturing kindergartners about fire safety. Imagine Dennis Rodman giving a talk to a high school basketball team about good conduct and good sportsmanship. Now imagine Bill and Hillary lecturing America about the moral dangers of greed and selfishness.

The point is this: The Reagan 1980s were not about greed and selfishness. It's not greedy to want to keep more of what you have earned through your own labor. That's only sensible, fair, and just. Greed is wanting to grab money, possessions, and power you haven't earned and have no right to. Greed is stealing and accepting laundered bribes and cheating the government and attacking an entire industry, diminishing the retirement investments of millions of people just to line your own pockets.

The decade of the 1980s was not a gilded age—it was a genuine, solid, 24-carat golden age. It was the real thing. Far from being an age of greed and selfishness, it was an age of burgeoning generosity, when charitable giving (which had been growing steadily at a compound annual rate of 3.3 percent from 1955 to 1980) suddenly spurted to a compound annual rate of 5.1 percent, resulting in a 56 percent growth in charitable giving (an additional $121 billion in constant 1990 dollars) during my father's eight years in office. The Reagan 1980s were the era of lower taxes, reduced government interference, expanded opportunity, greater self-reliance, increased optimism, and enlarged freedom. That's what America is all about. That's the essence of "life, liberty, and the pursuit of happiness." There's nothing greedy or selfish about it.

Whenever you hear people talk about the greedy 1980s, don't let them get away with it. Call them on it. Tell them what the Reagan 1980s were truly all about. Above all, tell them that we are once again going to build a society where "life, liberty, and the pursuit of happiness" are fostered and celebrated.

We're going to build the Shining City on a Hill.

PART FOUR

THE

CITY

SQUARE

The fourth cornerstone
of the City on a Hill is
Government

CHAPTER EIGHT

A

City

Secure

TO BEGIN
THE WORLD OVER AGAIN

Evil is powerless if the good are unafraid.
Ronald Reagan
Speech before the Conservative
Political Action Conference
Washington, D.C., March 20, 1981

There is one sign the Soviets can make that would be unmistakable, that would advance dramatically the cause of freedom and peace. General Secretary Gorbachev, if you seek peace, if you seek prosperity for the Soviet Union and Eastern Europe, if you seek liberalization: Come here to this gate! Mr. Gorbachev, open this gate! Mr. Gorbachev, tear down this wall!
Ronald Reagan
Speech before the Brandenburg Gate
West Berlin, June 12, 1987

Dad sat behind the microphone, patiently drumming his fingers on the table and gazing out the window of his Santa Barbara ranch house while the sound engineer checked his equipment. In a few minutes, Dad would be on the air with his weekly Saturday radio address. "Let's take a mike check, please, Mr. President," said the engineer.

"Okay," said Dad.

Most people would do a mike check by saying something inane like "Testing, one, two, three, testing. . . ." But not Dad. Instead, he leaned toward the mike, grinned mischievously, and said, "My fellow Americans, I am pleased to tell you today that I've signed legislation that will outlaw Russia forever. We begin bombing in five minutes."

Now, that was funny—and typical of the way Dad has always clowned around. But the comment got out in the press, and you know what? The Russians didn't laugh! Throughout the 1980s, the Soviet leaders viewed Ronald Reagan as a trigger-happy cowboy—and that was just fine with him. "It was part of Reagan's strategy," recalled then national security advisor Richard Allen, "to get the Soviets to think he was a little crazy."[1] A lot of people forget this, but the truth is that Ronald Reagan went to Washington, D.C., with a goal of putting an end to Soviet Communism. For eight years, the Reagan White House pursued that goal. Soon after he left office, Ronald Reagan's dream came true. Soviet Communism collapsed.

Does Ronald Reagan get credit for this accomplishment? Certainly not in the dominant media. Read the newsmagazines, listen to the commentators, and even listen to what history teachers are telling our schoolchildren, and you'll hear, again and again, that the credit for the collapse of Communism goes to Mikhail Gorbachev. It was Gorbachev, not Reagan, whom *Time* magazine named its Man of the Decade, because Gorbachev supposedly engineered the internal changes that led to the end of Communism.

Let's understand exactly who and what Mikhail Gorbachev was. First and foremost, he was a Communist. The last thing in the world any Communist would want to see is the collapse of Communism. Gorbachev's *glasnost* ("openness") and *perestroika* ("restructuring") policies—which liberals claim were an attempt to reform and de-Communize Soviet society—were actually a last-ditch effort to *save* the Soviet system from collapse and open revolt. Gorbachev hoped that by giving the people a little bit of freedom, he could quell the growing discontent against the totalitarian Soviet government—the kind of rebellion that was already under way in Poland and other parts of Eastern Europe. Gorbachev learned too late that he couldn't just give people a little bit of freedom. All people everywhere have an instinctive sense that freedom is their God-given birthright, so when

Gorbachev gave the Russian people a little freedom, they proceeded to pry the lid off the system and take all the freedom they could grab.

Second, Mikhail Gorbachev was the prize chump of history. The fall of the Soviet system was no accident. It was the direct result of a deliberate strategy conceived within the Reagan White House and carried out around the world by a renewed American military and intelligence community. The U.S. waged a silent but devastating war against the Soviet Union—an economic, technological war that aided groups fighting for freedom in places like Nicaragua, Afghanistan, and Poland. This controversial but highly successful strategy became known as "the Reagan Doctrine."

Ronald Reagan was not content simply to contain the advance of Soviet power as it marched through the Third World. He believed that, in spite of the Soviet Union's vaunted military power, Soviet society was fundamentally weak at the core, and crumbling fast. He was convinced that by strategically attacking the weak points of the system, he could bring about a complete internal collapse, and he announced his intentions right from the outset of his administration.

Speaking at the commencement exercises of the University of Notre Dame in May 1981, he told the students, "The years ahead will be great ones for our country, for the cause of freedom and the spread of civilization. The West will not contain Communism; it will *transcend* Communism. We will not bother to denounce it. We'll dismiss it as a sad, bizarre chapter in human history whose last pages are even now being written." And in his toughly worded speech to the British House of Commons, June 8, 1982, he declared that the Soviet Union

> runs against the tide of history by denying human freedom and human dignity to its citizens. It also is in deep economic difficulty. The rate of growth in the [Soviet] national product has been steadily declining since the fifties and is less than half of what it was then. The dimensions of this failure are astounding: a country which employs one-fifth of its population in agriculture is unable to feed its own people. . . .
>
> Overcentralized, with little or no incentives, year after year the Soviet system pours its best resources into the making of instruments of destruction. The constant shrinkage of economic growth combined with the growth of military production is putting a heavy strain on the Soviet people. What we see here is a political structure that no longer corresponds to its economic base, a society where productive forces are hampered by political ones.

The decay of the Soviet experiment should come as no surprise to us. . . . Any system is inherently unstable that has no peaceful means to legitimize its leaders. In such cases, the very repressiveness of the state ultimately drives people to resist it, if necessary, by force.

While we must be cautious about forcing the pace of change, we must not hesitate to declare our ultimate objectives and to take concrete actions to move toward them. . . . What I am describing now is a plan and a hope for the long term—the march of freedom and democracy which will leave Marxism-Leninism on the ash heap of history.

It's easy to forget, looking back almost twenty years later, what the world was like when Ronald Reagan boldly consigned the Soviet system to "the ash heap of history." The leading intellectuals and social critics of the time thought Ronald Reagan couldn't have been more wrong. "Those in the U.S. who think the Soviet Union is on the verge of economic and social collapse," said Arthur Schlesinger in 1982, "[are] . . . only kidding themselves." And in 1984, economist John Kenneth Galbraith asserted, "The Russian system succeeds because, in contrast to the Western industrial economies, it makes full use of its manpower."[2]

When Ronald Reagan took office, it looked as if America was headed for the ash heap and the Soviets were king of the hill. Following America's soul-sickening humiliation in Vietnam, the Soviet influence in the world expanded and America's retreated. The entire world saw an America in economic and military decline, while the Soviets become bold and adventuristic around the world. Soviet power was projected around the globe, in Asia, in Nicaragua and Cuba, in the Middle East, in Iraq, in Ethiopia, in Angola, in North and South Yemen. In December 1979, an overemboldened Kremlin invaded Afghanistan, a brazen act of war against a sovereign nation, while the U.S. stood by, wringing its hands. Moreover, the Soviet move into Afghanistan appeared to be a major step toward capturing the strategic Persian Gulf region and the rich oil fields of the Arabian peninsula. Another four years of aimless U.S. foreign policy would have probably allowed the Soviets to gain a stranglehold on the faltering economies of the West.

To look around at the Soviet presence throughout the world in the early 1980s, it certainly didn't look like the USSR was about to topple onto the ash heap of history. It took a man of rare vision and insight to see that the potential existed to completely alter the course of history, to "begin the world over again" (as Thomas Paine once put it, and as Dad loved to quote).

It took a man of rare conviction to decide that the time had come to end the stalemate between the superpowers and to liberate half of the globe from totalitarian oppression. Looking back on that time, Ronald Reagan recalled:

> When I came into office, I believed there had been mistakes in our policy toward the Soviets in particular. I wanted to do some things differently, like speaking the truth about them for a change, rather than hiding reality behind the niceties of diplomacy. . . . I even called them an evil empire. That woke everybody up. . . .
>
> In retrospect, I am amazed that our national leaders had not philosophically and intellectually taken on the principles of Marxist-Leninism. We were always too worried we would offend the Soviets if we struck at anything so basic. Well, so what? Marxist-Leninist thought is an empty cupboard. Everyone knew it by the 1980s, but no one was saying it. . . .
>
> I've always believed . . . that it's important to define differences, because there are choices and decisions to be made in life and history.[3]

Ronald Reagan did more than simply speak about choices and decisions—he made them. He set the machinery in motion that would, within a few years, topple the evil empire and begin the world over again. He selected people who shared his view of the world and his confidence in America's ability to tackle the Soviet challenge—Al Haig (later succeeded by George Schulz) as secretary of state, Caspar Weinberger as secretary of defense, and William Casey as CIA director. It was a calculated, multipronged approach: Domestically, Ronald Reagan advanced an agenda of tax cuts and deregulation to unleash the American economy and rev up the engine of American military technology. He called for a bold, new technological concept, the Strategic Defense Initiative, which not only promised to render nuclear missiles obsolete, but also engaged the Soviets in a costly research and development race they could not hope to win. He called upon Cap Weinberger to engineer the rebuilding and modernization of the American defense infrastructure, and he unleashed Bill Casey to plot and execute a massive scheme to attack the Soviet weak points and undermine the top-heavy Soviet system.

Casey's role in toppling the USSR is especially fascinating. At the time, many critics attacked the appointment of Casey to head the American spy agency. Having served as one of Ronald Reagan's closest, most trusted advisors and as chairman of the Reagan campaign, Casey was viewed by some as a political hack, not a master spy. Casey himself didn't want the job when it was first offered to him. He had been angling for one of the plum cabinet assignments, such as secretary of state or secretary of defense. He finally accepted the directorship on condition that it be made a cabinet-level position, with open access to the Oval Office. As it turned out, that was exactly the kind of powerful, activist CIA chief the new president wanted.

Ronald Reagan knew that Bill Casey was a not just a political hack. Before becoming an attorney-financier and serving in the Nixon and Ford administrations, Casey had been a master spy with an impressive list of achievements. He was a heavy hitter in that Great War against another evil empire, Hitler's Germany. As a young, but high-ranking OSS officer (the Office of Strategic Services was the forerunner of the modern CIA), Casey assembled a two-hundred-man intelligence network behind Nazi lines. He specialized in waging technological and economic warfare against Hitler— exactly the same kind of warfare Ronald Reagan planned to conduct against the USSR. Like Ronald Reagan, Casey (a devout Catholic) believed in the struggle between good and evil and in the need for bold action to change the course of human events.

Casey immediately went to work, reinvigorating an agency that had been neutralized under Jimmy Carter's CIA director, Stansfield Turner. In his black, unmarked, 007ish private jet, Casey flew around the world, personally visiting CIA stations and visiting with heads of state, gathering information, shoring up morale, searching out the weaknesses of the evil empire. The following strategies emerged:

- Working with the Saudis to reduce the worldwide price of oil, which would not only help the U.S. economy but reduce the amount of hard currency flowing into the USSR on its own oil exports. (During the enormous oil price increases of the Ford-Carter 1970s, the Soviets had increased hard currency earnings 272 percent while increasing exports only 22 percent. Casey's goal was to reverse that trend.)[4]
- Pressuring U.S. allies in Europe and technology companies in America to withdraw from the Soviets' East-West Urengoi gas pipeline, a project that the Soviets hoped would bring large amounts of hard currency into the country.
- Baiting Soviet engineers with disinformation, false blueprints, and sabotaged computer equipment supplied by CIA front companies, which

in turn sabotaged development of the Urengoi pipeline and various Soviet military projects.

- Cutting off Western trade, credit, and technology flowing to the USSR. (Both legal and illegal technology transfers from the West to the Soviet Union had kept the Soviet economy afloat throughout the Ford and Carter years.)

- Generating uncertainty among Soviet leaders about U.S. intentions in order to head off Soviet expansionism.

- Covertly assisting the anticommunist Solidarity movement in Poland, the mujahideen freedom fighters in Afghanistan, and the anticommunist Contras in Nicaragua (the Reagan Doctrine).

In late 1982, National Security Advisor Bill Clark (a trusted Reagan aide from his Sacramento days) and Clark's top aide, Richard Pipes, drafted a top-secret National Security Decision Directive for President Reagan's signature. Designated NSDD-75, this document outlined a fundamental shift in U.S. foreign policy, a switch from coexistence with and containment of the USSR to *a deliberate attempt to collapse the Soviet system.* No longer would the U.S. tolerate the existing projection of Soviet power around the world; the U.S. would roll that power back. No longer would the U.S. prop up the ailing Soviet economy; in fact, the U.S. would undermine the Soviet economy in any way possible.

The real genius of the Reagan strategy for victory in the East-West competition was that it was rooted in principles, values, and a vision for the future. Ronald Reagan started with the principles that good cannot coexist with evil, that evil must be defeated, and that Soviet Communism was clearly an evil system. He started with values, with the belief that all people have a God-given right to be free. And he started with a vision, a vision of a world in which communism had been transcended and consigned to the ash heap of history. Every presidential directive, every policy, every action that flowed from the White House originated from that matrix of principles, values, and vision.

As a result, there were great consistency and reliability in U.S. foreign policy. The U.S. followed precisely the same course of action in Poland as it did in Afghanistan as it did in Nicaragua. Instead of sending American boys off to fight protracted Vietnam-style wars of containment, we gave freedom-loving people the tools to fight their own war and to win their own freedom.

And in every instance, in Poland, Afghanistan, and Nicaragua, freedom-loving people won.

The only military setback America suffered in that era occurred when we strayed from that course and posted soldiers in the middle of a Bosnia-like civil war zone in Lebanon. It was a region that was peripheral to American security concerns, and the goals were not well defined. As in Bosnia, our forces were interposed between two hostile forces, Israel and Syria, and there was no clear plan for withdrawal. Before the operation was over, a truck loaded with over two thousand pounds of TNT blew up at the U.S. military compound, killing 241 American servicemen who were sleeping in their barracks. It was the worst disaster of my father's presidency, and his deepest regret. That was in 1983, fairly early in his presidency; Ronald Reagan learned from that experience and never placed our fighting forces in such a position again.

In 1984, Congress attached an amendment to an omnibus appropriations bill. That amendment—called Boland II after the liberal Massachusetts congressman who introduced it—banned any government agency from "supporting, directly or indirectly, military or paramilitary operations in Nicaragua by any nation, group, organization or individual." Congressman Boland and his fellow liberals mistakenly thought that by cutting off aid to the anticommunist Contras, they were keeping America out of a "Vietnam in Central America." Ronald Reagan was trying to help Nicaragua throw out the Soviets without sending in American troops.

Forced to find ways around Boland II in order to stop the communist advance just below our borders, the Reagan administration sought creative ways of funding the Contra resistance, including soliciting funds from other nations, such as Israel and Saudi Arabia, as well as from private donors within the United States. On October 5, 1986, an American cargo plane was shot down in Nicaragua while on a secret mission dropping supplies to the Contras. The only survivor, ex-marine Eugene Hasenfus, was captured and put on display by the pro-Soviet Sandanistas. What became known as the Iran–Contra scandal began to unravel. At around the same time, CIA director Casey was diagnosed with a brain tumor; he died in early 1987. Caspar Weinberger resigned. Much of the impetus behind the plan to dismantle the evil empire began to dissipate as the controversy over Iran–Contra commanded more and more White House attention.

It didn't matter. The strategy Ronald Reagan set in motion in the early

1980s had already succeeded. The Soviets began withdrawing from Afghanistan in May 1988; that defeat shook the foundations of the entire Communist bloc. Poland held free elections in 1989, throwing off the yoke of Soviet domination. In February 1990, Violeta Chamorro and the National Opposition Union (UNO) soundly defeated the ruling Sandanistas in the first free Nicaraguan election in years. Also in 1990, the two Germanys were reunited, and the Berlin Wall came tumbling down. A piece of that Wall was given to Ronald Reagan as a gift from the grateful free people of Germany and can be viewed today at the Reagan Library in Simi Valley, California.

Finally, in mid-1991, Ronald Reagan's dream became a reality. The Soviet Union collapsed onto the ash heap of history, replaced by a free Russia and a host of smaller independent states. The evil empire had been defeated, just as Ronald Reagan had prophesied.

No one in American politics, nor anyone else on the world stage, had articulated such a vision—only Ronald Reagan. If there had been no Ronald Reagan, no SDI, no campaign of technological warfare, no campaign of economic warfare to turn the Russian ruble into worthless paper, the Soviet bloc would be alive and well today. As Peter Schweizer observes in *Victory: The Reagan Administration's Secret Strategy that Hastened the Collapse of the Soviet Union,* "The irony of course is that current historiography has given Mikhail Gorbachev the lion's share of the credit for the dawning of the post-Cold War era. This is a most curious development, giving the vanquished more credit than the victor."[5]

Someday, a generation of historians who have no liberal, ideological ax to grind will reexamine these events. On that day, the judgment of history will be clear: Ronald Reagan slew the Soviet Bear.

PEACE THROUGH STRENGTH

Our status as a free society and world power is not based on brute strength. When we've taken up arms, it has been for the defense of freedom for ourselves and for other peaceful nations who needed our help. But now, faced with the development of weapons with immense destructive power, we've no choice but to maintain ready defense forces that are second to none. Yes, the cost is high, but the price of neglect would be infinitely higher.

Ronald Reagan
Speech, Recommissioning of
the battleship USS *New Jersey*
Long Beach Naval Shipyard
December 28, 1982

A lot of changes have taken place in our national defense system since Ronald Reagan spoke those words. The battleship *New Jersey* is decommissioned once more. The shipyard in Long Beach, where the recommissioning ceremony took place, is closed and boarded up. Even more humiliating for America, Bill Clinton personally intervened on two occasions to strike a deal that allows the Chinese Communists to take over the historic Long Beach Naval Shipyard and convert it into a way station for the Chinese merchant fleet. He did so after receiving $366,000 in suspicious campaign contributions that likely came from China (laundered through a Chinese-American businessman) and after meeting with officials of the Chinese shipping company during the now infamous White House fund-raising coffees.[6]

When Ronald Reagan gave that speech, recommissioning the *New Jersey*, he announced America's intention to build "a 600-ship fleet, including fifteen carrier battle groups." Of the "gallant lady" herself, he said that putting the *New Jersey* back in service "represents a major step toward fulfilling our pledge to rebuild America's military capabilities. It marks the resurgence of our nation's strength. . . . [The *New Jersey*] will truly fulfill her mission if her firepower never has to be used." By the time he left office, Ronald Reagan succeeded in building that six-hundred-ship navy, but George Bush and Bill Clinton have steadily dismantled it. Today our navy is down to about 350 ships and falling, the smallest fleet America has put to sea since 1938.

Even after the fall of Soviet Communism and the end of the Cold War, the world is still a very dangerous place. The greatest danger of all is that we will need to use America's firepower once more—and it won't be there. This brings us to the central responsibility of what I call the City Square, the governmental district of our Shining City on a Hill. The most fundamental duty of the City Square is spelled out in the Preamble to the Constitution:

We the People of the United States, in Order to form a more perfect Union, establish Justice, insure domestic Tranquility, provide for the common defence, promote the general Welfare, and secure the Blessings of Liberty to ourselves and our Posterity, do ordain and establish this Constitution for the United States of America.

According to this Preamble and the rest of the Constitution (see especially Article I, Section 8, and Article II, Section 2), our government exists primarily, fundamentally, and almost exclusively to provide American citizens with a just, tranquil, secure, stable, free society, so that we and our children and our children's children may enjoy the blessings of liberty. The Constitution is like railroad tracks that keep the train of government moving in the right direction. If government steps outside the constitutional boundaries—by doing what the Constitution doesn't call for or by neglecting what the Constitution demands—then government has gotten derailed. And that's a train wreck.

As I write these words, our federal government has completely jumped the tracks. It spends billions on centralized education, on social engineering, on corporate subsidies and art subsidies—none of which are delineated in the Constitution as the responsibilities of our government. At the same time, our government is neglecting the very responsibilities that are spelled out for all to see in the Constitution: defending the security of the United States of America. Friends, this government is completely off the tracks. If we fail to act now, a train wreck is coming—and it's gonna be bad.

Two of my friends in Congress, Duncan Hunter (R-California), chairman of the House National Security Subcommittee on Military Procurement, and his colleague Randall "Duke" Cunningham (R-California), were shocked to discover in 1996 that the Marine Corps does not have enough ammunition to fight two wars. The Corps—our crack 911 military force in times of international emergencies—had about a $365 million shortfall in such basic supplies as rifle rounds for the M16. If both Saddam Hussein and the North Koreans decided to kick sand in our face at the same time—a not-unlikely scenario—marines on one side of the globe would have no choice but to point their guns at the enemy and yell, "Bang! You're dead!" The ammo just wouldn't be there. During my father's administration, America was prepared to fight and win a two-front war in Europe and Korea, and still have enough firepower left over to defend the Middle East oil fields. That is no longer the case.

Duncan Hunter tells me that William Perry, Bill Clinton's secretary of defense until 1996, would come before Hunter's subcommittee every year and tell the members of Congress, "Everything is fine; we've got everything taken care of; we have all the ammunition and equipment we need to secure the country; don't give us any more money." Fortunately, Duncan Hunter and Duke Cunningham (a decorated fighter pilot who has flown F-14s) didn't take the assurances of the Clinton administration at face value. They knew that Bill Clinton and William Perry had cut the defense budget by $150 billion, and with such deep cuts it was unlikely that everything was "fine" and "taken care of" and "secure." So they went beneath the glossy cover of the Clinton defense budget to crunch the numbers. They talked to marines in the field, they asked what kinds of problems and shortages had arisen in the past few years. What they learned was nothing less than frightening.

Compared to 1985, military budgets have been cut 35 percent, research and development has been cut 57 percent, and military procurement has been slashed by 71 percent. For the first time in seventy years, the navy does not have a single aircraft of new design in development or production. Training has suffered. Marines at Camp Pendleton, California, walk seventeen miles to training grounds in order to conserve fuel and equipment. Tank crews of the Second Armored Division, First Battalion, Sixty-seventh Armor, conserve fuel by conducting platoon training exercises without tanks. Soldiers actually walk around wearing cardboard signs that read I'M A TANK.[7]

Most unforgivable of all, the Clinton military cutbacks have reduced the safety margin for our military aircraft. In the first five months of 1996 alone, an epidemic of military air crashes killed scores of military and civilian personnel:

- Three separate crashes destroyed three marine VTOL Harrier jump jets. (Duncan Hunter notes that, even after these crashes, the Clinton administration refuses to fund safety upgrades on the Harrier airfleet that would make the planes 50 percent safer to fly.)
- The navy lost four F-14 jet fighters in four separate crashes, including one horrible incident in Nashville, Tennessee, that killed both crewmen and three civilians on the ground. The F-14 is the high-performance, 1,240 mph fighter featured in the movie *Top Gun*. During the Clinton administration the number of F-14 crashes (8.55) per 100,000 flying hours was more than double the rate during the Reagan-Bush years, a fact for which navy officials offer no public explanation.[8]

- A navy EA-6B Prowler radar-jamming jet crashed off the California coast less than a week after an F-14 went down in the same area.
- On April 3, 1996, a U.S. Air Force passenger jet slammed into a mountain near Dubrovnik, Croatia, killing thirty-five civilian and military passengers, including Bill Clinton's commerce secretary, Ron Brown.
- A Sikorsky CH-53E helicopter crashed in Stratford, Connecticut, shortly before delivery to the Marine Corps, where it was slated to serve as a cargo lifter for the White House. Four crewmembers died.
- The day after the Sikorsky crash, two marine helicopters—an AH-1 Cobra attack helicopter and a troop-loaded CH-46 Sea Knight—collided and crashed during maneuvers at Camp Lejeune, North Carolina, killing fourteen marines.

According to Reuters News Service, military officials claimed there was "no common thread" linking the crashes, most of which involved navy and marine fighter jets.[9] But Duncan Hunter and Duke Cunningham see an *unmistakable* common thread: decreased funding for maintenance, repair, and upgrading of military aircraft. The military services' modernization budget has shrunk from $124 billion in 1986 to $39 billion (not adjusted for inflation) in 1996. As a result, military planners can no longer keep existing aircraft in the air while also obtaining newer aircraft and weapons to maintain a tactical edge. The Clinton cutbacks have forced them to confront potentially deadly choices.

Today, car sales by the Ford Motor Company are three times as great as the total amount of money allocated by the Defense Department to the procurement of new weapons systems, and investment in new weapons systems is 71 percent below what was spent in 1986. What is truly amazing is that the Department of Defense spent nearly $250 billion in 1996, yet the air force did not purchase a single new fighter or bomber, and the army did not buy a single tank. Where is the money going? Too much of it is going to pay for the UN peacekeeping mission in Bosnia, for the occupation of Haiti, for Russia's dismantling of its nuclear stockpile, and for bogus studies showing all the wonderful benefits of women in combat.

The mainstays of our air force are aging F-14s, F-16s, and even thirty-year-old-plus B-52s. Production of the new F-22 and the B-2 Spirit has been repeatedly delayed by lack of funding, and the air force has no plans to buy any new bombers until after the year 2001. Purchase of new helicopter gunships, including the advanced Comanche, has also been shelved for budgetary reasons. The army has no plans to purchase any new tanks until after the year 2010! The navy is retiring attack submarines faster than it builds them. We now have eighty attack subs in the water, but by the turn of the century, that number will be cut nearly in half. Under pressure from the Clinton White House, the Pentagon has delayed plans for every new weapons system that has been under development.

According to Bill Clinton's budget plans, defense spending in 1999 will reach the lowest point since the sneak attack on Pearl Harbor. The Clinton administration argues that because the Cold War is over we don't need to spend as much on defense and that what we do spend should be shifted to social causes and nation-building rather than weapons systems. In fact, much of the so-called defense budget for 1995 actually was disguised social spending: $35 million for environmental scholarships, $23 million for AIDS research, $65 million to hire teachers, $15 million in aid to African-American colleges, $210 million for breast cancer research, and on and on. How such expenditures come under the heading of national defense is a mystery to me.[10]

Compare Bill Clinton's defense budget with that of his hero and role model, John F. Kennedy. At a time when America was at peace (the Korean War was a memory and Vietnam was still in our future), JFK insisted on a strong national defense. During his presidency, we spent fifty-five cents of every federal dollar and 9 percent of the gross national product on military spending. Today, under Bill Clinton, we spend sixteen cents of every federal dollar and less than 3 percent of the GNP on the military.[11] I'm not asking Bill Clinton to be more like my father; I'd be happy if he'd just be a little more like JFK!

Duncan Hunter concludes:

> We are seeing aircraft accidents and ammo shortages. It's a replay of the late 1970s when Jimmy Carter told us everything was fine until it really began to unravel. The failed hostage rescue attempt in Iran—the Desert One fiasco that killed eight brave American servicemen—was the direct result of mechanical failures in three out of eight helicopters on that mission. We are approaching the same hollow military today. By some measures, Clinton's hollow force has already out-hollowed Carter's. In 1978 under Carter, 23 percent of the federal budget went to defense; today, 20 percent.
>
> When we defeated Saddam Hussein in Desert Storm, we had 18 Army

divisions. We now have ten divisions—slightly more than half the Army strength we had in 1991. During Desert Storm, we had twenty-four fighter air wings, we now have thirteen, nearly a 50 percent cut. This is a dangerous situation. History teaches us that world events can change very quickly in a short period of time.

After World War II, our military underwent a similar so-called "demobilization" to what we are seeing today, only not as drastic. In 1947, General Marshall was asked how the demobilization was going. He said, "This isn't a demobilization, it's a rout." Just a few years later, in 1950, American forces were driven down the Korean Peninsula by a third-rate power that wouldn't have withstood us for two days in World War II. We got whipped in the early part of that war because we were unprepared, because we had discarded all our equipment. We did the same thing after Desert Storm, and it is continuing right now. I know that pocketbook issues are important to the people, but I hope the American people remember that the most important duty government can carry out for its people is to protect them and maintain national security.[12]

In his address on defense and national security, March 23, 1983, Ronald Reagan staked out a cogent plan for arriving at a reasonable and responsible defense budget. One doesn't arrive at a defense budget by pulling numbers out of the air (as the Clinton administration has done) and lopping back the military until it fits within those numbers. No, one first looks at the potential risks and challenges to America's national security—then does whatever has to be done and spends whatever has to be spent in order to reduce those risks and meet those challenges. He explained:

> We start by considering what must be done to maintain peace and review all the possible threats against our security. Then a strategy for strengthening peace and defending against those threats must be agreed upon. And, finally, our defense establishment must be evaluated to see what is necessary to protect against any or all of the potential threats. The cost of achieving these ends is totaled up, and the result is the budget for national defense.
>
> There is no logical way you can say, "Let's spend X billion dollars less." You can only say, "Which part of our defense measures do we believe we can do without and still have security against all contingencies?" Anyone in the Congress who advocates a percentage or a specific dollar cut in defense spending should be made to say what part of our defenses he would eliminate, and he should be candid enough to acknowledge that his

cuts mean cutting our commitments to allies or inviting greater risk or both.

The defense policy of the United States is based on a simple premise: The United States does not start fights. We will never be an aggressor. We maintain our strength in order to deter and defend against aggression—to preserve freedom and peace. . . . "Deterrence" means simply this: making sure any adversary who thinks about attacking the United States, or our allies, or our vital interests, concludes that the risks to him outweigh any potential gains. Once he understands that, he won't attack. We maintain the peace through our strength; weakness only invites aggression.

Bill Clinton's way of looking at the defense budget is 180 degrees out of whack. He starts by telling the Congress and the secretary of defense, in effect, "Look, we're gonna cut defense spending by X amount because I need that money to buy votes. I told the people I'm gonna give 'em healthcare even if it kills 'em, so if we've got to cut some tanks and ships and bombers, so be it." That's not the way to defend America. That's the way to destroy it. As Congressman Robert K. Dornan once said on my show, "Liberals don't understand the reason we have a military. They think that the purpose of the military is to kill people. They don't understand that when our military is at its toughest, as under Eisenhower or Ronald Reagan, our soldiers don't have to kill people. When wielded by freedom-loving people, overwhelming military strength deters aggression and prevents the need for killing people. It is every mother's dream for her son or daughter serving in the military to never have to kill another mother's son or daughter. That's why America must be strong." Tragically, America is growing weaker by the day. And weakness invites miscalculation and war.

THE CHILDREN'S DEFENSE INITIATIVE

A certain amount of mythology grew up around the Strategic Defense Initiative, the program I announced in 1983 to develop a defensive shield against nuclear missiles. It wasn't conceived by scientists, although they came on board and contributed greatly to its success.

I came into office with a decided prejudice against our

*tacit agreement with the Soviet Union regarding nuclear mis-
siles. I'm talking about the MAD policy—"mutual assured
destruction"—the idea of deterrence providing safety so long
as each of us had the power to destroy the other with nuclear
missiles if one of us launched a first strike. Somehow this
didn't seem to me to be something that would send you to
bed feeling safe. It was like having two westerners standing
in a saloon aiming their guns at each other's head—perma-
nently. There had to be a better way.*

Ronald Reagan
An American Life
(New York: Simon & Schuster, 1990, p. 547)

Ronald Reagan has always been a visionary.

He looked into the future and saw things few other people could see. He
envisioned a world in which Soviet Communism was transcended and left
in the dust, and it came to pass. He envisioned the counterintuitive possibility that cutting taxes would actually bring *more* money into the Treasury—
and he was proved right. He envisioned a world in which technology ren-
dered nuclear weapons obsolete—and that technology is in our grasp today,
even though small political minds have blocked its deployment. While most
politicians of our time can't even adequately deal with the world as it is,
Ronald Reagan possessed the wonderful ability to see the world as it *might*
be.

Shortly after Neil Armstrong and Buzz Aldrin landed on the moon in
1969, America's elite air carrier, Pan Am, announced it was taking reserva-
tions for the first commercial flight to the moon. Scheduled departure time:
The year 2000. One of the first people to book a seat was—you guessed it—
Ronald Reagan. "One of his magics is looking to the future," said Ronald
Reagan's secretary of state, George Shultz.[13] And reporter Lou Cannon, who
chronicled Dad's career since his Sacramento days, said, "He was at once
old-fashioned and forward-looking, and frequently sounded as if he wanted
to go back to the future."[14] The most visionary and futuristic of all of Dad's
ideas, of course, was SDI—the Strategic Defense Initiative, or "Star Wars."
And let there be no mistake: It was Dad's idea right from the beginning.

As governor of California, Dad once met with a group of students who
complained that his generation was out of touch. "You don't know what it's
like," one student told him, "to grow up in an age of atomic bombs, space
travel, and high-speed computers." And Dad replied, "You're right. My

211

generation didn't grow up with such things. We *invented* them." In a very real sense, Ronald Reagan invented SDI. It was not a concept that was circulating in the scientific or military journals. It came straight out of the mind and soul of Ronald Reagan, not in a single flash of insight, but as a result of decades of observing, reading, and thinking about the seemingly insoluble problem of nuclear weapons.

Like most visionary ideas, SDI had its roots in science fiction. One of the main reasons we have computers, space shuttles, footprints on the moon, robot spacecraft mapping the outer planets, communication satellites, and the like is that today's scientists and engineers were once ten-year-old science fiction fans. Dad was no different. Like many boys of his generation, he grew up reading Edgar Rice Burroughs's novels about the Martian adventures of earthman John Carter and his Barsoomian princess girlfriend, Deja Thoris. After going to Hollywood, he enjoyed the science fiction adventure films and serials of the '40s and '50s. He even starred in one of them— *Murder in the Air* (1940), in which he played Secret Service agent Brass Bancroft, who cracks a spy ring attempting to steal a death ray projector that can shoot down enemy aircraft from a distance. (Sounds a lot like SDI, doesn't it?)

Since the day the first atomic bomb exploded over Hiroshima, Ronald Reagan worried about the doomsday potential of such weapons. After the Soviets acquired a nuclear capability and MAD became the ruling policy of the nuclear age, he concluded that the world situation was indeed mad, totally nuts, and certainly unsustainable over the long haul. Ultimately, someone has to blink, miscalculate, make a mistake—and the entire human race will pay the price. There had to be some way out of the stalemate. But what?

In 1967, the then governor of California was invited by the Hungarian-American physicist Edward Teller—known as the father of the hydrogen bomb—to attend a briefing on defensive technologies at the Lawrence Livermore National Laboratory in California. Teller later recalled that Ronald Reagan asked "good and fundamental questions" about the possibilities for an antimissile defense.[15] Clearly, the seeds of SDI were planted long before Ronald Reagan went to the White House.

After his inauguration, the potential for nuclear holocaust weighed on him even more heavily—because he carried the key to mankind's fate around with him in his own pocket. In his autobiography, Dad recalled,

Wherever I went, I carried a small, plastic-coated card with me, and a military aide with a very specialized job was always close by. He or she . . . carried a small bag everyone referred to as "the football." It contained the directives for launching our nuclear weapons in retaliation for a nuclear attack on our country. . . . The decision to launch the weapons was mine alone to make.

We had many contingency plans for responding to a nuclear attack. But everything would happen so fast that I wondered how much planning or reason could be applied in such a crisis. The Russians sometimes kept submarines off our East Coast with nuclear missiles that could turn the White House into a pile of radioactive rubble within six or eight minutes.

Six minutes to decide how to respond to a blip on a radarscope and decide whether to unleash Armageddon! How could anyone apply reason at a time like that?[16]

The awesome weight of that little plastic-coated card pressed on his mind. He couldn't accept the nuclear doctrine that had tied the hands of six presidents before him—a doctrine of mutually assured destruction. He desperately wanted to replace MAD with a completely new doctrine for the nuclear age—a doctrine of mutually assured survival. Out of that desire, together with decades of thought, questioning, reading, and observing, came the nucleus of a radically new way of looking at the problem of nuclear weapons: SDI. One of the keys to the concept of mutually assured survival was his commitment to sharing SDI technology with the world. Although many of Ronald Reagan's opponents—and many of his friends too—thought it was crazy to develop SDI then give it away to the Soviets, Ronald Reagan believed the right to survival in a nuclear age belonged to all mankind. If only one side or the other had SDI, the result would be catastrophic destabilization. If all sides possessed it, the result would be the final obsolescence of nuclear weapons.

Many critics doubted Ronald Reagan's sincerity in proposing SDI. They thought it was nothing but a bargaining chip, a throwaway to get a few extra concessions in arms control talks with the Russians. They couldn't have been more wrong. Ronald Reagan was as committed to SDI as he was to tax cuts, rebuilding the military, or any of his other deeply held convictions and goals. Proof of his intense commitment to SDI is the fact that during his summits with Gorbachev—in Geneva in 1985 and Reykjavik in 1986—the Russian leader pressured, cajoled, charmed, and offered concession after concession if Ronald Reagan would just give up SDI.

Dad never budged an inch.

In his mind, the dream of a world beyond MAD was nonnegotiable. SDI was no bargaining chip. It was, to Ronald Reagan, the future of humankind. In some ways, he saw it as the crowning achievement of human ingenuity. On February 7, 1983, during a White House ceremony commemorating the 200th anniversary of air- and spaceflight, he said, "God gave angels wings. He gave mankind dreams. And with His help, there's no limit to what can be accomplished." Six weeks later, in his defense policy speech of March 23, 1983, he revealed his dream for SDI to the nation:

> Would it not be better to save lives than to avenge them? Are we not capable of demonstrating our peaceful intentions by applying our abilities and our ingenuity to achieving a truly lasting stability? I think we are. . . . Let me share with you a vision of the future which offers hope.
>
> It is that we embark on a program to counter the awesome Soviet missile threat with measures that are defensive. Let us turn to the very strengths in technology that spawned our great industrial base and have given us the quality of life we enjoy today. . . . I call upon the scientific community in our country . . . to give us the means of rendering these nuclear weapons impotent and obsolete. . . . Is it not worth every invest-ment necessary to free the world from the threat of nuclear war?

It wasn't important to Dad exactly what shape SDI should take. It didn't matter to him whether it used lasers or charged particle beams or some as-yet-unknown technology. He didn't care whether it was ground-based or space-based. He only insisted on two things: (1) that SDI be nonnuclear and (2) that it work.

Small-minded critics dismissed SDI as impractical. "Like trying to shoot a bullet with a bullet," they jeered. "Impossible to make it leakproof—some nukes are bound to get through." The critics tried to shoot SDI down with words, even calling it "Star Wars," to make it seem like a far-out fantasy rather than a practical alternative to Armageddon. Dad didn't care what they called it. He knew it would work. His faith in American technical ingenuity was boundless. After all, he was born just seven years after the Wright brothers first flew at Kitty Hawk, and he had seen men walk on the moon. During his days as a spokesman for General Electric, he had pitched the slogan "Progress is our most important product"—and he truly believed it.

In 1972, when Richard Nixon negotiated the Anti-Ballistic Missile (ABM) Treaty, MAD was the only nuclear policy available to the superpowers, because SDI technology did not yet exist. Today, however, there is simply no excuse for pursuing MAD. Yet this is the course Bill Clinton and his fellow liberals have committed us to, the Nixon nuclear policy. How strange that the liberals, who always portray themselves as morally superior and infinitely more compassionate than conservatives, advocate Armageddon over SDI's approach of rendering nukes obsolete! What a bizarre picture: Bill Clinton in bed with Dr. Strangelove.

A vestige of SDI still remains under Bill Clinton—a shadow of the aggressive missile defense program set in motion by Ronald Reagan. In 1993, the Clinton administration changed the name of SDI to Ballistic Missile Defense Program (BMDP), cut funding by around $3 billion, pushed back deployment dates, and placed the program on the back burner of the national agenda. Funding for one extremely promising SDI program, Brilliant Pebbles, was cut from $300 million to just $73 million shortly after Clinton came to office. It was cut again just a few weeks later by another $50 million when Clinton went rummaging through the defense budget for money to fund his botched nation-building mission in Somalia.

The gutting of SDI comes at a particularly dangerous time for the United States, a time when the threat of a direct ballistic missile attack upon American cities is becoming more, not less, likely. Rogue states such as Libya, Syria, Iran, and Iraq don't even have to develop their own ballistic technologies anymore. They can now purchase ready-to-fire long-range delivery systems on the open market. The North Koreans have already tested a ballistic missile that can reach Hawaii and Guam, and the Chinese have missiles capable of hitting the western continental United States. Some twenty-five nations (including all the world's most dangerous rogue states) either have or are now acquiring ballistic missiles capable of delivering nukes, chemical weapons ("the poor country's nukes"), or biological weapons. Over seventy-five nations in the world now possess cruise missiles; twenty more nations are building them; and the cash-strapped Russians are now selling SS-25 long-range mobile missiles (in violation of U.S.-Soviet disarmament agreements) that could be used by terrorists or pariah states to hit American soil.

What do the American people think of the danger they are in? They don't even know! A 1995 poll conducted nationally by Luntz Research for the Coalition to Defend America found that nearly six out of ten Americans think they are already protected against a missile attack! They couldn't be more wrong. We are completely nuke-naked! We have *no* defense—none, zero, zip, nada—against a missile attack. And what did people want as soon as they found out the danger they were in? According to the Luntz poll, as soon as people were informed about the situation, 81 percent immediately and emphatically wanted to be protected! My friend Frank Gaffney, director of the Center for Security Policy, adds,

> A focus group subsequently conducted by Luntz in Columbia, South Carolina, and observed by the House National Security Committee's chairman, Rep. Floyd Spence (R-South Carolina), brought forth even more dramatic results: Every one of the participants assumed their city was defended against missile attack. They were visibly shaken and became angry when told that today a missile attack against Columbia could not be stopped. They wanted to know who was responsible and insisted that corrective action be taken.[17]

Who's responsible? Right now, the one person most responsible is Bill Clinton. His love affair with the 1972 Anti-Ballistic Missile (ABM) Treaty leaves us all completely exposed to the most horrible, deadly, destructive weapons—nuclear, chemical, and biological—that any rogue nation or terrorist group would love to lob at us. Right now, today, we have the technical know-how to defend America from missile attack—but we choose not to. It is not technology, but leftist ideology that keeps us in a state of utter helplessness.

The Preamble to the Constitution (which Clinton has sworn an oath to preserve, protect, and defend) states that one of the primary obligations of the government is to "provide for the common defense." Bill Clinton, in choosing to leave America naked against missile attack, places the cramped restrictions of the 1972 ABM Treaty (which Clinton calls "the cornerstone of strategic stability") above the demands of the Constitution. The ABM Treaty is the very essence of MADness, an archaic hangover from the Cold War that makes no sense in today's world. Even crazier, Clinton has agreed with Boris Yeltsin to impose constraints on U.S. antimissile systems (such as the navy's Upper Tier system) that are not even limited by the ABM Treaty.

Because of Clinton's stance on Upper Tier, we face the absurd situation that if the commander of a navy cruiser detects a North Korean ballistic missile headed for Japan, he can shoot it down, but if it is headed for American soil, he must let it pass unmolested! This is not some accidental policy oversight, but the result of deliberate planning. Bill Clinton has made a conscious decision to keep America undefended. He is committed to the MAD policy of holding America's entire population hostage.

And Clinton's MADness doesn't stop there. He has placed America in a position where we won't have even the deterrence of "mutually assured destruction" in a few years. If nothing is done to reverse Bill Clinton's policy of unilaterally disarming the United States, our nuclear forces will evaporate early in the next century, leaving America naked to nuclear attack, unable even to retaliate. In his book *The Next War* (which I strongly urge you to read), my father's longtime friend and secretary of defense, Caspar Weinberger, explains:

> In March 1993 [just weeks after Bill Clinton took office] the Department of Energy (DOE) formally closed the Office of New Production Reactors, a body charged with ensuring the nation's long-term need for tritium. . . . Tritium is a radioactive gas critical to the proper operation of every modern nuclear weapon in the American arsenal. Without this gas, these weapons will not perform reliably and as specified. Tritium decays very rapidly, losing 50 percent of its radioactive charge over a twelve-year period. And unless it is periodically replaced, nuclear weapons become inoperable and useless. Because of the Clinton administration's shutdown of our tritium program, we may be incapable of securing adequate supplies for at least a decade or more. Imagine—a U.S. president may face a nuclear crisis in 2007 and be uncertain as to whether he can truly respond to a nuclear strike. Even worse—imagine that the enemy knows.[18]

Of all the lies Bill Clinton has told the American people, the most monstrous is the one he has repeatedly used to lull our nation into a false sense of security: "For the first time since the beginning of the Cold War, not a single Russian missile is pointed at America's children." First, Bill Clinton can't possibly state that as a fact, because we have no way of verifying what is programmed into the targeting computers of Russian missiles. Second, if it is true, it is nothing Bill Clinton can take credit for. Third, supposing it's true that not a single Russian missile is targeted on American soil right now, that situation could change in a few heartbeats. Altering the target selection on a nuclear missile takes about thirty seconds, max. Fourth, missiles never point at children. Missiles sit in silos and point straight up at the sky. If you want to protect children from nuclear missiles, forget where they are "pointed." Instead, build SDI and make sure those missiles can never *reach* our children. As Frank Gaffney once observed on my show, "The way President Clinton likes to couch everything in terms of 'let's do it for the children,' perhaps we ought to rename SDI the 'Children's Defense

Initiative.' Because that's really what SDI is all about, isn't it? Protecting America's future—our children—from nuclear annihilation."

If Bill Clinton insists on keeping America stuck in the MAD years of the 1970s, Congress will have to seize the day and drag America's strategic thinking into the twenty-first century. The 105th Congress should hold hearings on the abrogation of the ABM Treaty, and candidates for the 106th Congress should run on a campaign pledge to end MAD and return America to a Reaganite course of mutually assured survival for the next century. Americans need to be informed that they are completely defenseless against nuclear attack, and that their president is the reason why.

Meanwhile, we can have an extremely effective SDI system up and running cheaply and immediately. As a nation, we have already invested $50 billion to build the navy's AEGIS Upper Tier fleet air-defense system, complete with ships, radar, and missile systems. For another $2 billion to $3 billion, spread over five years, we could equip Upper Tier surface-to-air missiles on twenty-two AEGIS cruisers to provide antimissile protection for most of the United States. This would be a very effective stopgap to buy time until a permanent, space-based SDI system is up and running.

Ultimately, a space-based SDI would offer complete protection to America via a layered, 100 percent nonnuclear defense, exactly as Ronald Reagan envisioned. Hostile launches from any point on the globe could be detected by small satellites operated by the U.S. Air Force's Space Missile and Tracking System (aka *Brilliant Eyes*). These satellites would alert space-based and ground-based defenses to swing into action. Space-based, ground-controlled interceptors called *Brilliant Pebbles,* which would take out the missiles by simply ramming them at high speeds, would intercept long-range ballistic missiles of three hundred- to seven thousand-mile capability. Ground-based and sea-based interceptors would tackle short-range missiles (including cruise missiles). Total cost of building and deploying such a system: about 2 percent of the annual defense budget.

In March 1997, Bill Clinton and Boris Yeltsin met in Helsinki and agreed to extend the boundaries of the ABM Treaty to cover defense systems not previously prohibited under the 1972 treaty. Boris wanted to make sure we wouldn't build any defense systems that could stop his long-range nukes, and Bill said, in effect, "Boris, ol' buddy, don't give it another thought. We're sittin' here fat, dumb, and happy, and if you unload your silos on us, there ain't thing one we can do about it!" Clinton's obsession with the ABM Treaty is so indefensible it borders on treason. The MAD nuclear doctrine should have died in the early years of the Reagan administration; the fact that Bill Clinton has resurrected it and plans to extend it into the twenty-first century is a crime against the American people and all humanity.[19]

As Ronald Reagan observed on the occasion of the tenth anniversary of SDI, March 23, 1993:

> Unfortunately, there is a stubborn contingent of policy makers who insist on abiding by the obsolete ABM Treaty and support only extremely limited missile defenses, or even none at all. Yet I believe their efforts will not stop the progress we have made and the progress we have yet to make. The wisdom of the program we launched a decade ago will prevail, and America will not remain forever defenseless against ballistic missile attack.

Dad, you've always been right before. I hope you're right on this one. As Winston Churchill once said during World War II, "You can always count on the Americans to do the right thing—but only after they exhaust all other options."

CHAPTER NINE

A
CITY OF
THE WORLD

NO MORE VIETNAMS
OR BOSNIAS

*There was a time when our national security was based on a
standing army here within our own borders and shore batter-
ies of artillery along our coasts, and of course, a navy to keep
the sea-lanes open for the shipping of things necessary to our
well-being. The world has changed. Today, our national security can be threatened in faraway places. It's up to all of us
to be aware of the strategic importance of such places and to
be able to identify them.*

Ronald Reagan
Televised address on events in Lebanon and Grenada
Oval Office, October 27, 1983

At a White House State dinner honoring François Mitterrand, Dad and
Nancy and the president and first lady of France had just finished greeting
guests in the receiving line. Together, the two couples walked from the East
Room to the State Dining Room. All the guests stood at their tables, waiting
for the two presidents and the two first ladies to be seated. As was the
custom at White House State dinners, Nancy guided Mr. Mitterrand to one
table, while Dad was to host Mrs. Mitterrand at another table. But Mrs.
Mitterrand suddenly stopped, as if her shoes were nailed to the floor.

Dad leaned over, gestured toward their places at the table, and whispered, "We're supposed to be seated over there."

Mrs. Mitterrand leaned in his direction, said something softly to him in French, and stayed rooted to the spot. Dad didn't understand French, so he spread his hands helplessly and said, "I'm sorry, I don't understand. . . ." Mrs. Mitterrand repeated the same message in French, and all Dad could do was shake his head. Again he gestured toward their table but Mrs. Mitterrand remained frozen where she was.

Just then, an interpreter stepped to Dad's side and, in a low voice, explained, "Madame Mitterrand says that you are standing on her gown."

Well, a minor misstep in foreign relations—certainly nothing to compare with the major foreign policy stumbles we have witnessed in the past few years.

Elected on a platform of it's-the-economy-stupid, Clinton has been recklessly inattentive in his conduct of foreign policy. Like the captain of the *Titanic*, he has seen to the comfort of his passengers while steering the ship of state into dark, icy waters. He seems to pay attention to the rest of the world only when it offers an opportunity to surrender U.S. sovereignty to the United Nations (as in Somalia or Bosnia), or when Asian officials come to the White House for coffee, check in hand. Clinton got off pretty lightly in his first term, and he seems to think he can get away with his minimalist approach to foreign policy in Clinton II. In the course of his entire, long-winded Second Inaugural address, he didn't bother to raise a single foreign policy issue.

Americans should be extremely concerned over the long-term repercussions of the fact that Bill Clinton has repeatedly sold U.S. foreign policy to the highest bidder. Bill Clinton's message to the world is "Show me the money." Here is a partial list of people from foreign countries who gave questionable or illegal contributions in order to gain leverage over U.S. foreign policy:

- **Mochtar Riady** is the billionaire CEO of Indonesia's Lippo Group and one of the richest men in the world. Over the years, Riady has steered an untold amount of money into various Clinton campaigns, including over $1.5 million in clearly illegal, scarcely disguised foreign contributions during the 1996 presidential campaign. That kind of money buys a lot of influence.

In the entire world, only two places supply a certain kind of clean-burning coal that is acceptable under the EPA's new environmental standards. One of those places is in Utah; the other is the Indonesian island of Kalimantan, which is controlled by Riady's Lippo Group. Sales of the Kalimantan coal are expected to boost the Indonesian economy by an astounding 8 percent a year far into the next century. In 1996, Clinton signed an extraordinary executive order, which created the Grand Staircase–Escalante National Monument, placing 1.7 million acres in southwest Utah off-limits to development and mining. That action locked up seven billion tons of clean-burning coal valued at over $1 trillion, cost thousands of American jobs, robbed Utah's public education system of $62 billion in taxes over forty years, and robbed the federal treasury of additional millions.

Investigative reporter L. J. Davis of *Mother Jones* magazine has made an intensive study of Mochtar Riady and his long-standing connection with Bill Clinton, concluding that Riady is "a front man for the Indonesian government. [The Indonesians] regard the United States government as a regime much like their own"—that is, a corrupt "banana republic" that operates on greed and political payoffs for the acquisition of power and political favors.[1]

- **James Riady** is the son of Lippo Group's Mochtar Riady. The friendship between James Riady and Bill Clinton goes back to around 1979. After the Lippo Group bought an interest in Little Rock's Worthen National Bank, Riady operated the bank, seeing that then governor Bill Clinton received last-minute loans whenever needed for his gubernatorial and presidential campaigns. In 1992, for example, when Bill Clinton floundered badly in the New Hampshire primaries and the campaign was dead broke, Riady and Worthen revived the campaign with a $2 million infusion. Riady also contributed $175,000 to the DNC and the Clinton Inaugural Fund in 1992. He's had at least three White House meetings with Bill Clinton.[2]

- **John Huang** is a Chinese-born Lippo operative whom James Riady introduced to Bill Clinton. He moved to Little Rock in the early 1980s to establish Lippo operations in Arkansas. He later became a top official in the Clinton administration and the Democratic Party. Huang maintained ties with the Lippo Group throughout the time he was a high-ranking official with the Department of Commerce and a top fund-raiser for the Democratic National Committee (DNC). He was put in the Commerce slot by then secretary of commerce Ron Brown, who personally ordered that Huang be given a top-secret security clearance with no background check by the FBI or the State Department's security office. Huang had access to highly classified U.S. intelligence information and accompanied Brown on a 1994 trade mission to Beijing that resulted in $5.5 billion in trade deals. There is strong evidence to suggest that Huang is part of a Chinese espionage effort to gather intelligence and tilt U.S. trade and foreign policy in China's favor. Huang illegally raised hundreds of thousands of dollars for Bill Clinton's reelection campaign.[3]

- **Arief and Soraya Wiriandinata** earned little more than minimum wage as green-card-holding gardeners in the United States. After making a $450,000 donation to the DNC, they returned home to Indonesia, beyond the reach of American investigators and subpoenas. It turns out that Arief is the son-in-law of a top Lippo Group executive and shareholder. The only reasonable conclusion is that the Wiriandinatas were a conduit for laundered Lippobucks.[4]

- **John K. H. Lee** is chairman of South Korea's Cheong Am America, Inc. He arranged for a quarter-million-dollar illegal donation to the DNC in exchange for a personal meeting with the president at the White House.[5]

- **Yogesh Gandhi** is a man who falsely claimed kinship to the great Indian leader Mahatma Gandhi and who gave Bill Clinton the dubious distinction of the Gandhi Peace Prize, a life-size bust of "Uncle" Mahatma plus a $325,000 contribution to the DNC. Clinton smilingly received the bust during a White House ceremony. Yogesh claims to be penniless, owes $10,000 in back taxes, and lives off his brother's credit card.[6]

- **Jorge Cabrera** is a convicted Cuban drug smuggler with links to Fidel Castro. Cabrera contributed $20,000 to the Democratic National Committee in exchange for invitations to dinners with Vice President Al Gore and Hillary Rodham Clinton. The donation was solicited during a November 1995 rendezvous at a Havana hotel between Cabrera and a prominent Democratic fund-raiser, **Vivian Mannerud**, president of Airline Brokers Co., Inc., of Miami. Mannerud's air charter company specializes in flying people to Cuba by indirect means, such as Miami to Cancun to Havana, to circumvent the embargo on U.S.-Cuba passenger flights.

Cabrera says he dropped off the money at Mannerud's Miami office and soon received an invitation to a Miami dinner honoring Vice President Gore; less than two weeks after the Gore dinner, Cabrera attended a White House party hosted by Mrs. Clinton. Cabrera was well known to law enforcement officials, having previously been convicted of drug-related felonies in the 1980s. Three weeks after meeting the first lady, he was arrested for importing over a ton of Colombian cocaine into the United States; he was convicted and is serving a nineteen-year sentence in a Florida prison. When confronted by reporters about her role in soliciting the donation, Vivian Mannerud replied, "Let's suppose I did meet him in Cuba and asked him for money. So what?"[7]

- **Grigori Loutchanski** is a Latvian businessman and reputed master criminal who operates Nordex, an international conglomerate linked to drug trafficking, international arms sales, and money laundering. He has been implicated in the smuggling of nuclear weapons materials out of the former Soviet Union. *Time* magazine calls him "the most pernicious unindicted criminal in the world." He met privately with Bill Clinton during a 1993 fund-raiser.[8]

Bill Clinton is at the center of the biggest international shakedown operation in the history of mankind. Before coming to Washington, he ran the state of Arkansas like a Third World banana republic, peddling influence for campaign cash, maintaining power through machine-politics and corruption. (For additional discussion of Clinton's corruption as governor of Arkansas, see Chapters 4, 5, and 6 of my previous book, *Making Waves*.) As the president of the United States, Bill Clinton is now applying the same political methods to raise money and maintain power. He has turned America into a "banana superpower."

Clinton's foreign policy performance has unnerved our friends and emboldened our adversaries. The world knows that with Bill Clinton in charge, America's word can't be trusted. As a result, our relationships with allies are badly frayed. This was demonstrated when Clinton launched a salvo of cruise missiles at targets in southern Iraq just weeks before the 1996 election. Almost all the members of the thirty-two-nation coalition assembled for the 1991 Gulf War either tried to talk Clinton out of the attack, or simply sat on the sidelines. Clinton's foray into Iraq was much like earlier forays into Somalia, Bosnia, and Haiti. When the dust cleared, Clinton announced that "our mission has been achieved"—yet at no time did he ever define what the mission was or exactly what was achieved.

There is a fundamental reason why American foreign policy is adrift under Bill Clinton: Liberals, like Clinton, do not understand the function of the military and the foreign policy apparatus. They think the army and the marines are just like the Peace Corps, only they ride in tanks and Humvees. That is not the way to use the military.

Both Reagan and Bush understood that military force should only be used (1) when our vital national interests are at stake and (2) when domestic political support is strong and dependable. If freedom and U.S. interests are threatened in some part of the world, but the people don't favor overt military intervention, then the U.S. should lend strong support to democratic forces or freedom fighters within those regions. If our interests are at stake, if popular support is strong, and if the decision to use military force receives the green light, then the military must be sent in with swift, overwhelming, and decisive force. Those were the criteria applied when we undertook military operations in hot spots ranging from Panama and Grenada to Iraq during the Gulf War.

The world is too complex and dangerous a place to allow an aimless, amateurish foreign policy to drag us from one calamity to the next, flailing around for a rationale. The same foreign policy principles that served us so well in the Reagan 1980s are still valid today: Maintain peace through strength. Be consistent and keep your word among your allies. Don't make threats you don't intend to keep. Keep the expansion of freedom and democracy around the world as the guiding principle. Use the military only to defend U.S. interests and with popular support—and use it decisively.

No more Vietnams, Lebanons, or Bosnias.

STORM CLOUDS
ON THE HORIZON

America's strength is the bedrock of the free world's security, for the freedom we guard is not just our own.

Ronald Reagan
Speech, Recommissioning of
the battleship USS *New Jersey*
Long Beach Naval Shipyard,
December 28, 1982

Throughout most of his presidency, Dad was in the radio talk show business. Every Saturday, at noon Eastern time, he gave a five-minute radio address. Over his two terms in office, he did 331 radio commentaries on a variety of subjects ranging from current issues and crises to warm human-interest stories. On Christmas Day 1982, he went on the air and said:

> One of my favorite pieces of Christmas mail came early this year, a sort of modern American Christmas story that took place not in our country's heartland, but on the troubled waters of the South China Sea last October. . . . It's a letter from Ordnance Man First Class John Mooney, written to his parents from aboard the aircraft carrier *Midway*. . . .
>
> "Dear Mom and Dad," he wrote, "today we spotted a boat in the water, and we rendered assistance. We picked up sixty-five Vietnamese refugees. It was about a two-hour job getting everyone aboard, and then they had to get screened by intelligence and checked out by medical and fed and clothed and all that. . . . Their boat was sinking as we came alongside. They'd been at sea five days and had run out of water. . . . It took a lot of guts for those parents to make a choice like that to go to sea in a leaky boat in hope of finding someone to take them from the sea. So much risk! But apparently they felt it was worth it rather than live in a communist country. . . .
>
> "As they approached the ship, they were all waving and trying as best they could to say, 'Hello, America sailor! Hello, freedom man!' . . . It reminds us all of what America has always been—a place a man or woman can come to for freedom. I know we're crowded and we have unemployment and we have a real burden with refugees, but I honestly hope and pray we can always find room. We have a unique society, made up of castoffs of all the world's wars and oppressions, and yet we're strong and free. We have one thing in common—no matter where our forefathers came from, we believe in that freedom. . . ."
>
> Well, I think that letter just about says it all. In spite of everything, we Americans are still uniquely blessed, not only with the rich bounty of our land but by a bounty of the spirit—a kind of year-round Christmas spirit that still makes our country a beacon of hope in a troubled world.

Under Ronald Reagan, America rediscovered what it means to be a beacon of hope and freedom in the world. But in recent years, it seems we've lost our way again. We've forgotten what it means to be "freedom men" and "freedom women" in a world where people are in bondage.

As the land of liberty, "the last best hope of man on earth," America has a special obligation to remain strong and to lead in world events. We cannot simply place our armed forces at the beck and call of that global bureaucracy over on the East River in New York. That's not leadership. That's the complete *abdication* of leadership. In order to truly lead in world events, we must define what our vital national interests are—and then we must assertively, aggressively defend those interests. In so doing, we will also be defending the interests of freedom-loving people throughout the world.

During the Reagan and Bush years, America's leaders had a much clearer, surer definition of our vital interests around the world. Those interests can be reduced to just four basic categories.

FOUR VITAL FOREIGN POLICY INTERESTS

1. Defend the security of the United States of America. Or as the Preamble to the Constitution puts it, "provide for the common defense." That's primary. That's basic. Nothing supersedes that. We must protect our nation's people, borders, land, waters, and airspace. Once we recognize that national security supersedes all other considerations, many of our choices as a society become clear. We must secure the skies against incoming missiles, from wherever they may be launched. We must maintain a state of military readiness that is capable of deterring or defeating any threat on land, sea, or air. We must secure our borders against encroachment. The security of the United States is nonnegotiable. This vital American interest was central to the defense buildup under Ronald Reagan.

2. Defend freedom and oppose expansionist tyranny around the world. Ronald Reagan pursued this vital American interest through a direct invasion of Grenada (a small island nation in our own hemisphere, that had been subverted by Soviet-Cuban expansionism). He also pursued this vital American interest through quiet, covert assistance to freedom fighters in Afghanistan and Nicaragua and to the Solidarity movement in Poland, who were all seeking freedom from Soviet domination. George Bush pursued this vital American interest in kicking the expansionist Iraqis out of Kuwait. This does not mean we should send in the marines every time there is instability, poverty, or a nasty dictator in power somewhere in the world. Inserting U.S. troops between warring factions in Somalia or Bosnia does not qualify under this definition of a vital American interest. Nor does using the marines to remove one Haitian strongman while installing another. In such cases, neither our people nor our security interests are at stake.

It does mean, however, that America needs to keep its forces strategically placed around the world, in places like Europe, the Middle East, and the Far East—not merely to defend those nations over there, but to stop trouble before it gets to our shores. When we put defense dollars into the defense of Europe or South Korea or India, we are also defending California, Maine, and Iowa. Though the threat from Russia may have diminished, it has certainly not disappeared (especially if the Russian government falls into the hands of a dictator). Additional threats are emerging from North Korea, Iran, and especially China. We must continue to be a powerful force for stability around the world.

3. Defend the lives and well-being of American citizens around the world. The United States government has an obligation to defend American lives not only against the actions of hostile states but also against the actions of international terrorists. The U.S. must not only react forcefully when terrorists strike, but must conduct itself proactively, using intelligence assets to intercept terrorists before they strike and enforcing sanctions and even reprisals against governments that arm and sponsor terrorists (such as Iran, Iraq, Syria, Libya, the Sudan, Cuba, and North Korea).

4. Defend U.S. access to world markets for products, commodities, matériel, and energy. In wartime, this means that we must defend American merchant vessels in international shipping lanes. In peacetime, it means that America must maintain free trade relationships with other nations—including free trade in energy commodities, such as oil, gas, and coal. The engine of American freedom and prosperity runs on energy, and our primary form of energy is oil. Foreign oil comprises over half of all oil consumed in the U.S. today, and that percentage will surely rise in the future. As we saw in the 1970s, interruptions in the supply of oil threaten American freedom and security.

Ironically, one of the biggest impediments to genuine free trade is the proliferation of so-called free trade agreements, such as the North American Free Trade Agreement (NAFTA) and the General Agreement on Tariffs and Trade (GATT). Both agreements are numbingly long and complex. NAFTA is 1,500 pages long, while GATT—sometimes called "NAFTA on steroids"—runs 22,000 pages long. NAFTA contains over 200 pages of regulations and formulas defining what the "origin" of various products shall be, so that it can be determined whether or not each product is subject to a tariff. The paperwork needed to comply with these formulas forces manufacturers to add 3 percent to 5 percent to the cost of the product covered by those regulations.[9] Added to all the complexity contained in these bloated agreements are the multitudinous side agreements, covering everything from labor demands to environmental issues, plus all the international commissions, arbitrating bodies, and courts, which supersede American sovereignty and cannot be challenged in American courts.

We don't need free trade agreements. We just need free trade, period. Free trade is easy to accomplish. Simply drop tariffs, end import quotas, and abolish the Jones Act (which senselessly overregulates shipping in and out of U.S. ports). If other nations refuse to lower tariffs or grant access to their markets, we simply tell them, "Fine. Our trade policy toward you will be a mirror of your trade policy toward us. If you drop your tariffs and import quotas on our goods, we'll drop them on yours." Put the ball in the other country's court—and give the other country the incentive to play ball on a level field.

These, then, are our four vital foreign policy interests: (1) Defend America's national security; (2) defend freedom and oppose expansionist tyranny around the world; (3) defend American citizens around the world; and (4) defend U.S. access to world markets and trade. The careful but assertive pursuit of these four vital American interests guided U.S. foreign policy in the Reagan and Bush years, and largely accounted for the foreign policy successes of the Reagan and Bush years. We have deviated from these four simple principles during the Clinton years—and look what we have to show for it: failure and mire in Somalia, Bosnia, and Haiti, plus the emerging threat of Red China. In fact, there are foreign policy storm clouds forming all across the horizon of the future. Following is a brief checklist of emerging foreign policy problems that could darken the skies over our Shining City during the next decade.

EMERGING FOREIGN POLICY PROBLEMS

Asia

The continent of Asia is brimming with economic promise and bubbling with political turmoil. China and India are showing economic growth that is three times the growth in the U.S., Europe, and Japan. But enormous social instability and military expansion are also taking place in these nations.

China. For the next few decades, China is likely to present America with its most dangerous challenge since World War II, in large part because of events Bill Clinton set in motion in the 1990s. As a candidate in 1992, Clinton was highly critical of the Bush White House policy toward China and promised to take a hard line on China regarding human rights, trade, regional stability, and nuclear proliferation. Once in office, however, Clinton pursued a policy of appeasement. Early in his presidency, he "delinked" China's trading privileges from its abysmal human rights record so that Hillary Rodham Clinton could address the UN Conference on Women in Beijing.

More recently, he has simply been selling out for cold, hard cash. As the *London Daily Telegraph* observed, "It is dawning on the public that their President may have sold foreign policy to a manipulative and potentially hostile foreign power. . . . The Clinton Doctrine on Asia has involved focusing on trade and selling China military technology. The fear is that this policy was molded by Chinese agents handing cash in buff envelopes to the President's party. Sucking up to Beijing is also demanded by U.S. business, which fears exclusion from [a Chinese] economy [that is] growing by 12 percent a year."[10]

The very real danger for future world stability is that the U.S. is now arming and energizing the next great superpower and setting the stage for a new Cold War, this time between China and the West. Ronald Reagan brought Soviet Communism down by restricting the flow of technology and hard currency to the USSR. For his own short-term political gain, Bill Clinton is rapidly expanding the flow of military hardware, aircraft, computer and communications technology, and hard currency to China. It is no secret that America's China policy during the Clinton years has been shaped more by the Department of Commerce (which was corrupted under Ron Brown and John Huang) than by Warren Christopher's ineffectual Department of State.

Cash-strapped Russia is also helping to elevate China to superpower status by selling off its military, missile, and nuclear technology to China. The Chinese are increasing their military budget by 10 percent a year at the same time the U.S. is severely cutting military spending and reducing its presence in the Philippines, Japan, and elsewhere in the Pacific, creating a power vacuum the Chinese are eager to fill. In contrast to Clinton's campaign promises, the White House has muted its criticism of Chinese human rights abuses to near silence. Many China-watchers (including myself) are convinced that America's next war will be with China. It is likely to be a very hot and bloody war—*and it is doubtful, given our current military readiness, that we would win.*

Taiwan. The bone of contention in the next war with China could well be Taiwan. China has never given up its plans to reacquire Taiwan. Knowing that the United States no longer possesses the capability to fight more than one war at a time, the Chinese may be waiting for the United States to be distracted in some other part of the world before pouncing on Taiwan. To head off Chinese expansionism, the U.S. must reassert its military presence in the region, reaffirm its commitment to the Taiwan Relations Act and to Taiwan's sovereignty and security, and strongly state its position that any attempt to alter the government of Taiwan by force will be considered a threat to vital American security interests. We must also provide Taiwan with a *theater missile defense* (a mini-SDI designed to defend a localized region or theater) to protect the Taiwanese people from a growing missile threat from the Chinese mainland. And we must restore our lost ability to fight—and win—a two- or three-front war.

North Korea. It is an unstable, rogue state, one of the few Communist dictatorships left after the fall of the Soviet Union. The country already wields missiles capable of reaching targets in Alaska and Hawaii and may possess nuclear weapons as well. The North Koreans tested Bill Clinton's resolve in 1994, violating the Nuclear Nonproliferation Treaty by refusing to allow international inspectors into its nuclear power plants. Waste from the North Korean plants could be processed into weapons-grade plutonium. After Bill Clinton's warnings went unheeded, Jimmy Carter stepped in and privately negotiated with the Koreans (while publicly embarrassing Clinton and his secretary of state, Warren Christopher). The result was an agreement in which the U.S. taxpayers would buy North Korea brand-new light water nuclear power plants, and the Koreans promised to let the inspectors into the old nuclear plants at some unspecified future date.

The Clinton-Carter policy didn't solve the problem of a nuclear-armed North Korea. It only shifted it slightly into the future. Clinton or some future president will undoubtedly have to revisit that policy. The only prudent policy toward North Korea is a *tough* policy, combining a strong regional military presence, a strongly worded commitment to defending the people of Japan and the Republic of Korea (South Korea) from attack, a stern warning to North Korea that the U.S. will defend its vital security interests in the region, and a theater missile defense to protect Japan, South Korea, and the Pacific sector of the United States from the growing North Korean missile threat.

Europe

The security of Europe is indispensable to the security of America, and Europe cannot remain secure without the assistance of the United States.

NATO. The NATO Alliance is the cornerstone of America's relationship with Europe—and the linchpin of European freedom and stability. The real gains in European security, which Ronald Reagan achieved by ending the Cold War, have to be built upon in the post-Cold War world. In deference to Russian objections, Bill Clinton has retarded the process of integrating former Warsaw Pact nations (Poland, Hungary, the Czech Republic, and the Slovak Republic) under the NATO security umbrella. Eastern Europe, still fearful of potential future aggression by the Russian Bear, is eager to merge its security interests with those of the existing Atlantic alliance.

Russia. Even fragmented, Russia presents a tough challenge to American foreign policy, a challenge that has clearly overwhelmed the current leadership in the Oval Office. I vividly recall the summer day in 1976 when my father lost the Republican presidential nomination to Gerald Ford at the convention in Kansas City. I had never seen Dad lose at anything before. So I asked him, "What are you feeling right now, Dad? What are you going through?"

"You know, Mike," he said, "the thing I regret most is that I won't get to sit down and negotiate with Secretary General Breshnev. Over the years, I've seen American presidents kowtow to the Russians and give them whatever they demand. I've wanted the chance to negotiate with the Soviets from a position of American strength. I was going to let Mr. Breshnev pick the size and shape of the negotiating table, and I was ready to listen patiently as he listed everthing America would have to give up in order to get along with the Russians. Then I was going to get up, walk to Mr. Breshnev's side of the table, and whisper one word in his ear: 'Nyet!' The Russians haven't heard that word in a long time from an American president, and I wanted to be the president to tell them *nyet*."

Ten years later, almost to the month, Dad got his chance to say *nyet* to the Russians—not to Breshnev, but to Mikhail Gorbachev at a summit in Reykjavik, Iceland. Gorbachev told Ronald Reagan that to get along with the Russians he would have to give up SDI. And Ronald Reagan leaned across the table and did what he had waited ten years to do: He said *nyet* to the Russians. It was a *nyet* heard round the world.

Bill Clinton is a no-nyet president. Guided in large part by his longtime pro-Soviet pal, Strobe Talbot, Clinton has pursued a course of accommodation toward the post–Cold War Kremlin. He rationalized his lack of response to Russian brutality in the breakaway republic of Chechnya by comparing Boris Yeltsin to Abraham Lincoln going to war to maintain the Union (an offensive comparison if there ever was one). Clinton's passivity in the bloody Chechnya crisis, where tens of thousands died, only invited an increase in Russian repression.

While America has a clear, vital interest in keeping a working relationship with democratic Russia, U.S. aid and friendship with Russia must be built on a basis of accountability. Russia must be held to its treaty obligations and must stop arming rogue nations. We need strong, courageous leadership in the White House in order to hold Russia to those standards of accountability. And we cannot expect Russia to stop arming China unless we do the same.

Russia's transition to a democratic society and a free market economy will be long and difficult, and the Russian people are understandably vulnerable to the demagoguery of nationalistic leaders. It remains to be seen whether the Russian people will have the patience to allow democratic reforms to produce a better way of life or whether a nostalgic longing for totalitarian stability (and food trains that run on time) will bring communism back to the Kremlin.

Bosnia. This little country will be a thorn in America's side for years to come. In 1992, candidate Bill Clinton promised to lift the arms embargo on Bosnia, an embargo that was originally imposed on Yugoslavia, a political entity that ceased to exist in 1991. Once in office, Clinton betrayed his promise and allowed Serbian genocide against Bosnian Muslims to go unchallenged for three years, at great cost to our relations with Muslims around the world. Had he lifted the arms embargo (as the Republican-led Congress voted to do, stopped only by a Clinton veto), Bosnian Muslims could have defended themselves and the U.S. never would have had to send troops to Bosnia. (That's the Reagan Doctrine.)

Incredibly, while opposing the Republican effort to lift the arms embargo, Clinton secretly facilitated a deal to allow Iran—an outlaw nation—to supply arms to the Bosnian Muslims, turning Bosnia into Clinton's own version of the Iran–Contra affair. At the advice of National Security Advisor Anthony Lake and Deputy Secretary of State Strobe Talbott, Clinton handed Iran a powerful wedge of influence in the region while passing up the opportunity for America to build a stronger relationship with the Muslim world by giving Bosnian Muslims the tools to defend themselves.

The Middle East

About three-quarters of the world's oil reserves are located in the Muslim world, a source of concentrated wealth amid societies of rampant poverty, political unrest, and social instability. Most of those reserves are in the Persian Gulf region, which is controlled by nondemocratic regimes. Gulf reserves are expected to last for a century or more, after which new forms of energy will be needed to power the engines of the world. Demand for oil from the Middle East—particularly in newly industrialized East Asia—is expected to squeeze supplies and drive up prices early in the next century.[11] Meanwhile, America and the rest of the West will continue to be dependent on Gulf oil and to be vulnerable to supply disruptions and petro-blackmail. These facts make the Middle East the single most vital region to the security and stability of the world. Unfortunately, the Middle East is also the most volatile region in the world. American foreign policy goals in the region must be focused on:

1. Maintaining secure access to oil resources at market prices.
2. Maintaining the security of Israel, our most reliable ally in the region and a nation of strategic importance.
3. Promoting freedom, security, and political self-determination for *all* people in the region—Muslim, Jewish, and Christian.

The challenge of the Middle East requires leadership that is strong, courageous, and principled. One of the most sobering political realities we face in the coming century is the fact that most of the world's oil flows through a choke point that is hemmed in by religious and political extremism, mounting terrorism, the escalating danger of nuclear, chemical, and biological warfare, and the destabilizing influence of rogue states such as Syria, Iran, Iraq, and Libya.

Under Bill Clinton, our military preparedness has sunk to such a low level that we could not prosecute the 1991 Gulf War again today. We simply do not have the air strength, naval strength, and army and marine manpower we had back then (see Chapter 8). The Middle East is more of a powder keg now than it ever was. American military weakness today invites trouble in the region tomorrow. Peace through strength must continue to be the centerpiece of U.S. policy in the Middle East.

Iran. This Islamic fundamentalist theocracy hasn't gotten much press lately, despite the fact that it is emerging as one of the greatest threats to our interests anywhere in the world. Iran continues to advance Islamic fundamentalism throughout the region while quietly undermining and destabilizing neighboring countries such as Algeria, Egypt, and the Sudan. The president of Egypt, Hosni Mubarak, has openly warned of a possible war with Iran if that country continues to seek strategic control of the Red Sea and Gulf of Aden. Iran's capital city, Tehran, is a hub of international terrorist activity and assassination, sponsoring such groups as the radical Lebanese Shi'ite Hizbollah (Party of God), Hamas, and the Islamic Jihad. Iran was a state sponsor of the World Trade Center bombing in New York.

One of the most underreported stories of the last few years is the Iranian acquisition of an atomic bomb. When U.S. secretary of defense William Perry went to Israel in 1995 to browbeat the Israelis into signing the Nuclear Non-Proliferation Treaty, the Israelis tried to warn Perry that Iran was about to have its own bomb. Perry insisted the Iranians were seven to fifteen years from possessing the bomb; the Israelis insisted Iran was a year away. A year later, it became clear that Iran did, indeed, possess all the elements of a bomb, thanks to assistance from Russia, China, and North Korea. Tehran has also acquired medium-range Nodong missiles from North Korea, easily capable of hitting Israel.[12]

Even before Perry brushed off Israeli fears, there were reports that Iran had already acquired up to seven nuclear warheads from Kazakhstan as early as 1991 to 1993, capable of being launched on either Scud or Nodong missiles—plus highly paid nuclear scientists from the former Soviet Union to provide technical know-how. Tehran has also received advanced radar, air defense, and missile technology, plus chemicals used to manufacture deadly nerve gas, from China. This sale violates numerous international agreements, as well as a 1992 U.S. law that requires the U.S. government to impose strict sanctions on any nation that sells destabilizing conventional weapons to Iran or Iraq.

Iran has a number of motivations for developing its own Islamic bomb:

- Advancing its own regional and global prestige and influence.
- Holding a powerful threat over its oil-rich rivals, Iraq and Saudi Arabia.
- Replacing Western and U.S. influence in the Middle East with a dominating Iranian presence.
- Threatening the existence of Israel.

Tehran is eager to shed its backward image and assert itself as the leading power in the Middle East.

As we try to protect the flow of oil and defend the existence of Israel, we will confront a nuclear-armed Iran with a precarious economy, dangerous social instability, and intensely anti-Western religious fanaticism. In order to maintain its survival amid internal crises, Iranian leaders will look outside their borders to stir up distractions and keep the Iranian people whipped up into a revolutionary mind-set.

Iraq. Saddam Hussein still has his eye on the oil fields of Kuwait—and Saudi Arabia. His forces continue to train for a future invasion of Kuwait, and there is evidence that, in the old Babylonian tradition of his ancestors, Hussein plans his military and political actions according to astrological calculations (his invasion of Kuwait occurred on August 2, 1990, when Mars and Pluto squared a lunar eclipse). In other words, his thinking is not like our thinking, and the fact that Hussein governs according to astrological portents while the West expects him to think rationally means that there is an enormous risk of miscalculation on both sides. Saddam is a loose cannon on the rolling deck of the Middle East. The only way to render a loose cannon harmless is to securely tie it down. If Saddam faces an American leader whom he does not fear or respect, or whose word or resolve he doubts, the chances increase dramatically that Saddam will miscalculate (or worse, calculate correctly) and touch off a new round of war.

Iraq has never fully complied with all the UN Security Council resolutions that were imposed by the international coalition after the Gulf War. An outbreak of hostilities involving Iraq could quickly spread elsewhere in the Middle East. For example, an Iraqi attack on Kuwait could be rapidly followed by a Syrian attack against Israel, with Iraqi, Palestinian, and even Iranian forces quickly added in. Israel, Iran, and Pakistan could turn the conflict into a nuclear exchange, and almost any country in the region could introduce chemical and biological warfare.

Saudi Arabia. One of the seemingly more stable nations in the region is actually in a more fragile condition than most people realize. A struggle for the right to succession in Saudi Arabia is already going on. One branch of the Saudi family, the Prince Abdallah faction, is bent on seizing power, kicking the United States out of the region, and shifting oil exports toward East Asia at the expense of the West.

Israel. The nexus of all disputes in the Middle East is Israel. Despite any agreements that have been signed over the years between Israel and her neighbors, the aim of the Arab world remains one of isolating Israel internationally, surrounding her militarily, and if not annihilating her, then at least using the threat of annihilation to force Israel to meet Arab demands (including the surrender of Jerusalem). As Arab military power expands, the Arabs might use a combination of nuclear (or chemical or biological) warfare and economic (oil boycott) warfare to prevent the West from intervening while a new all-out attack is conducted against Israel—all the more reason the United States needs SDI. We cannot afford to have our foreign policy hamstrung by nuclear blackmail.

As Ronald Reagan said in a speech to the nation regarding Lebanon and Grenada, October 27, 1983, "Since 1948 our nation has recognized and accepted a moral obligation to assure the continued existence of Israel as a nation. Israel shares our democratic values and is a formidable force an invader of the Middle East would have to reckon with." In order to help Israel defend herself and to maintain stability throughout the region, the U.S. must continue planning for worst-case scenarios. That means we must provide Israel with a reliable theater missile defense (smarter and more leakproof than the Patriot system that was stretched beyond its design capabilities during the Gulf War).

The Clinton administration has repeatedly interfered in Israel's security affairs, tilting toward agreements that offer Israeli land in exchange for hollow promises. We need leadership in America that will recognize Israel's right to assess its own security needs and arm itself accordingly. While we must support the peace process between Israel and her neighbors, our leaders must recognize that for Israel to place all her hopes for the future in paper treaties would be wishful thinking at best—and suicide at worst. Negotiations between Israel and her neighbors should generate not only peace but also security.

Africa

Africa is a continent moving in two directions at the same time. Many African nations, such as South Africa, Ghana, Botswana, Senegal, Uganda, and Mozambique, are moving slowly toward democracy, economic reform, and social stability. Other African nations, meanwhile, are sliding toward chaos.

African economies are hindered by the cost of importing oil to fuel their emerging industrial economies and by the bureaucratic incompetence of their often-corrupt governments. Bribery is considered a simple cost of doing business, and that creates a major impediment to foreign investment in African economies. African instability is perpetuated by the lack of an educated middle class, which is so essential to maintaining democracy. Even in majority-ruled South Africa, the dramatic move toward democracy is threatened by the gulf between the haves and the have-nots. Unless there are opportunities for people at the bottom of society to move upward and form a strong middle class, the chances for a return to civil unrest and repressive government are great in South Africa and other emerging democracies.

On the whole, Africa has benefited from the end of the Cold War. Prior to the collapse of Soviet Communism, much of the competition between East and West was concentrated in places like Angola, Ethiopia, and Somalia. The end of the Cold War allows African nations to focus on their own problems without meddling from the superpowers. But the withdrawal of the superpowers also creates a power vacuum, unleashing bloody internal struggles in such countries as Somalia, Liberia, the Sudan, Rwanda, and Burundi.

Latin America

Ultimately, America's most vital foreign interests are right here in our own hemisphere—a principle spelled out in the 1823 Monroe Doctrine, which warned European powers not to interfere in the affairs of the Americas. Ronald Reagan invoked the Monroe Doctrine in his successful offensive against communism in Nicaragua, El Salvador, Grenada, and elsewhere in the Americas. As he said in a speech before Congress on Central American issues, April 27, 1983, "If the Nazis during World War II and the Soviets today could recognize the Caribbean and Central America as vital to our interests, shouldn't we, also?" Not only did Reagan policies halt the advance of Soviet expansionism in Latin America, they helped produce real economic and political reform, diminishing the power of tinhorn totalitarianism.

Latin American progress toward democracy, stability, and prosperity has stalled since 1993. Some may think it coincidental, but during the tenure of the "I-didn't-inhale" president, the forces of narco-corruption have taken over the government of Colombia and subverted the government of Mexico. The drug trade threatens the stability and integrity of every government in the Western Hemisphere, including that of the good ol' U.S. of A. The drug trade not only shreds our social fabric here, north of the border, but also causes increased crime, government and police corruption, and social breakdown south of the border. NAFTA—the North American Free Trade Agreement, which went into effect at the beginning of 1994—has only exacerbated the problem by allowing trucks loaded with drugs to cross the border into the States completely sealed and uninspected.

Mexico. This is a nation of 100 million people right on our border, our third largest trading partner, and a powder keg with a fuse sizzling down to the nub. While the Clinton administration and the Mexican government claim that Mexico has recovered from the economic crisis of 1994–1995, the value of the peso has fallen as flat as a tortilla, pointing to the fact that Mexico is still in enormous political and social trouble. Like Africa, Mexico suffers from the lack of a middle class. While the fifteen wealthiest individuals in Mexico control fortunes equal to almost a tenth of Mexico's gross domestic product, fully 70 percent of the people live in poverty. The country is going through its worst depression since the 1920s, resulting in a loss of about a million jobs a year in 1995 and 1996. After sixty years of relative stability, the Mexican social system is teetering on the edge of collapse.

In Mexico, the foundations of an old and proud society have been shaken by a destructive guerrilla war that has gone largely unreported by American media. Some knowledgeable Mexico-watchers consider that country to already be in a state of civil war. According to Diego Cevallos of the Inter Press English Service News Wire, "At least 1,500 paramilitary groups are currently operative in Mexico, where crime rose by more than 30 percent from 1994 to 1995 and police corruption led the government to sack dozens of agents and put the military in charge of the security forces." The paramilitary groups in Mexico serve the interests of drug traffickers and corrupt political bosses.[13]

The civil disorder of Mexico is already spilling onto the streets of America. Not all illegal immigrants from Mexico are fleeing crime, drugs, and social squalor. Some are bringing it with them. The freedom and vast opportunities of life in America are attracting far more people here than our society and social institutions can support. Instead of opening the floodgates of illegal immigration (which only burdens our taxpayers, dilutes our prosperity, and multiplies our crime and poverty problems), we need to find ways to export freedom and the free market system to Mexico. We need to export our way of life around the world and make the world want what we have—not just our prosperity, but the freedom that makes prosperity possible.

Central and South America. Unemployment and economic instability plague the entire region. From Mexico to Colombia to Argentina, children are sold into prostitution, people crowd church sanctuaries to pray for jobs, and once-honest farmers grow coca to make crack and powder cocaine for American streets. Of Latin America's 460 million people, over 200 million are poor (up from around 140 million in the 1980s). Throughout Latin America, the scare word on everyone's lips is *desempleo,* unemployment. Millions of jobs have been lost throughout Latin America in the last few years, and the two dominant emotions that reign today in the *villas miserias*—the urban slum-villages—are rage and despair. Crime is exploding.

Terrorism, long dormant in Latin America, is returning to the forefront, as groups like the dreaded Shining Path and Tupac Amaru (which stunned the world with a 1996 mass hostage-taking at an embassy residence in Lima, Peru) recruit new followers among the desperate poor.

Though education is essential for turning Latin America's economic and social decay around, it is becoming increasingly hard to keep kids in school. Half of all students in Central and South America drop out of school before reaching high school, and only one in eight Latin American schoolchildren enrolls in high school. The lack of an educated, skilled workforce is making it increasingly hard for Latin America to compete in the world economy.

Brazil and Chile. The Latin nations with the strongest economies are products of free market reforms and economic freedom. Chile's economy is growing at a rate of more than 4 percent, and Brazil's at more than 6 percent. Brazil and Chile are more competitive in the global economy because of higher worker productivity. Overseas firms are more willing to invest in countries with higher productivity, even if the laborers demand a higher wage and higher standard of living. A decently paid, highly productive laborer is much more valuable than a poorly paid, unproductive laborer. To remain competitive, Latin American economies must focus on building a competitive workforce. That means having better education, keeping kids in school, and creating incentives to make workers more productive.

Cuba. This island nation remains what it has been for nearly four decades—a totalitarian dictatorship just ninety miles from our shores. In March 1996, Cuban dictator Fidel Castro personally ordered two unarmed American single-engine Cessna planes shot out of the sky over international waters, killing four American citizens of the Cuban exile group Brothers to the Rescue. Had Ronald Reagan been president during this outrage, every MiG in Castro's air force would have been a smoking hole in the tarmac by the next day. Clinton's response? Nothing but talk. He sends the U.S. military on nation-building missions to Haiti and Somalia—but when American citizens are murdered, he does nothing.

Prior to the shootdown, Clinton was pursuing a policy of *constructive engagement* (translation: "appeasement") with Castro, following the standard liberal philosophy that if you are nice to murdering tyrants, they will be nice in return. Though the embargo implemented under the Cuban Democracy Act of 1992 was working and causing Castro's power to crumble, Clinton began easing sanctions after he came to office in order to open a dialogue with the dictator. (As any Cuban exile will tell you, the only dialogue a man of Castro's record deserves is, "Blindfold— sí or no?")

Clinton continued his dialogue with Castro even after July 1994, when Cuban ships rammed a slow, overloaded boat crammed with refugees, sinking it and drowning thirty-seven men, women, and children at sea. Clinton continued his dialogue after Castro crushed Concilio Cubano, Cuba's version of the Solidarity freedom movement. And in early 1995, Clinton even aided Castro in oppressing the Cuban people by sending back freedom-seeking Cuban refugees who had made it to American shores. As Castro's reign of death and terror increased in ferocity, Clinton spoke of Cuba's "peaceful transition to a free and open society." When Bill Clinton reaches out to the monster that Cuban exiles call "El Diablo," "Bola de Churre," and several names unprintable in any language, he only delays the day of *Cuba Libre,* "Free Cuba."

After the Brothers to the Rescue shootdown, the U.S. passed the Helms-Burton Act, tightening the economic noose around Castro by punishing companies that do business with Cuba. It says, in effect, "You can do business with Castro and his socialist paradise, or you can do business with the U.S.—but not both." Clinton didn't want to sign Helms-Burton, but it soon became clear that if he vetoed Helms-Burton, he would not only be embarrassed by a veto override but he would appear to be "coddling dictators" (the same charge he used against George Bush in the campaign).

So Clinton bit his lower lip and said, "I sign this bill into law in the name of the four men who were killed when their planes were shot down—Armando Alejandre, Carlos Costa, Mario de la Pena, and Pablo Morales. In their memory, I will continue to do everything I can to help the tide of democracy that has swept our entire hemisphere finally, finally reach the shores of Cuba." Then, almost immediately after signing Helms-Burton, he turned right around and signed an executive order suspending the key provision of the act![14]

The Soviet Union was brought down because Ronald Reagan did everything in his power to destabilize and weaken the Soviet system. Bill Clinton could and should be taking the same action to produce the same results in the remaining communist states, China, Korea, and Cuba. Instead, he engages in policies that strengthen, prop up, and artificially extend the life span of these oppressive, murderous regimes. The collapse of Cuba's sponsor state, the USSR, demonstrated the true weakness of the Cuban system.

Castro cannot remain in power without outside help. The Cuban sugar crop has failed, and Cuba no longer receives Soviet oil, military assistance, and funding. Unfortunately, other Western nations have rushed in to fill the void left by the fallen USSR, and Bill Clinton refuses to do anything about it.

The future of American foreign policy requires leadership that is visionary and principled. A president who lacks a clear sense of vision, purpose, and direction in foreign policy is doomed to remain in a reactive rather than proactive role. Until we elect principled, visionary leadership to watch the stormy horizon of America's future, we deserve what we get.

SHINING CITY— OR GLOBAL NEIGHBORHOOD?

Our own sovereignty is not for sale.

Ronald Reagan
First Inaugural Address
January 20, 1981

It was leadership here at home that gave us strong American influence abroad, and the collapse of imperial Communism. Great nations have responsibilities to lead, and we should always be cautious of those who would lower our profile, because they might just wind up lowering our flag.

Ronald Reagan
Speech before the
Republican National Committee Annual Gala
Washington, D.C., February 3, 1994

The brightest symbol of hope for the world is found in New York City. No, it's not that glass-walled, slab-shaped building on the East River. It's the lady with the torch in New York Harbor. America, not the UN, is the Shining City on a Hill. We need to be reminded of Ronald Reagan's words when he rededicated the Statue of Liberty in 1986:

Call it mysticism if you will, but I have always believed there was some divine providence that placed this great land here between the two great oceans, to be found by a special kind of people from every corner of the world, who had a special love for freedom and a special courage that enabled them to leave their own land, leave their friends and their countrymen, and come to this new and strange land to build a new world of peace and freedom and hope.

America's mission in the world is to point the way to peace and freedom and hope. The blessings of liberty are the birthright of all people, all around the world. That is why Abraham Lincoln called this great land "the last best hope of man on earth." Here in this country, we have been called to show the world what freedom means, what freedom costs, and what freedom accomplishes in the world. America is industrious, brilliant, and prosperous because she is free.

Yes, the UN and international cooperation and multinational peacekeeping forces do have a place in the world. But we should never view the UN as a supergovernment to which America owes allegiance. America is a sovereign nation and Americans are a sovereign people. While we care about the world, we should not be the caretakers of the world. We must not submit our sovereignty to the UN or to any other power, nor should we isolate ourselves from the rest of the world. We must lead the world. That is our mission as citizens of the City on a Hill.

The Clintonistas don't see America as a Shining City. The vision of Bill Clinton and his team of globalists is not to magnify the light of America's freedom but to magnify the power of what they call "the world body," the United Nations. The organization that was chartered in 1945 as a cooperative family of nations is on its way to becoming a supergovernment. The Clinton vision of the New World Order was spelled out by Strobe Talbott, Clinton's Oxford roommate and deputy secretary of state, in a magazine piece he wrote shortly before Clinton was elected. In "Birth of the Global Nation" (*Time*, July 20, 1992), Talbot predicted, "Nationhood as we know it will be obsolete; all states will recognize a single global authority. . . . 'Citizen of the world' will have assumed real meaning."

It is understandable that the idealists of the left would romanticize this idea of a "borderless world." After all, if there were no nations, there would be no need for nukes. Maybe this utopian ideal is one reason the left is so stubbornly opposed to what is an obviously good idea, SDI. A Star Wars missile defense is designed to preserve national sovereignty and security. If we render nukes obsolete with SDI technology, we dilute the urgency to unite the world under a single socialist government.

From Rush Limbaugh to Bill Clinton, today's opinion leaders scorn "conspiracy kooks" who worry about globalism. They lump all discussion of a one-world government in the same category with black helicopters, the Illuminati, Elvis sightings, and UFOs hiding in the tail of the Hale-Bopp comet. But the fact is, right here in the real world, the United Nations Commision on Global Governance has completed a three-year study with plans to implement global governance by the year 2000. You won't read about it in your newspaper or hear about it on CNN, but you can read the entire plan for yourself in a 410-page UN report, *Our Global Neighbourhood,* published by Oxford University Press ($14.95)—or you can download the entire document from the Global Governance website at http://www.cgg.ch/contents.htm. It begins with a disclaimer that the UN global governance plan "does not imply world government or world federalism," but the rest of the book is a blueprint for exactly that—a one-world government built around a "global civic ethic" based on "a set of core values that can unite people of all cultural, political, religious, or philosophical backgrounds." Believe it. The New World Order is gonna be in your face before you know it. Following is how the one-worlders plan to do it.

They will impose socialism and equality of outcome on an entire planet through *global trade and economic policy.* GATT is a first step in that direction, but plans are being drawn for the creation of a UN Economic Security Council that would centralize all international finance, industry, and trade policy under one global authority. Existing agencies such as the World Bank, the World Trade Organization, and the International Monetary Fund would function under the aegis of the Economic Security Council, consisting of twenty-three individuals chosen from around the world.

The globalists will impose *global taxation* to fund the UN and redistribute wealth on a global scale. Global tax schemes range from individual income taxes on the entire world's population to taxes on all international financial transactions (which is projected to produce $1.5 trillion annually—about 150 times the current UN budget). America was founded as a revolt against taxation without representation; the day an American president, an American Congress, and the American people submit to global control and global taxation, America is history, sayonara, outta here, gone.

The globalists plan to overrule national sovereignty through *global environmental policy.* This is a stealth process of chipping away at our national sovereignty through such seemingly laudable goals as protecting the ecosystem. We see it taking place through global "nongovernment organizations" (or NGOs)—the International Union for the Conservation of Nature

(IUCN), the United Nations Environment Programme (UNEP), the World Resources Institute, the Earth Council, and ultimately a proposed "Assembly of the People," which would be elected by the world at large and would promote environmental policy in the UN. We see our national sovereignty being chipped away through the policies and pronouncements from the United Nations Conference on Environment and Development (the Rio de Janeiro "Earth Summit," 1992) and its follow-up conferences. We see it promoted in such documents as the Earth Summit's "Agenda XXI" and the Conventions on Climate Change, Biodiversity, Ozone Depleting Substances, Desertification, Endangered Species, Wetlands, and World Heritage Sites.

The globalists' agenda is embedded in such buzzwords as *re-wilding* and *sustainable development,* which sum up the global environmentalists' belief that industrialized human society is a cancer on the planet, and that the only hope for Mother Earth is a return to a planetwide preindustrial, Third World standard of living; radical cuts in the consumption of energy, raw materials, food, and water; central planning of the world economy; global eco-indoc-trination and family planning goals; and of course the abolition of national sovereignty. Globalists talk about a "growing gap between the world's rich and poor" and the "environmental jeopardy" caused by "unbridled con-sumerism in the North" that "despoils the integrity of the earth." Their solution is to impoverish America and spread the misery around the planet.

Most Americans are unaware that global environmentalism has already resulted in a UN takeover of many of our national parks and historical sites. The takeover began with the World Heritage Treaty drafted by the UN Educational, Scientific, and Cultural Organization (UNESCO) in 1972. (UN watchers consider UNESCO to be one of the most corrupt agencies in the entire UN bureaucracy.) Under the World Heritage Treaty, the UN has al-ready taken over eighteen so-called "World Heritage Sites." An additional forty-eight Biosphere Reserve sites have been handed over to UNESCO's Man and the Biosphere program by the U.S. State Department without any treaty or congressional oversight whatsoever. Natural Heritage sites include Carlsbad Caverns, Glacier National Park, the Florida Everglades, and Yel-lowstone National Park. Cultural Heritage sites include—are you ready for this?—the Statue of Liberty and Independence Hall in Philadelphia!

We can expect to see even more *UN-ization of our military*—the use of our own young men and women, our own tax-bought matériel, in causes other than our own national defense and security. This is an insult and a dishonor to all those who, over the past two hundred-plus years, gave their last measure of devotion to the defense of America's freedom and security. Our freedom is so sacred that thousands of American soldiers have willingly suffered dismemberment or death to defend it, and the liberal one-worlders in our own government are willing to surrender our sovereignty, security, and fighting forces to foreign powers without a whimper.

The globalists are also using *food and population scares* to give the UN leverage over national sovereignty. The 1996 World Food Summit in Rome produced mountains of stupidity but not an ounce of real hope for the hungry people of the world. If adopted, the Food Summit's agenda would produce *less* food in the world, not more. The Food Summit focused on sustainable growth plans for more population control, more abortions, the placement of usable land off-limits to farming and development, and world-wide adoption of organic food production. (Organic methods are wasteful and ineffective because they reject the use of pesticides and require more land to produce smaller yields.) Almost nothing was said at the Summit about using new high-yielding hybrid seeds and environmentally friendly fertilizers and pesticides to double food production in the have-not nations. According to *USA Today,* the star of the Food Summit was that beloved humanitarian, Fidel Castro, who spoke glowingly of the need for more government-imposed birth control.

The Food Summit hyped a crisis where no crisis exists. The world is not getting hungrier every day. While the world population has doubled since 1960, the percentage of those without enough to eat has dropped from 35 percent to 20 percent. Food has become about 40 percent cheaper (in real, adjusted-for-inflation terms) throughout the world. The doomsayers claim the world is running out of room and resources. The truth is that the entire population of the planet could be comfortably housed within the borders of the state of Texas by placing only eight people to an acre—and each family could sustain and feed itself by devoting as little as 20 percent of its space to raising food with artificial light and hydroponics (the raising of food in nutrient-enriched water). Thanks to rapid advances in agricultural technology, food can be produced more abundantly and efficiently today than ever before, but the UN's World Food Summit would put a stop to that.[15]

The solution to world hunger is not centralized control of food production or the elimination of pesticides. Nor is the solution to abort more of the world's children. The solution is *freedom*. Nicholas Eberstadt of the American Enterprise Institute put it this way: "Political freedom is the enemy of famine. And economic liberty is the foe of hunger." He points to Vietnam as proof of the value of freedom in feeding people. For years after the end of the Vietnam War, the collective, state-controlled farms of Communist Vietnam could not produce enough rice to feed the people of the country. In 1986, the government conducted an economic experiment, breaking up collectives and giving people their own land to farm while allowing food prices to find their own level. Three years later, Vietnam had become the third-largest exporter of rice in the world. That's the power of freedom. If you want to feed the world, get rid of government price controls, import quotas, and subsidies; feed the world with freedom.[16]

The UN also plans to *strip America of its world leadership position.* In the UN's "global neighborhood," veto power and permanent status would be stripped from the five permanent nations of the UN Security Council—China, France, Great Britain, Russia, and the United States. This would dilute, if not abolish, the leadership role of America. Also, the Economic Security Council would collect the wealth produced by the citizens of developed nations and redistribute it to developing societies. The Clinton administration is helping to sponsor the 1998 World Conference on Global Governance, and can be expected to campaign hard to elect liberal Democrats to Congress in 1998 so that the UN global governance treaties and agreements can be more easily ratified. The world needs the illumination and moral leadership of the Shining City on a Hill, but there are those in many nations and within our own government who want to place a shroud over the City and hide its light from the world.

"Shut up and pay up" is the message of the global bureaucracy to the Shining City. The United Nations doesn't want our influence—just our affluence. From former UN secretary general Boutros Boutros-Ghali to new secretary general Kofi Annan, from Bill Clinton to Newt Gingrich, we have been hearing about a U.S. "debt" of $1.4 billion to the United Nations. Some in the UN bureaucracy have been floating plans to cut off our UN voting rights, slap us with late charges, and ban U.S. citizens from holding UN jobs if the Congress doesn't cough up. The fact is, the U.S. doesn't owe the UN a dime. Instead, the UN owes the American taxpayers—big time.

Our globalist president, Bill Clinton, has tried to shame his own country, calling America "the biggest piker in the UN."[17] But the U.S. has always been more than generous with the bloated, wasteful, and anti-American world bureaucracy. Our normal UN assessments are 25 percent of the operating budget and 31 percent of peacekeeping costs. (The next largest contributor is Japan, with an assessment of 14 percent of the budget; only

Russia, Germany, France, Great Britain, Italy, Spain, and Canada contributed more than 2 percent.) But on top of our normal assessment, the U.S. provided some $6.6 billion in logistical and other support to the UN from 1992 to 1995. Of that money, the global bean counters on the East River credited $1.8 billion against our so-called debt! Of the remaining $4.8 billion, the UN reimbursed us for less than $80 million. Those are General Accounting Office figures.[18] So we should not write a check for $1.4 billion to the UN. We should deduct that amount from the $4.8 billion credit the UN now owes us, then submit an invoice for $3.4 billion!

Who has been spending all this American money on dubious UN peacekeeping missions? It wasn't the U.S. Congress, through the legal appropriations process. No, this money came out of the budgets of various federal agencies (including the Department of Defense) without congressional approval—which is at least improper and probably illegal. The Clinton administration looted the budgets of these agencies in order to support the global governance of the UN.

At a White House press conference on March 8, 1997, Sarah McClendon of the McClendon News Service lobbed this mushball question to Bill Clinton: "Large segments of our citizens believe that the United Nations is taking over whole blocks of counties in Kentucky and Tennessee. They believe that you're going to give our army to Russia and all that baloney. Can you do something about this? Because it's hurting the unity of the United States."

The question set off gales of laughter throughout the White House press corps and put a smile on Clinton's face. "I dunno." Clinton chuckled. "Because the people who believe that think I'm the problem. We're all laughing about it, but there is a not-insubstantial number of people who believe there's a plan out there for world domination and I'm trying to give American sovereignty over to the UN. Let me just say this: For those that are worried about it, I would say there is a serious issue here that every American has to come to grips with. The issue is, we live in an interdependent world. We have to cooperate with people. We're better off when we do. We're better off with NATO, we're better off with the United Nations, we're better off when these countries can work together. So I just think, for folks that are worried about this out in the country, they need to be thinking about how—We're not going to give up our freedom, our independence. But we're not going to go it alone into the twenty-first century, either. We're going to work together, and we have to."

President Clinton's answer is not a denial. It's an admission. We live, he says, in an interdependent world and we're better off with the UN and we can't go it alone. He laughs at the suggestion that he is ceding American sovereignty to the UN—but he doesn't deny it. Because he can't. His actions show that this is *exactly* what he is doing—surrendering to an alien power our hard-won leadership position in the world, our wealth, our young men and women in the armed forces, our national parks and historical sites, our authority over our own environmental policies, food policy, population policy, economic and trade policies, and more.

America must make a choice, because there is no middle ground. We can either become the Shining City on a Hill that Ronald Reagan envisioned, or we can cross Bill Clinton's bridge to the twenty-first century, a bridge to a Brave New World of global governance, in which the light of the Shining City is snuffed out by the darkness of a global socialist bureaucracy. Will America continue to be the "last best hope of man on earth"? Or will America become a memory of what almost was and what could have been?

My friend, *we* will decide that question.

CHAPTER TEN

BUILDING

THE CITY

TOGETHER

HE BROUGHT US
ALL TOGETHER

*In this springtime of hope, some lights seem eternal;
America's is.*

Ronald Reagan
Acceptance speech
Republican National Convention
Dallas, Texas, August 23, 1984

Dad was having lunch at the White House with the network TV anchors, briefing them in preparation for the State of the Union address later that evening. In the middle of the briefing, several members of the White House staff rushed in, interrupting the briefing. "It's the space shuttle *Challenger*," one of them said breathlessly. "It exploded in midair!"

"Oh, no," said Dad in a stricken voice. "It's the shuttle with the teacher aboard." Ashen-faced, he rose from the table. Trailed by his aides, he strode quickly down a hallway to an office with a television set. There, along with millions of stunned Americans, he watched the video of the explosion as it was played and replayed, again and again. Silent and horror-struck, he thought back to the day the teacher-astronaut, Christa McAuliffe, stood beside him at a White House ceremony, her face beaming with excitement as he introduced America's first teacher in space.

251

The State of the Union address was canceled. Dad placed calls to the families of the astronauts, offering what little comfort he could. Every one of the family members stressed to him that America's space program had to continue despite the disaster. That is what the astronauts themselves would have wanted. That evening, January 28, 1986, Dad went before a single television camera in the Oval Office and told the nation,

> We mourn seven heroes: Michael Smith, Dick Scobee, Judith Resnik, Ronald McNair, Ellison Onizuka, Gregory Jarvis, and Christa McAuliffe. We mourn their loss as a nation together.
>
> For the families of the seven, we cannot bear, as you do, the full impact of this tragedy. But we feel the loss, and we're thinking about you so very much. Your loved ones were daring and brave, and they had that special grace, that special spirit that says, "Give me a challenge and I'll meet it with joy." They had a hunger to explore the universe and discover its truths. They wished to serve, and they did.
>
> I want to say something to the schoolchildren of America who were watching the live coverage of the shuttle's takeoff. I know it is hard to understand, but sometimes painful things like this happen. It's all part of the process of exploration and discovery. It's all part of taking a chance and expanding man's horizons. The future doesn't belong to the fainthearted; it belongs to the brave. The *Challenger* crew was pulling us into the future, and we'll continue to follow them. . . .
>
> Nothing ends here; our hopes and our journeys continue. The crew of the space shuttle *Challenger* honored us by the manner in which they lived their lives. We will never forget them, nor the last time we saw them, this morning, as they prepared for their journey and waved good-bye and "slipped the surly bonds of earth" to "touch the face of God."

You could see the profound pain in my father's eyes as he said those words. It was genuine. It was America's grief and agony, etched in the face of one American man. Though he only spoke for five minutes, he placed the shock and grief of the nation's loss in an eternal perspective. As he spoke those closing lines, borrowed from the poem "High Flight" by John Gillespie Magee Jr.,[1] the camera pulled back. Seated alone behind his Oval Office desk, he seemed more wounded than when I saw him in that hospital bed after he was shot.

The red light on the television camera winked out. Dad sat back in his chair and sighed. Several White House aides stepped forward, saying, "Wonderful job, Mr. President."

Dad shook his head, the anguish of the nation still written across his features. "I don't know," he said sadly. "I don't think I did it very well."

"It was perfect, Mr. President. Just what the nation needed to hear."

"I don't think I did it justice," Dad insisted. "Of course, what can you do with words at a time like this?"

It's said that Lincoln had the same sense of letdown, of failure, after delivering the Gettysburg Address, yet today schoolchildren memorize Lincoln's powerful words. After his address to the nation on the *Challenger* disaster, Dad felt he had failed. But in the hours that followed his televised speech, telegrams and phone calls flooded the White House. Over the next few days, the White House mail room was also overwhelmed with response. "Thank you, Mr. President, for your words of comfort at such a sad time," said the people of America. "Thank you for helping our family, and especially our children, deal with this terrible loss."

In a time of unspeakable national trauma, Ronald Reagan brought us all together. He brought us together when 248 soldiers of the 101st Airborne died in a crash near Gander, Newfoundland, on their way home for Christmas after peacekeeping duties in the Middle East. He brought us together after a terrorist bomb at a marines barracks in Lebanon killed 240 marines and one sailor—more American servicemen killed than in any single engagement of the Vietnam War.

We remember Ronald and Nancy Reagan, their arms wrapped around the ones whose loss was beyond words. We remember the little boy who reached out to the president at the memorial service for his daddy, who was killed when an Iraqi fighter jet fired a missile into the U.S.S. *Stark* on patrol in the Persian Gulf. "Sir," the little boy said, "please bring my daddy home." And Ronald Reagan could do nothing but hug the boy, trying to absorb some of the boy's loss and pain. When the sorrow of our nation has seemed too deep to be borne, Ronald Reagan embraced America. He brought us all together.

The day my father first stood on the west side of the Capitol to take his oath of office, America was a deeply anguished, divided nation. We had gone through the long national nightmare of the Iranian hostage crisis. We had endured years of oil embargoes, double-digit inflation, unemployment, national malaise, and entrenched pessimism. America seemed weak and impotent, hemmed in by enemies, a once-great power succumbing to the inevitability of decline. We were divided over what to do about the Soviet Union, about our hollow military, about our deepening economic crisis. But over the next eight years, Ronald Reagan brought us all together.

The day of his inauguration as the fortieth president of the United States, my father placed his left hand upon the well-worn, well-marked Bible of his late mother, raised his right hand, and took the oath of office as prescribed by the Constitution. The Bible was open, and his hand rested on the words God spoke to King Solomon in 2 Chronicles 7:14:

> If My people who are called by My name will humble themselves, and pray and seek My face, and turn from their wicked ways, then I will hear from heaven, and will forgive their sin and heal their land.

In the margin next to that verse, his mother had written, *A most wonderful verse for the healing of the nations.* And America did undergo a miraculous healing over the next eight years—in large part, I believe, because America was led by a president who had dedicated his life and his presidency to serving God.

When we listened to Ronald Reagan describe his vision of the Shining City on a Hill, we were all inspired with a sense of our destiny as an American people. He truly made us believe that God placed America between the two great oceans to be a beacon to the world. He inspired us with the sense that America is more than just a place on a map, more than just a time line in a history book. America is a great people with a great idea, carrying out a great purpose by pointing the way to hope and freedom on this dark and troubled planet.

In a time of national malaise, despair, and darkness, Ronald Reagan brought us together. His wise words and his vision for America are still fresh and alive. He brought us together in those days; his vision for America can bring us together in the days ahead.

YOU AIN'T SEEN NOTHIN' YET!

They say the world has become too complex for simple answers. They are wrong. There are no easy answers, but there are simple answers. We must have the courage to do what we know is morally right.

Ronald Reagan
"A Time for Choosing"
Televised speech on behalf of
presidential candidate Barry Goldwater
October 27, 1964

The blueprint for the Shining City on a Hill is actually quite simple. Ideally, the City has four districts, and each is the same size. One district does not dominate any of the other three. They are equal in influence and responsibility. The four equal districts are:

- "The Neighborhood" (the American family)
- "The Corner of Faith and Charity" (the religious and civic sector)
- "Main Street" (the business and industrial sector)
- "The City Square" (the government)

According to liberal Big Brother ideology, it is the all-powerful government that solves the vast majority of society's problems. But as Ronald Reagan said throughout his career, "Government does not solve problems. It subsidizes them." And, "Government is not the solution to our problem; government *is* the problem." And, "In America, *people* solve problems." The agenda I've presented in this book is a plan for taking the problem-solving responsibility away from the government and giving it back to the people. It's a plan for taking the money and power that government has usurped, and redistributing it to the other three districts of the city where it belongs.

We'll dismantle the welfare state, load the pieces into a big U-Haul truck, and move it to the Corner of Faith and Charity. We'll take a wrecking ball to the Department of Education, and we'll build our local schoolhouse out in the Neighborhood where it belongs, and where it can be responsive to

255

local values and needs. We'll drive a steamroller through the center of the City and flatten the tax rates so that families in the Neighborhood can keep more of what they earn. We'll slay the regulatory monster and balance the budget. Then we'll watch the wealth-producing dynamos on Main Street roar to life.

Government—the City Square—will always have a crucial role to play in our Shining City on a Hill. But we will carefully limit that role. The federal government will not perform functions that can be managed at the state or local level, and no level of government will do what people can do for themselves. That will leave the federal government free to concentrate on its primary functions: establishing justice, ensuring domestic tranquillity, providing for the common defense. As government shrinks, taxes will fall, the budget will balance, and the national debt can finally be paid down.

And the futures of our children and our children's children will finally be secured.

It's time to open a national dialogue about personal responsibility, smaller government, empowered families, a thriving business sector, and a compassionate society. It's time to begin the world again.

This is not some idealistic vision of a utopian future. This is a realistic and achievable blueprint for a new society. It is not merely what we *can* do. It is what we *must* do. As currently structured, our overtaxed, top-heavy society is destined to collapse from the weight of its own bureaucracy, debt, and social decay. As it now stands, America can last a few decades at most. If we do not begin *right now* to return our nation to its constitutional form of small government, strong families, active charities, and thriving businesses, we cannot expect America to survive into the next millennium.

The Shining City on a Hill is a simple blueprint, but it is not simplistic. It's easy to understand, but it won't be easy to build. Why? Because it represents change—and there will always be people who resist change, even when it is clearly a change for the better. There will be opposition and criticism. There will be fear. But I believe we can withstand the opposition. We can counter the criticism; we can allay the fear. We can build the Shining City on a Hill. I know we can.

As my father told the nation on the day he took office, the task of renewing America requires "our best effort, and our willingness to believe in ourselves and to believe in our capacity to perform great deeds; to believe that together, with God's help, we can and will resolve the problems which now confront us. And, after all, why shouldn't we believe that? We are Americans."

Americans are by nature a responsible, self-reliant, and compassionate people. If government will get out of our way, we'll get the job done. As we expect less of government and more of ourselves, Ronald Reagan's vision for America will finally be fulfilled. With the Shining City on a Hill as our vision, we can face the uncertain future as my father faced it, even in the shadow of a terrible illness, confident that whatever happens in this life, for America there will always be a bright dawn ahead.

As Dad so often said, "You ain't seen nothin' yet!"

ONE MORE
FOR THE GIPPER

And I hope that someday your children and grandchildren will tell of the time that a certain president came to town at the end of a long journey and asked their parents and grandparents to join him in setting America on the course to the new millennium—and that a century of peace, prosperity, opportunity, and hope followed. So, if I could ask you just one last time: Tomorrow, when mountains greet the dawn, would you go out there and win one for the Gipper?

Ronald Reagan
Speech at a campaign rally for
Vice President George Bush
San Diego, California,
November 7, 1988

In December 1979, at the request of the Reagan campaign, I went to Iowa to campaign for Dad. The Iowa caucuses in January would be the first battleground of the primaries. Dad's campaign head, John Sears, was running him as if he were already the president, having him make only a few appearances while his chief rival, George Bush, relentlessly crisscrossed the state.

I spent four or five days in Iowa, going to coffee klatches and bridge clubs, downing fourteen cups of coffee and nineteen doughnuts before 8:00 in the morning. I shook hands until my palms were raw. I talked to the

Reagan supporters in Iowa, and they were worried about how Dad was doing in the state where he had been a favorite son since his days on WHO radio in Des Moines. "We've been trying to get ahold of your dad," they said, "because he's got big problems here in Iowa. He needs to get out here and campaign. But every time we try to call your dad, we get John Sears, and he says Ronald Reagan isn't available."

I said, "I'll see what I can do." So I called Dad at home. "Dad," I said, "I'm in Iowa."

"Iowa? What are you doing in Iowa, Michael?"

"Campaigning for you. Your campaign office asked me to come out here, so here I am. And Dad, I have to tell you, you're gonna get beat by George Bush if you don't make an appearance."

"Why do you say that?"

"I say that because I've been all over the state, talking to people, and the word out in the cornfield is that people think you've forgotten your roots. They say you think you're better than the good people of Iowa. Dad, George Bush doesn't speak the language of Iowa, he can't communicate with these people like you can—but he's gonna win because he's here and you're not."

"Well, Michael," said Dad, "I just got off the phone with John Sears and Charlie Black, and they say things look very good for me in Iowa, and there's no reason for concern. I'm paying these fellas a lot of money for their professional opinion, so I have to be guided by what they tell me."

"Dad, I just want to be on record about this."

"Okay, Michael, you're on record. And thank you for all you're doing."

Well, Dad got beat in Iowa, just like I said he would. George Bush roared out of Iowa caucuses with a lot of momentum—"the Big Mo," he called it. Suddenly the New Hampshire primary on February 26 had become a make-or-break situation. If Ronald Reagan didn't score big in New Hampshire, his quest for the White House was over.

Dad would have to do two things to win the nomination and the White House. First, he had to get mad. Most of us in the Reagan family, from Nancy to Maureen and myself, felt that Dad needed to show more fire. Ronald Reagan is an amiable man who almost never shows anger—a frown of disappointment is about as wrathful as he gets. We thought a little righteous indignation now and then would give him that aura of decisiveness all presidents must project.

A few days before the New Hampshire primary, Dad and George Bush were scheduled to debate in Nashua. When the other candidates—Bob

Dole, John Anderson, Howard Baker, John Connolly, and Phil Crane—
learned that the *Nashua Telegraph* was sponsoring a debate excluding them,
they were incensed. Dole filed a complaint with the Federal Elections Commission, claiming the newspaper's sponsorship amounted to a donation to
the Bush and Reagan campaigns.[2] The FEC agreed, so Dad suggested to the
Bush camp that they simply split the cost of the debate between them. The
Bush people refused, so the Reagan campaign offered to pay the entire cost,
a few thousand dollars. Bush accepted.

Since Dad was footing the bill, he figured he could invite anyone he
wanted—so he invited the other candidates. All but Connolly showed up.
When the Bush people saw the other candidates, they went ballistic! No way
would their guy debate five other candidates—Bush was here to debate
Reagan, period. Bush sat in his chair with his arms folded. Dad sat in the
other chair at the table. The four wanna-be debaters stood fidgeting behind
Dad. It was an embarrassing standoff in front of a few thousand restless New
Hampshirites who wanted to get this show on the road! As Dad's people and
Bush's people argued, the audience began hooting and stomping.

Hoping to quiet the crowd, Dad leaned toward his microphone and
attempted to explain. But as Dad was talking, the moderator—*Nashua Telegraph* editor Jon Breen—shouted to the sound engineer, "Turn Mr. Reagan's
microphone off!"

Well, Mr. Breen may have been the moderator of the debate, but he
didn't pay the sound engineer's salary—Dad did. There was a spark of ire in
his voice as he growled, "I'm paying for this microphone, Mr. Breen!" (Actually, Dad called him "Mr. Green"—he was never very good with names.)

As soon as Dad said that, the entire audience erupted in cheers and
applause. It was an electric moment in the campaign. People thought, *Hey,
there's a tough side to Ronald Reagan!* Dad said his campaign turned the
corner during those moments in a Nashua high-school gymnasium.

The second thing Ronald Reagan needed to do to win the nomination
and the White House took place on the very day of the New Hampshire
primary. I was awakened very early that day by a phone call from Dad. He
rarely calls unless I've embarrassed the family in some way. So when I
answered the phone and heard Dad say, "Hello, Michael, it's Dad," I
thought, *Ohmigosh, what have I done now?*

A little hesitantly, I replied, "Hi, Dad. How're you doing?"

"Fine, fine," he said. "I'm calling from New Hampshire. You know,
they're voting in the primary today."

"Yeah," I said. "It's in all the papers."

"Well, I have a statement I'm preparing to release to the press, and I just wanted to get your approval before I did so."

I was shocked. "My approval?" I asked. "Why in the world would you need my approval on a statement to the press?"

"Because, Michael, you're the only one who would understand it."

Still baffled, I said, "Okay, Dad."

So he read the statement to me. It was an announcement that he had asked for the resignations of John Sears and Charlie Black. He was replacing Sears with William Casey, former chairman of the Securities and Exchange Commission. After reading the statement, he said, "What do you think?" I was really touched. Dad came from a generation that didn't say to their kids (even their adult kids), "You were right and I was wrong." But in his own way, that's what he had just told me: I was right about John Sears and the loss in Iowa.

"Dad," I said, "I think it's terrific."

"Then I have your approval to release this to the press?"

"Yes, Dad, you have my approval. But can I ask you another question?"

"What's that?"

"Are you gonna win the primary today?"

"Oh, yes," he replied, "we're going to win. In fact, we knew we were going to win right after the Nashua debate. That night, as we were walking out of the gymnasium, it was as if we were walking on crickets, because the ground was littered with Bush buttons. The opinion polls only confirmed what we already knew."

After the polls closed later that day, Dad was proved exactly right. In a seven-way race, he finished with 51 percent of the vote. From then on, he campaigned hard, and he won almost every primary. By the end of the road, he had defeated the GOP hierarchy's handpicked candidate, George Bush.

There's a lesson in that for all of us who want to see Ronald Reagan's dream fulfilled. In order to keep the Reagan vision alive, the Republican Party must regain the confidence of grassroots America. It must become once more the party of Lincoln and Reagan. To do that, we must take the party out of the hands of these anything-for-a-buck consultants who work only for greed and not for principle, and we must hand the party over to a new generation of vibrant young people who are committed to the vision.

The people who nearly sank Ronald Reagan's campaign—people like John Sears and Charlie Black—are still around. To this day, their résumés claim that they helped Ronald Reagan get elected. They helped by walking out the door after Ronald Reagan *fired* them! And where are those guys today? John Sears worked as a strategist for Steve Forbes's '96 primary campaign and for Bob Dole's '96 general election campaign. After the election, he signed on as a consultant to Jack Kemp for a presidential bid in the year 2000. Advice to Jack Kemp: Go ahead and listen to John Sears—as long as you do the *opposite* of everything he tells you.

It was Sears who counseled candidate Dole to avoid the "character issues"—Clinton's lack of honesty, and his ethical problems with Whitewater, Filegate, and Lippogate. Late in the campaign, when Dole finally started hitting those issues, it smelled of desperation. When both the media and Bob Dole gave Clinton a free ride on those issues, voters concluded that character and truth don't matter.

And what about Charlie Black, whom Ronald Reagan fired the same day he fired John Sears? He's CEO of the PR and lobbying firm of Black, Manafort, Stone, & Kelly. He's also the "genius" (note the quotes) who steered both the Bush-Quayle '92 campaign and Phil Gramm's '96 primary bid straight into a brick wall. Charlie Black, Paul Manafort, and Roger Stone have largely worked with GOP candidates, but also with Democrats. And their partner, Peter G. Kelly, is a prominent Democrat who has worked for liberal candidates and causes—including serving as Al Gore's top fundraiser!

From what I've seen, people like John Sears and Charlie Black don't give a rodent's rear bumper about the Republican cause or conservative values. They care about accounts receivable, period. So why do Republicans like Forbes, Gramm, Kemp, and Dole keep hiring these hucksters? For the life of me, I couldn't tell you. But I'll tell you this: We need people who care about the City on a Hill—people who want to *advance* the conservative agenda, not pimp it.

We don't need more media manipulation. We just need more leaders with character and conviction. We don't need more consultants and focus groups. We just need a few people with the courage to stand up for what they believe, people like—

Well, like Ronald Reagan.

He brought the Republican Party back from the black hole of Watergate, and gave the common, decent people of America reason to believe in the Republican Party once more. But the Grand Old Party has not been paying attention lately to either the Reagan legacy or grassroots Americans. The good people of this nation have begun to feel (deservedly so) that the Republican Party is taking them for granted.

Republican presidential candidates have twice been defeated by a Democratic candidate who is clearly the most corrupt and scandal-plagued president in American history, a candidate with a proven record of lies and broken promises, a candidate who has never commanded a majority of the popular vote. A lot of Republicans blamed the loss in '96 on special prosecutor Kenneth Starr. They ask, "Why didn't Starr keep Clinton from being re-elected? He's got the goods on Bill and Hillary—why didn't he indict them before the election?"

Wait a minute! It's not Kenneth Starr's job to win the election for the Republicans. That's the Republicans' job. If the Republican Party couldn't get the job done, we have to ask ourselves: Why not? Clearly, one of the reasons the Republicans lost the '96 election was that they had lost touch with grassroots America.

In March of 1997, I shocked a lot of people by announcing that I was leaving the Republican Party. There were stories in the *London Telegraph* and the *Washington Times,* and I got calls from CNN and Fox News inviting me to come on the air and explain what it all meant—a Reagan leaving the Republican Party! A lot of people told me that, because my name is Reagan, I owed an allegiance to the party my father made popular. But you know what? A lot *more* people cheered me. They were ecstatic that something was happening to shake up the party, that someone was desperately trying to return the GOP to its Reaganite ideals. I had struck a responsive chord with Ronald Reagan's America.

It's just like what happened to Dad when he was a New Deal Democrat. He realized that while he was giving speeches about the decline of America, he was voting for the very people who contributed to that decline. One day, he woke up and realized that he hadn't left the Democratic Party—the party had left him! In 1962, while Dad was giving a speech in Pacific Palisades, a woman stood up in the middle of his speech and asked him if he had registered Republican yet. Dad said, "No, but I intend to," and the woman walked up the aisle, shoved a registration form at him and said, "I'm a registrar. Sign here." So Dad signed and became a Republican right on the spot—then continued on with his speech.

In 1997, I found myself in a similar situation. I didn't leave the Republican Party, the party left me. I'm right where I was all along, right where Ronald Reagan led this party. It's the party that's jumped the tracks, not me.

I'm not a politician looking for votes. I'm a talk show host looking for truth. And the truth is that Republican leaders have forgotten why they were sent to Washington in the first place. On issue after issue, they've walked away from the very principles that gave them the majority in both houses.

I didn't quit the party over one issue, but over a whole cloud of issues, adding up to what I saw as an attitude of retreat and defeat within the GOP. The Republican Speaker, Newt Gingrich, caved to the liberal Democrats by declaring that the most fundamental of all grassroots issues—tax cuts—were off the table for 1997. He went on to announce that there would be no Republican legislative agenda until the year 2000. The congressional committees looking into illegal campaign financing capitulated to the Democrats, agreeing to examine legal Republican campaign practices alongside illegal contributions to Democrats. The Republicans also bailed out on defunding the Department of Education, on defunding the National Endowment for the Arts, on raising the minimum wage, and so much more.

Every day I open the newspaper, hoping for some sign that the Republicans have grown a backbone—and every day I find that the Republican majority has caved on yet another issue. Haven't Republicans learned why the Rockefeller Republicans, the moderate-to-liberal Republicans like George Bush and Bob Dole—keep losing elections? George Bush watched grassroots Republicanism in action for eight years and learned precisely nothing from it. As soon as he was in office, he purged all the Reaganites. He mowed down the grass roots. He brought in the East Coast establishment Republicans and promptly began dismantling the Reagan legacy. Four years later, Bill Clinton was knocking on Bush's door with an eviction notice.

The Republicans won the Congress, but the Democrats are winning every issue. Today's Republican Party is rudderless, leaderless, and in full retreat from the conservative values and vision of Ronald Reagan. So I'm taking a leave of absence from the Republican Party—but I hope to return soon. It all depends on whether or not the Republicans can find their way back to the people who elected them, and to the principles and the vision that elevated them—the principles of Ronald Reagan and his vision of the Shining City on a Hill. When the Republicans are ready to come back to grassroots America, I'll come back to the Republican Party.

In one of his most famous film roles, Dad played football star George Gipp in *Knute Rockne—All American*. In an emotional scene, the Gipper was on his deathbed, dying of an advanced infection in his throat. With his last few breaths, Gipp told Notre Dame coach Knute Rockne, "I've got to go,

263

Rock. It's all right. I'm not afraid. Sometime, Rock, when things are tough and the breaks are going against the boys, ask them to go out there and win just one for the Gipper. I don't know where I'll be, Rock, but I'll know about it and I'll be happy."

Knute Rockne listened, and he remembered. In 1928, when underdog Notre Dame went to play unbeaten Army in Yankee Stadium, Rockne related the Gipper's last words in his pregame pep talk. "The day before he died," said Rockne, "George Gipp asked me to wait until the situation seemed hopeless—then ask the team to go out and win one for him. Well, fellas, this is the day and you are the team." Notre Dame won it, 12 to 6. Those who saw the game said it was the most amazing exhibition of inspired football ever played.

We can do the same thing for America, right now. This is the day, and we are the team. The Gipper is our inspiration. All we need now is a smart coach to map our game plan, and a tough quarterback to carry the ball. Who will our coach be? "Knute" Gingrich? Trent Lott? Dick Armey?

And who will our quarterback be? Jack Kemp? Fred Thompson? Steve Forbes? J. C. Watts? Steve Largent?

Whoever leads us, let's make sure our goal is the same one Ronald Reagan had his sights on—the Shining City on a Hill.

I'm ready to take the field. How about you?

Let's get the job done. Let's go out and win one more for the Gipper.

NOTES

Chapter 1

1. CATO Policy Analysis No. 147, February 4, 1991, "The Profligate President: A Midterm Review of Bush's Fiscal Policy" by Stephen Moore, electronically retrieved on the Internet.

Chapter 2

1. *National Review*, November 7, 1994, pp. 28–29.
2. "Bauer Challenges the GOP," press release on Gary Bauer's speech before the Heritage Foundation, November 20, 1996, electronically retrieved from the Michael Reagan Information Interchange at www.reagan.com.
3. Peggy Noonan, *What I Saw at the Revolution* (New York: Random House, 1990), p. 160.
4. Lou Cannon, *President Reagan: The Role of a Lifetime* (New York: Simon & Schuster, 1989), p. 229.
5. Quoted by Michael Ryan, "How to Stand for a Child," *Parade Magazine*, February 8, 1997, p. 10.
6. Brian Tumulty, "Administration's Vaccine Program Labeled Wasteful," Gannett News Service, June 15, 1995; and Millicent Lawton, "Distribution snag means free-vaccine program is delayed indefinitely," *Education Week*, vol. 14, October 19, 1994, p. 18.
7. Robert M. Goldberg, op-ed piece in *Wall Street Journal*, June 20, 1994, electronically retrieved at "The RNC Truth Test" at www.rnc.org/news/talking.
8. John Hanchette, "Plans to Vaccinate Needy Children in Shambles," Gannett News Service, April 16, 1995, electronically retrieved at www.elibrary.com.
9. Joseph C. Koenenn, "Too Liberal: Clinton's well-intended vaccination program falls victim to ideological rigidity," *Newsday*, June 28, 1995, p. A28.
10. "Facing sad facts about the American family," *Washington Times*, National Weekly Edition, Oct. 30–Nov. 5, 1995, p. 37.
11. Larry B. Stammer, "A crusade to save marriages," *Los Angeles Times*, March 17, 1997, pp. A1 and A15.
12. "Facing sad facts about the American family," p. 37.

Chapter 3

1. Facts on the Washington, D.C., school system are from "A Well-Financed Failure" by Sari Horwitz and Valerie Strauss, *Washington Post*, Sunday, February 16, 1997, p. A01; and from "Who Truly Values Kids Most?" *Investor's Business Daily*, November 18, 1996, electronically retrieved from the Idea House website of the National Center for Policy Analysis at www.public-policy.org.
2. Samuel Blumenfeld, "Education as a Political Issue," *Vital Speeches*, vol. 61, January 15, 1995, p. 208.
3. Ibid.
4. Linda Chavez, "Promises Don't Help Kids Read," *USA Today*, September 4, 1996, electronically retrieved from the Michael Reagan Information Interchange at www.reagan.com.
5. Robert J. Barro (Hoover Institution), "Teachers' Unions Don't Deliver Quality," *Wall Street Journal*, September 27, 1996, electronically retrieved from the Idea

House website of the National Center for Policy Analysis at www.public-policy.org.

6. Richard Vedder, "School Vouchers to the Rescue . . . or to the Ruin?" *Washington Times*, August 18, 1996, electronically retrieved from the Michael Reagan Information Interchange at www.reagan.com.

7. Peter Schrag, "The New School Wars: How Outcome-Based Education Blew Up," *American Prospect*, no. 20, Winter 1995, pp. 53–62, electronically retrieved at http://epn.org/prospect/20/20schr.html.

8. Associated Press, "Study Shows Voucher Pupils Thriving in Private Schools," *New York Times*, August 13, 1996, electronically retrieved from the Idea House website of the National Center for Policy Analysis at www.public-policy.org.

9. Janet R. Beales (Reason Foundation), "Educating the Uneducatable," *Wall Street Journal*, August 21, 1996, electronically retrieved from the Michael Reagan Information Interchange at www.reagan.com.

10. Patrick F. Fagan, "Why Religion Matters: The Impact of Religious Practice on Social Stability," *The Heritage Foundation Backgrounder,* no. 1064, January 25, 1996, electronically retrieved at www.townhall.com/heritage/library/categories/family/bg1064.html.

11. Joe Klein, "Parochial Concerns," *Newsweek*, September 2, 1996, electronically retrieved from the Michael Reagan Information Interchange at www.reagan.com.

12. David Popenoe, "Life Without Father," *Reader's Digest*, February 1997, pp. 66–67.

Chapter 4

1. John R. Lott Jr., "More Guns, Less Violent Crime," *Wall Street Journal*, August 28, 1996; Ian Katz, "Gun Law Cuts Crime Rate, US Study Finds," *Guardian*, August 3, 1996; and Dennis Cauchon, "Study: Weapons Laws Deter Crime—Fewer Rapes, Murders Found Where Concealed Guns Legal," *USA Today*, August 2, 1996, all electronically retrieved from the Idea House website of the National Center for Policy Analysis at www.public-policy.org.

2. Susan Estrich, "Violent Kids Can't Be Reformed," *USA Today*, August 8, 1996, electronically retrieved from the Michael Reagan Information Interchange at www.reagan.com.

3. Haya El Nasser and Desda Moss, "Teen Crime Tosses Ball to Parents' Court," *USA Today*, August 6, 1996, electronically retrieved from the Michael Reagan Information Interchange at www.reagan.com.

4. David A. Price, "Ganging Up on the Street Gangs," *Investor's Business Daily*, August 7, 1996, electronically retrieved from the Michael Reagan Information Interchange at www.reagan.com.

5. Quoted in *Investor's Business Daily*, June 26, 1996, electronically retrieved on the Internet.

6. Ambrose Evans-Pritchard, "Cocaine and toga parties: Clinton stands accused," *London Telegraph*, July 17, 1994, electronically retrieved at www.assumption.edu/WebVAX/ET/ambr17Jul94.html; and Jamie Dettmer, "Dan Lasater: A Friend of Bill," *Insight Magazine*, November 6, 1995, electronically retrieved at www.westol.com/speck/lasater.html.

7. Susan Schmidt and Lena H. Sun, "Clinton Calls Wang Meeting 'Inappropriate,' " *Washington Post*, December 21, 1996, p. A01.

8. Mike Reynolds, Bill Jones, and Dan Evans, *Three Strikes and You're Out!—A Promise to Kimber* (Fresno, Calif.: Quill Driver Books, 1996), pp. 33–34.

9. Stephanie Simon, "Angry 'Three Strikes' Supporters Vow to Fight Back," *Los Angeles Times*, June 21, 1996, p. A-20.

10. Dan Morain, "Impact of Three Strikes Less Than Expected," *Los Angeles Times*, October 25, 1996, page A3.

(Note the media spin of the headline: Though it sounds as if it is saying that Three Strikes failed, it actually refers to the fact that the opponents of Three Strikes were wrong and that the anticrime law did not result in a drastic need to build more prisons. The impact of Three Strikes on the *crime rate*, however, was far greater than anyone expected! The liberal press hates admitting that Three Strikes works.)

11. Interview with Mike Reynolds; statistics compiled by California Secretary of State Bill Jones.

12. Dale Buss, "Combatting Crime," *Nation's Business*, vol. 82, March 1, 1994, p. 16.

13. Edwin Meese and Robert E. Moffit, editors, *Making America Safer: What Citizens and Their State and Local Officials Can Do to Combat Crime* (Washington, D.C.: The Heritage Foundation, 1997), pp. 3–4.

14. Bill McCollum, "Interview: The Message Is Deterrence," *Michael Reagan Monthly Monitor*, February 1995, p. 5.

15. Koo Tsai Kee, letter to *Straits Times*, October 12, 1993, Forum page, electronically retrieved on the Internet.

16. Quoted by Mary Mostert, "Background: Misguided Values Cost Is Crime," *Michael Reagan Monthly Monitor*, February 1995, p. 4.

Chapter 5

1. Ronald Reagan, *An American Life* (New York: Simon & Schuster, 1990), pp. 32, 56.

2. Ronald Reagan, *Speaking My Mind: Selected Speeches* (New York: Simon & Schuster, 1989), p. 135.

3. Patrick F. Fagan, "Why Religion Matters: The Impact of Religious Practice on Social Stability."

Chapter 6

1. Charles Oliver, "The Real Cost of Big Government," *Investor's Business Daily*, November 15, 1996, electronically retrieved from the Michael Reagan Information Interchange at www.reagan.com.

2. Peggy Noonan, *What I Saw at the Revolution*, pp. 173–74.

3. Quoted by Deroy Murdock, "Private Alternatives to Public Assistance," *National Minority Politics*, August 31, 1995, electronically retrieved at www.elibrary.com.

4. Father Robert A. Sirico, "Terms of the Welfare Debate," *Washington Times*, April 19, 1995, electronically retrieved at www.washtimes.com.

5. Pete du Pont and Jeffrey Eisenach, "Poor Substitute," *National Review*, vol. 46, no. 25, December 31, 1994, p. 51.

6. Jennifer E. Marshall, "The Greatest of These Is Love: A Faith-Based Alternative to the Welfare State," electronically retrieved at www.townhall.com/townhall/FRC/fampol/fp95lwl.html.

7. Peter J. Ferrara, "What Really Happened in the 1980s?" *The Heritage Foundation—Issues '94: The Candidate's Briefing Book,* electronically retrieved at www.townhall.com.

8. "Special Report: The New Volunteers," *Newsweek*, July 10, 1989, p. 36.

9. David L. Haase, "Coats Hears from Religious Groups About Ways to Lend a Hand to Poor," *Indianapolis Star*, September 29, 1995, p. E-10.

10. Governor George W. Bush, Executive Order GWB 96-5: "Relating to Faith-Based Community Service Groups," issued May 2, 1996.

11. Quoted by Mike Rubinkam, "Victory Fellowship Founder Joining Debate on Welfare," *Houston Post*, February 3, 1995, p. A-27.

12. Luke 10:27.

13. Quoted by William Raspberry, "Distant Government Frustrates People," *San Antonio Express-News*, March 10, 1995, p. C-1.

14. Quoted by Ian Christopher McCaleb, "GOP Lawmakers Unveil Faith-Based Plan," United Press International wire story, February 27, 1996, electronically retrieved on the Internet.

15. *The American Enterprise*, vol. 6, no. 2, March–April 1995, p. 19.

16. James F. Hirni, "AmeriCorps: A $575 Million Boondoggle," *The Heritage Foundation Issue Bulletin*, no. 212, September 14, 1995, electronically retrieved at http://www.townhall.com.

17. Ronald Reagan, *An American Life*, pp. 30–31.

18. The story of Marcella is true, though names and details have been changed to protect the privacy of the individuals involved.

Chapter 7

1. Ronald Reagan, "Tax Cuts and Increased Revenue," syndicated newspaper column, October 8, 1976, quoted by Martin Anderson, *Revolution* (New York: Harcourt Brace Jovanovich, 1988), p. 151.

2. Though Bill Clinton disputes it, his $260 billion 1993 tax increase was the largest tax increase in U.S. history. When Republican challenger Bob Dole made that claim during the 1996 campaign, Clinton claimed that the largest tax increase in history was the 1982 Tax Equity and Fiscal Responsibility Act (TEFRA) that Bob Dole helped steer through the Senate, signed by Ronald Reagan. Most economists agree, however, that TEFRA was not a true tax hike but a reduction in the size and scope of tax relief contained in 1981's ERTA tax cut bill. TEFRA reduced ERTA's tax cuts by about one-third, according to the congressional Joint Committee on Taxation. Even after TEFRA became law, the economy still received more than a half trillion dollars of ERTA tax relief from 1982 to 1986, when the Tax Reform Act was passed. Ronald Reagan's critics predicted that the drastically lower tax rates of ERTA would cause tax revenue to fall disastrously. Yet throughout the 1980s, federal tax revenue *doubled*—not in spite of tax cuts but *because* of the economic stimulus of tax cuts. The Clinton tax hike is what it is: the biggest ever. Even prominent Democrats admit it. Senator Daniel Patrick Moynihan of New York has called the Clinton tax bill "the largest tax increase in the history of public finance in the United States or anywhere else in the world." (For this analysis, I am indebted to Daniel J. Mitchell of the Heritage Foundation, whose article, "The Biggest Tax Increase, Period," appeared in *Wall Street Journal*, September 10, 1996.)

3. Isabel V. Sawhill and Mark Condon, "Is U.S. Income Inequality Really Growing? Sorting Out the Fairness Question," Urban Institute Policy Bites, June 1992, quoted by Peter J. Ferrara, "What Really Happened in the 1980s?" (The Heritage Foundation—Issues '94: The Candidate's Briefing Book), electronically retrieved at www.townhall.com.

4. Statistical source on the Reagan 1980s: Peter J. Ferrara, "What Really Happened

in the 1980s?" (The Heritage Foundation—Issues 1994: The Candidate's Briefing Book), electronically retrieved at www.townhall.com/heritage/library/categories/budgettax/1980s.html.

5. John S. Barry, "How a Flat Tax Would Affect Charitable Contributions," *The Heritage Foundation Backgrounder*, no. 1093, December 16, 1996, electronically retrieved at www.townhall.com/heritage/library.

6. Electronically retrieved from the Western Journalism Center's website at http://www.e-truth.com.

7. The IRS has even come down on individuals who have shown an anti-Clinton bent, such as Patricia Mendoza, the Chicago woman who shouted at Clinton during a 1996 campaign stop, "You suck, and those boys died!" (The "boys" she referred to were the nineteen U.S. servicemen killed in the Saudia Arabian truck bombing.) Clinton ordered Secret Service agents to take her into custody; she was arrested, held in jail, and charged with "threatening" the president. Five months later the charges were dismissed—but not before the Mendozas received a letter from the IRS, threatening to take away their property over $200 in alleged "back taxes" (the Mendozas denied owing any back taxes). That letter arrived just one month after the Clinton incident. Coincidence?

8. William W. Beach, "The Case for Repealing the Estate Tax," *The Heritage Foundation Backgrounder*, no. 1091, August 21, 1996, electronically retrieved at www.townhall.com/heritage/library.

9. Bruce Bartlett and John C. Goodman, National Center for Policy Analyis briefing paper: "Dynamic Scoring: A Primer," electronically retrieved from the Michael Reagan Information Interchange at www.reagan.com.

10. Ronald Reagan, *An American Life*, p. 55.

11. Charles Oliver, "How Government Punishes Small Firms," *Investor's Business Daily*, November 20, 1996, electronically retrieved from the National Center for Policy Analysis archives at www.public-policy.org/ncpa/pd/regulat.

12. Senator Orrin Hatch, "A Secure Bridge to the Future Rests on a Balanced Budget," *Washington Times*, November 15, 1996, electronically retrieved from the Michael Reagan Information Interchange at www.reagan.com.

13. Ronald Reagan, *An American Life* p. 157.

14. Quoted in *Weekly Standard*, August 22, 1996, electronically retrieved at www.townhall.com/heritage/library.

15. Joe Urschel, "Whitewater, hypocrisy and the first lady," *USA Today*, January 20, 1994, p. 8.

16. Arnold Beichman, "What did Hillary trade and when did she do it?" *Washington Times*, April 24, 1995, p. 37.

17. Quoted by Doug Ireland, "Whitewater Rafting," *The Nation*, April 22, 1996, electronically retrieved at www.assumption.edu/WebVAX/Nation/Ireland22-Apr96.html.

18. Sister Mary Ann Walsh, "Clintons' market windfall invites many questions," *USA Today*, March 31, 1994, p. 12.

19. Arnold Beichman, "What did Hillary trade and when did she do it?", p. 37.

20. When selling short, an investor borrows stock from a broker and sells the stock at current market price, expecting the market value of the stock to decrease. Later, when the price does fall, the investor buys the cheaper stock and returns it to the broker. The investor profits from the difference in price.

NOTES

Chapter 8

1. Quoted by Peter Schweizer, *Victory* (New York: The Atlantic Monthly Press, 1994), p. 8.
2. Ibid., p. xiv.
3. Ronald Reagan, *Speaking My Mind,* pp. 135, 168.
4. Peter Schweizer, *Victory,* p. 105.
5. Ibid., p. 284.
6. Bill Clinton met on two occasions with officials of the City of Long Beach to promote a plan to lease the recently closed Long Beach Naval Station to COSCO, the China Ocean Shipping Company. The facility—prime port space—is valued at $65 million, though historic preservationists put its value at closer to $300 million. The U.S. government would turn the shipyard over to the city free of charge, and without a security review.

COSCO is a wholly owned subsidiary of the Chinese Communist government, and operates a six-hundred-ship merchant fleet. The White House is well aware of the troubled history of the Chinese company. In 1996, 2,000 illegal Chinese-made weapons were intercepted by U.S. agents during an attempt to smuggle the guns aboard a COSCO ship docked in Oakland, California. The guns were destined for U.S. street gangs. In December 1996, a COSCO ship rammed a dockside shopping complex in New Orleans, injuring 116 people. Six COSCO ships were detained for international safety violations in 1996, and the Coast Guard placed the company on a watch list for stepped-up monitoring. In 1993, the U.S. Navy stopped a COSCO ship in the Persian Gulf on suspicion that it was carrying chemical weapons cargo; after a standoff (when some of the cargo could have been dumped), the ship was searched and no contraband was found. In 1992, COSCO paid a $400,000 settlement over kickback and tariff-violation charges.

Knowing all this, Bill Clinton went to bat for COSCO, urging Long Beach officials to grant prime port space to a foreign shipping company with a dubious past and in direct competition with American shipping interests. Most important, he did so after receiving questionable donations and having White House meetings with Chinese officials, including officials of COSCO.

In 1996, Johnny Chung, a Chinese-American businessman from California, donated $366,000 to the Democrats and led a delegation of six Chinese officials (including one COSCO official) to the White House to watch Clinton broadcast his weekly radio address. (The $366,000 was returned by the Democrats after it was uncovered in press reports.) Also in 1996, Bill Clinton entertained the chairman of the Chinese arms company implicated in the COSCO weapons smuggling incident in Oakland.

COSCO already operates an 80-acre facility in the Port of Long Beach (the Long Beach Naval Shipyard would give COSCO a 145-acre cargo terminal). Perhaps it is coincidental that in March 1997, U.S. border agents seized two truckloads of military assault rifles and grenade launchers that had been smuggled through the Port of Long Beach. It is not known if they were shipped by COSCO or not, but the weapons clearly came from Asia, were destined for Mexico's drug cartels, and were being stored in a warehouse at the Otay Mesa border crossing (near San Diego) when they were seized. It is also known that other truckloads from this same weapons shipment crossed the border into Mexico. We have to wonder: How many illicit shipments have passed through the Port of Long Beach undetected? And how many more would result if the Chinese controlled the former naval base?

And then there's the bigger question: Was Bill Clinton *bought* by the Chinese government? Let me tell you something about money and politics: When big donors give big donations, the politicians who take the money *always* know who it comes from and what sort of quid pro quo is expected in return. Otherwise, the donors would never give the money. That's how the game is played, and anyone who thinks otherwise is naive.

On June 3, 1996, the FBI national security Division Five sent two agents to alert the White House to the fact that the Chinese government was shopping for influence among U.S. politicians, primarily Democrats. Communication intercepts showed that the Chinese were attempting to affect the 1996 election using laundered campaign contributions. The Division Five agents met with two National Security Council aides, Rand Beers and Ed Appel, and gave them the warning about Chinese influence. Months later, when the story broke, Bill Clinton claimed that the agents also told the NSC aides not to convey the information to higher-ups, so he was never told. This is as plausible as "but I didn't inhale" and "I just happened to get lucky in cattle futures." The *only* reason for sending the FBI Division Five agents to the White House was to alert the *president*! The FBI took the rare step of contradicting the White House, insisting that its agents never told the NSC aides to keep the information to themselves.

There is a very real danger that a huge COSCO facility—operated directly by the Chinese Communist government on U.S. soil—would pose a significant threat to U.S. security as a spy center and smuggling depot for guns and drugs. And there is a very real possibility that the president of the United States knowingly violated U.S. interests to bring the Chinese Communists to the Long Beach Naval Shipyard.

Sources: The Associated Press, "Clinton Helped Chinese Get Base," *Newsday*, March 9, 1997, p. A8; Richard Lacayo, "What Did China Want? The Contributions Made by Johnny Chung and Others to the Clinton White House Backfire on Beijing," *Time*, March 24, 1997, pp. 48ff.; Anne-Marie O'Connor and Jeff Leeds, "U.S. Agents Seize Smuggled Arms," *Los Angeles Times*, home edition, March 15, 1997, p. A19.

7. Facts on military cutbacks compiled from personal interviews with Duncan Hunter, Duke Cunningham, and Caspar Weinberger, and from Caspar Weinberger and Peter Schweizer's book, *The Next War* (Washington, D.C.: Regnery Publishing, Inc., 1996), pp. xiii–xxii.

8. Art Pine and Ralph Vartabedian, "F-14 Crashes Raise Questions of Age, Safety," *Los Angeles Times*, home edition, May 12, 1996, p. A1.

9. Charles Aldinger, "U.S. military dogged by air accidents this year," Reuters News Service, May 10, 1996, electronically retrieved at www.elibrary.com.

10. Richard Thompson, "Another pizza, another policy: Decision-making in the Clinton White House," *Contemporary Review*, vol. 267, October 1, 1995, p. 188.

11. Representative Curt Weldon (R-Pennsyvania), "Conference Report on H.R. 3230, National Defense Authorization Act," presented to the House of Representatives, July 31, 1996.

12. Duncan Hunter, conversation with the author.

13. Quoted by Lou Cannon, *President Reagan: The Role of a Lifetime,* p. 15.

14. Ibid., p. 23.

15. Ibid., p. 319.

16. Ronald Reagan, *An American Life,* p. 257.

17. Frank Gaffney Jr., "The 'Antimissile Gap,'" *World & I*, vol. 10, July 1, 1995, p. 74.

18. Caspar Weinberger and Peter Schweizer, *The Next War*, p. xxiii.
19. Information compiled from the following sources: John Meroney, "Will U.S. ever get a missile defense?" *Human Events*, vol. 51, June 30, 1995, p. 3; Sidney Graybeal and Michael Krepon, "It's not son of star wars," *Bulletin of the Atomic Scientists*, vol. 50, March 1, 1994, p. 16; Elizabeth Shogren, "U.S.–Russia Talks End in Arms Breakthrough; Summit: Clinton, Yeltsin resolve differences on ABM treaty," *Los Angeles Times*, home edition, March 22, 1997, p. A1; The White House, "Press briefing by Secretary Albright and National Security Advisor Sandy Berger," M2 PressWIRE, March 19, 1997; The White House, "Fact sheet—Joint statement concerning the anti-ballistic missile treaty," M2 PressWIRE, March 24, 1997; The White House, "Joint statement on parameters on future reductions in nuclear forces," M2 PressWIRE, March 24, 1997; and "Republicans warn Clinton against arms concessions," Reuters News Service, March 20, 1997, electronically retrieved at www.elibrary.com

Chapter 9

1. "Quid Pro Coal," excerpts from a transcript of the TV program *American Investigator* on NET: National News/Talk Television, electronically retrieved at www.reagan.com.
2. Ambrose Evans-Pritchard, "Clinton's Chinese takeaway," *London Telegraph*, February 16, 1997, electronically retrieved from the Electronic Telegraph at www.telegraph.co.uk.
3. Lena H. Sun and John Pomfret, "The Curious Cast of Asian Donors," *Washington Post*, January 27, 1997, p. A1; Anne Farris, "Unfolding Story Swelling Like a Sponge," *Washington Post*, April 6, 1997, p. A16.
4. Cynthia Osterman, "Clinton's Indonesian friend got govt deals—report," Reuters New Service, October 13, 1996; Steve Holland, "Clinton dodges questions on campaign contributions," Reuters News Service, October 14, 1996, electronically retrieved at www.elibrary.com.
5. Lena H. Sun and John Pomfret, "The Curious Cast of Asian Donors," p. A1.
6. Anne Farris, "Unfolding Story Swelling Like a Sponge," p. A16; Steve Holland, "Clinton says Indonesia policy not altered by money," Reuters News Service, November 8, 1996, electronically retrieved at www.elibrary.com; Andy Thibault and Jerry Seper, "They're back—and maybe to face the music; Hillary sought to hire Huang over Brown's objections," *Washington Times*, November 17, 1996, p. 1.
7. Hugh Davies, "Clinton aide 'in funds appeal' to drug smuggler," *London Daily Telegraph*, April 5, 1997, electronically retrieved at www.telegraph.co.uk; and Norman Kempster and Juanita Darling, "Clinton Outlines Sanctions on Cuba for Downing Planes," *Los Angeles Times*, February 27, 1996, p. A1.
8. Bob Woodward, "White House Gave DNC Top-Secret Intelligence; Information Used to Rescind Dinner Invitation," *Washington Post*, Tuesday, April 8, 1997; p. A1.
9. Martin Wooster, "Do free trade agreements slow free trade?" *American Enterprise*, vol. 6, July 1, 1995, p. 97.
10. Hugo Gurdon, "Americans wake up to the peril of appeasement," *London Daily Telegraph*, March 27, 1997, electronically retrieved from the Electronic Telegraph at www.telegraph.co.uk.
11. Hooshang Amirahmadi, "Oil at the turn of the twenty-first century," *Futurist*, vol. 28, June 1, 1996, pp. 433ff., electronically retrieved at www.elibrary.com.

12. Steve Rodan, "What the U.S. is whispering to Israel about Iran," *Jerusalem Post,* January 13, 1995, electronically retrieved at www.elibrary.com.

13. Diego Cevallos, "Mexico: On the Verge of War or Peace?" Inter Press Service English News Wire, September 3, 1996.

14. The Helms-Burton act was passed overwhelmingly by Congress and was aimed at discouraging foreign investment in Cuba that would prop up the Castro regime. The central provision of Helms-Burton is Title Three, which allows U.S. nationals and companies whose property was seized by Castro to sue foreign individuals or corporations who "traffick" (buy, lease, utilize, or acquire an interest) in that property. Clinton initially suspended Title Three for six months, barring U.S. citizens whose property was taken over during the Cuban Revolution from filing suit—and he promised to renew that suspension every six months as long as he saw "progress" in moving Cuba toward democracy. "I would expect to continue suspending the right to file suit," he said, "so long as America's friends and allies continue their stepped-up efforts to promote a transition to democracy in Cuba." Source: Jim Lobe, "U.S.–Cuba: Claiming victory, Clinton suspends Helms-Burton again," Inter Press Service English News Wire, February 19, 1997, electronically retrieved at www.elibrary.com.

15. Julian L. Simon (The CATO Institute), "What the Starvation Lobby Eschews . . . ," *Wall Street Journal,* November 18, 1996, electronically retrieved at www.reagan.com.

16. Anna J. Bray, "Hunger's Real Cure? Freedom," *Investor's Business Daily,* November 22, 1996, electronically retrieved at www.reagan.com.

17. Quoted by Patrick Worsnip, "UN, at 50, faces threat from U.S. Congress," Reuters News Service, October 16, 1995, electronically retrieved at www.elibrary.com.

18. Source: General Accounting Office Report to the Majority Leader, U.S. Senate, *Peace Operations—U.S. Costs in Support of Haiti, Former Yugoslavia, Somalia, and Rwanda,* March 1996, designated GAO/NSIAD-96-38.

Chapter 10

1. Pilot Officer John G. Magee Jr. was a young American pilot who joined the Royal Canadian Air Force in 1939 in order to join the fight against the Axis before the United States had entered the war. After making a test flight in a Spitfire over England in 1941, he was inspired to compose a poem, "High Flight," which he mailed home to his parents in America. That poem, which is in the public domain, is known by heart by thousands of military aviators the world over. It reads:

Oh, I have slipped the surly bonds of earth
    And danced the skies on laughter-silvered wings;
Sunward I've climbed, and joined the tumbling mirth
    Of sun-split clouds—and done a hundred things
You have not dreamed of—wheeled and soared and swung
    High in the sunlit silence. Hovering there,
I've chased the shouting wind along, and flung
    My eager craft through footless halls of air.
Up, up the long, delirious, burning blue
    I've topped the windswept heights with easy grace
Where never lark, or even eagle flew.
    And, while with silent, lifting mind I've trod

The high untrespassed sanctity of space,
Put out my hand, and touched the face of God.

On December 11, 1941, just days after mailing those words home to his parents in America, nineteen-year-old Lieutenant John G. Magee, 412 Squadron, RCAF, was killed in a midair collision.

2. In 1980, Bob Dole wanted a completely open, inclusive primary process, with all seven candidates included in the debates and on the ballots. Dole was incensed when he and his fellow also-rans were kept off the ballot in delegate-rich New York. In 1996, however, when the shoe was on the other foot, Bob Dole was the only name on the Republican ballot in the state of New York—Dole and New York senator Alphonse D'Amato completely locked all other candidates out of the process!

ABOUT THE AUTHOR

Michael Reagan grew up in Hollywood, the son of Ronald Reagan and actress Jane Wyman. He hosts the nationally syndicated *Michael Reagan Talk Show* and publishes *The Monthly Monitor* newsletter. The Michael Reagan Information Interchange (http://www.reagan.com) is one of the most active and influential websites on the Internet. He delivered the keynote address to the freshman class of the 104th Congress in 1994, and was one of only two Americans named as an honorary member of the 104th Congress. He is the author of *Michael Reagan: Making Waves* and *On the Outside Looking In.*